OBJECTIVITY IN LAW

Objectivity in Law

NICOS STAVROPOULOS

CLARENDON PRESS · OXFORD
1996

Oxford University Press, Walton Street, Oxford OX2 6DP
Oxford New York
Athens Auckland Bangkok Bombay
Calcutta Cape Town Dar es Salaam Delhi
Florence Hong Kong Istanbul Karachi
Kuala Lumpur Madras Madrid Melbourne
Mexico City Nairobi Paris Singapore
Taipei Tokyo Toronto
and associated companies in
Berlin Ibadan

Oxford is a trade mark of Oxford University Press

Published in the United States
by Oxford University Press Inc. New York

British Library Cataloguing in Publication Data
Data available

Stavropoulos, Nicos.
Objectivity in law/Nicos Stavropoulos.
p. cm.
Includes bibliographical references.
1. Law–Interpretation and construction. 2. Objectivity.
K290.S73 1996
340'.1–dc20 95–37001
ISBN 0–19–825899–2
1 3 5 7 9 10 8 6 4 2

Typeset by J&L Composition Ltd, Filey, North Yorkshire

Printed in Great Britain
on acid-free paper by
Bookcraft Ltd., Midsomer Norton, Avon

To my mother
and the memory of my father

Acknowledgements

This book started as a D.Phil. thesis. Joseph Raz, Anne deMoor, John Bell, and Michael Luntley all kindly offered help and advice on my work at Oxford. Special thanks are due to Susan Hurley and Adrian Moore, who read and commented upon several late drafts of a large part of the manuscript, as well as to Neil MacCormick and Anne deMoor for their suggestions on a recent draft. I have been greatly helped by long conversations with Mark Greenberg, who also commented on parts of a late draft. An anonymous reader for the Press helped me see where criticism is likely to focus.

My greatest debt is to Ronald Dworkin. Initially as thesis supervisor, subsequently as friend, he has found (or made) an extraordinary amount of time for my work. It is a special pleasure to acknowledge a great debt that keeps mounting.

I should like to thank my editor, John Whelan, for his patience and encouragement. *D. Damis and Associates* kindly made office facilities available to me throughout the production of this book.

N. S.

Contents

1. Introduction 1

1. Objective 1
2. Revisionist Semantics in Legal Theory 5
3. Strategy 7
4. Synopsis 8

2. The Semantic Framework 15

1. Introduction 15
2. Kripke on Names 17
   2.1 Modal Contexts 18
   2.2 Epistemic Contexts 22
   2.3 Practice, Empty Names, Substitution 25
3. Putnam and Natural Kinds 29
4. Burge and the Social Context 34
5. The Real Target of the Theories 38
6. Theoretical Terms and the Distinction Between Different Belief – Different Concept 44
7. Interim Parallels With Law 46
8. Classification? 48

3. Empirical Counterparts and Hart's Semantics 52

1. Introduction 52
2. Hart's Semantics 53
   2.1 Use 54
   2.2 Force 55
   2.3 Open-Endedness 62
   2.4 Counterparts 68
3. Hart's Target: Reductionism 69
4. Anti-realism and Ontic Commitment 77
   4.1 Ontological Liberalism 77
   4.2 Epistemic Distance and Doubt 80

4. Mind-Dependence and Cognitivism 83

1. Introduction 83
2. Mind-Dependence 84
3. Non-Cognitivism and Subjectivism 89
4. The 'Subjective' 92
5. Can There Be Principled Projections? 96
6. The Objective World 100
7. Naturalism 103
   7.1 Conceptual Independence 106
   7.2 Counterfactual Independence 109
8. Selective and Global Scepticism 111
9. Convergence 115
10. Ethical Error, Real Options, and Circularity 117
11. The Nature of Values and Law 121

5. Substantive Disagreement and Indeterminacy 125

1. Introduction 125
2. Substantive Disagreement in Law 127
3. Constraints: Practice *versus* Criteria 128
   3.1 Dworkin's Practices 129
   3.2 The Semantic Sting and K–P Semantics 129
4. The Threat of Indeterminacy: Raz's Version 136
5. Dworkin's Pre-Interpretive Agreement: Some Misunderstandings 137
   5.1 Extravagant Cases 139
   5.2 Easy Cases 140
6. Scepticism and Indubitability 143
7. Wittgensteinian Arguments 147
8. Interpretive Constraints 155
9. Indeterminacy Again 159
10. Is Dworkin a Metaphysician? 160
11. Interpretive Positivism 162

6. Conceptions of Practice 165

1. Introduction 165
2. Fish's Pragmatism 165
3. Moore on Discourse Autonomy 179
4. Concept Attribution and Law's Autonomy 186
   4.1 The Intention Connection 188
   4.2 Avoiding Intention Problems? 189
   4.3 Legal Examples 191

4.4 Is the Distinction Genuine? 195
5. Conservatism 198

References 202

Index 208

1

Introduction

1. OBJECTIVE

This is an essay in support of the idea that legal interpretation can be objective. Legal interpretation, in the simple sense in which I am interested, consists in making statements like 'under English law, a *bona fide* purchaser of chattels acquires a good title' or 'this plaintiff has a right to recover damages'. These sentences are propositions reporting what the law is, on some relatively general or some more specific question, respectively. In this essay I shall identify one important source of resistance to the idea that legal interpretation can be objective: a defective semantics that is very widely accepted. I shall try to establish the inadequacy of that traditional semantics and the superiority of an alternative framework. I shall argue that, once that alternative framework is accepted, most doubts about the possibility of objectivity in legal interpretation fade. Further, I shall argue that the alternative framework yields new insights into important jurisprudential puzzles.

Most lawyers would accept that semantic questions figure in legal interpretation. Law is largely expressed in canonical language, and most lawyers agree that what the canonical text of a statute, for example, means, bears upon a statute's impact on the law. The precise bearing of the statute's meaning on the law is controversial, and lawyers have to take a stand on the relation between the meaning of the canonical text and the content of the rest of the law: making assumptions about the *purpose* the statute is supposed to serve; the *intentions* of the legislature that passed it; the *principle* the statute may be thought to express. Whatever answer different lawyers give on how these items are related, they must hold a view on the semantic content of the canonical text.

What is the key semantic unit over which such semantic views range? Is it the words of the text, sentences or perhaps large pieces of text? I shall concentrate on *concepts* as the key semantic unit. Concepts are abstract entities, designated by concept-words, that have *extensions*, that is objects falling under them.[1] For

[1] I am here following the standard (Fregean) picture of concepts. I assume that the notion is clear enough, at least regarding these two characteristics: concept-words (or, more loosely, concepts) have

example, the word 'vehicle' stands for the concept vehicle, whose extension includes all motor cars and buses, and various other objects.[2] We may have concepts which are complex, in some sense, such as cruel punishment, whose extension includes amputation and the rack.[3] The principal semantic question I shall be discussing is: what determines the extension, or range of application, of legal concepts? That is, what makes it the case that A's agreement with B is correctly characterized as a contract—that the concept of a contract is correctly applied to that case?

Concept-words also have *senses*, i.e. the information dossier that speakers associate with the concept and use to specify a concept's content. For example, speakers may associate 'vehicle' with 'carriage used for land transport', and 'contract' with 'promise or set of promises between two parties, resulting from an agreement in consideration of something in return, which is normally enforceable in law'. Any theory of meaning must specify the relation between the sense of a concept-word and the extension of a concept. Traditional semantic theory holds that the sense of a concept-word determines the concept's extension: the concept applies to whatever satisfies the specification set out in speakers' information dossier.

A version of the traditional semantic theory is the *Criterial Model*.[4] The Criterial Model holds that corresponding to each concept there is some information dossier which is common among speakers, that is, a dossier consisting of descriptions of the properties commonly associated with the concept-word. That dossier—communal sense—supplies a list of criteria that determine a concept's extension. The criteria describe how the facts must be for something to count as, say, a contract. In its more sophisticated version, the Criterial Model treats only the experts'

senses and (the relevant concepts have) extensions. These two notions are clarified below. Throughout the essay I shall somewhat loosely be referring to 'concepts' (or conceptual) 'content' in the sense of conditions of correct application of concepts. This use is not unnatural, since, given the conditions determining correct application of 'contract', what it is for something to be contract follows. So 'objective content' means that correct application is determined objectively, 'stipulative content' means that correct application is determined by a stipulation, etc.

[2] I shall be using single quotes for expressions whose meaning is under consideration and ordinary typeface (or italics, for emphasis) for the concept, object, or class of objects they stand for.

[3] A different sense of conceptual complexity will be introduced in due course, and the latter sense will be intended in the text, unless otherwise indicated. That sense concerns cases of concepts, if any occur, whose content is interdependent with the content of other concepts. For example 'cruel punishment', 'dignity', 'human rights', and other concepts may be interdependent.

[4] The Criterial Model is not any particular philosopher's theory, but rather a set of semantic views that figure in many philosophers' understanding of language. It can be traced to Locke's view of concepts, figures in Carnap's logical positivism, and survives in much of the semantics inspired by the later Wittgenstein. So-called anti-realists also tend to align themselves with it. I shall not attempt to attribute it properly here. Aspects of it will be attributed to various theorists in due course. See Michael Moore's attribution of conventionalism in 'A Natural Law Theory of Interpretation', *58 S. Cal. L. R.*, 277–398, 291 ff, esp. n. 25. I intend that the Criterial Model capture what is considered to be philosophical common sense, the sort of semantics that has 'trickled down' and 'warped' lower-level theories and practices, e.g. of legal interpretation. These clarifications are in response to an anonymous reader's comments.

criteria as decisive. The Criterial Model draws two important conclusions. First, the truth that something is a contract if and only if it is x, y, and z, where x, y, and z are the relevant criteria, is a degenerate truth: that something is a contract if it fulfils these criteria is a matter of conventional arrangement. The fact that everyone (or every expert) agrees that contracts are x, y, and z makes x, y, and z criteria of contract-hood. It may be a substantive empirical matter, and thus open to doubt, whether something is x, y, and z. But, provided that it is, it is not a substantive matter that it is a contract: no competent user of the concept can coherently doubt that truth. Second, there will be cases in which the agreement among users that underlies the standard cases of application will break down. In those cases there will be indeterminacy over the application of the concept.[5]

It is widely assumed that, to the extent that the content of the law turns on semantic analysis, something like the Criterial Model must hold. I shall call this the *Semantic Assumption*. It is assumed, that is, that, insofar as questions of legal interpretation are questions about the meaning of the canonical language, they concern the shared beliefs of competent (or expert) users about the content of legal concepts; and those beliefs are criteria of concepts' correct application. Legal positivists are the obvious allies of the Semantic Assumption. But legal naturalists may also uphold it, by claiming that principles of natural justice are further criteria of the application of legal concepts. A less obvious way of endorsing the Semantic Assumption is by rejecting semantics *tout court*, in order to reject the Criterial Model. Pragmatists may argue against the idea that semantics is at all relevant to law, assuming that semantics cannot but be criterial semantics. Ronald Dworkin's critique of positivism may appear to endorse the Semantic Assumption: Dworkin's argument is directed against the adequacy of criterial semantics, but what he says is consistent with believing that, were semantics adequate, the Criterial Model would be entailed.[6]

The Semantic Assumption is unwarranted: the Criterial Model is not the only one in the field. There are competitive, and more plausible, theories of conceptual content which would yield an entirely different picture of legal content. An important group of such theories is found in the writings of Saul Kripke, Hilary Putnam, Tyler Burge, and Donald Davidson. The content of these theories, as well as the question whether and to what extent they can be grouped together, is

[5] The exact way in which indeterminacy comes about according to the Criterial Model is complicated and obscure. I shall discuss it in chapter 3. For present purposes it suffices that indeterminancy *will* come about, one way or another.

[6] In effect, Dworkin rejects the Semantic Assumption: he calls for rejection of the entire semantic approach, and argues for his interpretive method instead. His rejection has two motivations. In the first place, he does not accept the Criterial Model. In the second place, he appears to doubt whether all important problems of legal interpretation can *usefully* be stated in terms of questions about some concept's extension. The compatibility of Dworkin's interpretivism with the alternative semantics developed here is discussed in chapter 5. His worry to the effect that conceiving legal issues as semantic, and therefore as problems of 'classification', is not helpful, is discussed in chapter 2 section 8.

controversial. Yet they all raise challenges to the Criterial Model too important to be ignored. I shall develop an alternative view of semantics—hereafter, *K–P semantics*—drawing on these theorists' work, and argue for its applicability to questions of legal interpretation. The discussion of arguments for and against the alternative framework's applicability will serve the essay's *diagnostic* aim: I shall try to explain the prevalence of the Semantic Assumption by locating the philosophical assumptions that make it appear self-evident, or at least compelling, to many lawyers. The essay's other principal aim is *revisionary*: I shall try to defend the alternative framework not only as superior to the Criterial Model, but also as valuable for jurisprudence in its own right.

Developing a semantic framework for law is in some sense a modest project. A full theory of legal interpretation may need much more besides. For example, a full theory may need to include specific accounts of statutory and constitutional interpretation. Further, semantic theories are more readily understood to concern texts, so that precedent may pose further problems. Finally, there may be questions of legal interpretation that are awkward to construe as questions of application of legal concepts.[7] But the role of a semantic foundation is important: the Semantic Assumption has had a large impact on the law. Many persistent controversies in legal interpretation rest on little more than that, or closely related, semantic assumptions, the case for which is rarely argued. A clear view on the apparently simple question of concepts' application should help locate and expose these sources of controversy, and so help progress in the relevant debate.

A notable example of the effect the Semantic Assumption has had on the law is the 'originalist–interpretivist' controversy in US constitutional law. In this case, conservative pressure against civil rights is covered beneath supposedly obvious and politically neutral views about the content of constitutional concepts, namely that Framers' beliefs about the content of the concepts they used were part of their intention to use them. The liberal opposition has largely accepted this semantic 'truism', and has been trying to justify protection of rights through justifying changes in the content of the concepts involved. Both sides are agreed that a concept's content is determined by criteria, and therefore frame their dispute in terms of a choice over whose criteria are to apply—the Framers' or the Supreme Court's.[8]

The way the Semantic Assumption has misdirected legal practice—constitutional and otherwise—is well established in the literature.[9] Naturally, legal theory is itself plagued by unargued semantic prejudice. The chief problem the Semantic

[7] See chapter 2, section 8.

[8] Dworkin is a notable exception in the controversy: he has been urging for some time now the view that what determines the content of these concepts is really an important substantive issue.

[9] See David Brink's 'Legal Theory, Legal Interpretation, and Judicial Review', *17 Philosophy and Public Affairs*, 105–48, esp. 112 ff; Moore, 'A Natural Law Theory of Interpretation', 322 ff. The best known exposition of the connection between what I call the Semantic Assumption and warped legal practice is Dworkin's discussion of the 'semantic sting' and his analysis of statutory interpretation; see *Law's Empire*, chs. 2 and 9.

Assumption creates for legal theory is that disagreement cannot be adequately represented. If concepts' content is determined by shared criteria, then lawyers cannot genuinely disagree over whether something is, say, a contract. To disagree is to cease employing *shared* criteria. Therefore, disputing lawyers cannot be arguing on whether something is in fact within the extension of the concept of a contract, but only on whether the concept ought to be extended, for reasons independent of 'contracthood', to cover it. By contrast, disputing lawyers perceive themselves to be arguing about whether cases *in fact* fall under the relevant legal concepts. The Semantic Assumption renders that perception inexplicably wrong.[10]

More generally, fierce opposition to theories challenging legal positivism is often driven by semantic views perceived as too obvious to be worth discussing.[11] The Semantic Assumption works in favour of a form of strict positivism, defined by two theses: first, that a statute's impact on the law is fully determined by the meaning of the statute's words; second, that the words' meaning is determined by shared criteria. The Semantic Assumption amounts to the second thesis; and, once that is granted, it is very hard to resist the first. Those who want to challenge the first thesis—those who want to say that often legal problems about a statute are not about what words in it mean—should not fight their battles on their enemies' semantic territory.[12]

2. REVISIONIST SEMANTICS IN LEGAL THEORY

Michael Moore and David Brink have (separately) initiated a programme of exploring the implications for the law of Kripke and Putnam's theories. Aspects of both Moore's and Brink's work are discussed later in this essay. However, it may be useful to describe here the broad differences between their work and my own approach.

Moore's theory, to begin with, embraces what he calls metaphysical realism. On the whole, metaphysical realism contrasts with anti-realism, a philosophical doctrine—deriving from constructivism in the philosophy of mathematics and largely developed by Michael Dummett and his students—concerning a set of issues revolving around the concept of truth. There is by now a vast idiosyncratic literature discussing the real locus of difference between realism and anti-realism. Roughly, the leading idea is that the issue is focused on the question whether truth can transcend actual or potential decidability, and the related question

[10] Dworkin, Brink, and Moore, opp.citt., all focus their critique of legal positivism on its inability to make conceptual room for genuine disagreement. In philosophy, Kripke, Putnam, and Burge focus again on the respective inability of the Criterial Model. See Chapters 5 and 2, respectively.

[11] See chapter 5 for a discussion of the semantic assumptions underscoring the 'indeterminancy' objection to Dworkin's theory.

[12] I am borrowing this image from Jennifer Hornsby's 'Descartes, Rorty and the Mind-Body Fiction', in Malachowski, A. (ed.), *Reading Rorty*, 40.

whether bivalence and the law of the excluded middle (informally, the proposition that every sentence has a determinate truth value and the law of logic requiring that any proposition can either be true or not true, respectively) hold.[13]

Both realism and anti-realism are highly abstract, domain-independent doctrines: they aspire to cover every discourse. Provided there are no domain-specific obstacles, and if realism is right, there is scope for objectivity, whatever that means, for every domain—for physics as well as law. Conversely, if anti-realism is right, there is no scope for objectivity, whatever that means, for any domain—again, physics and law included.

In fact, however, the central questions in jurisprudence are domain-specific, not global. Arguments against the possibility of objectivity in law are not to do with the concept of truth *in abstracto*, but with the nature of law in particular. To 'earn' objectivity in law, one has to succeed in showing, not that truth can transcend effective or other decidability—that may be true in general, yet not for law—rather, one must show that there can be objectivity in law (and indeed flesh out the notion of objectivity involved), having taken into account whatever peculiarities the legal domain has, and having deflected objections that invoke such peculiarities.

This, then, is a broad difference between Moore's and my own approach: instead of starting from a general, technical characterization of objectivity like that provided by metaphysical realism, I start by sketching domains, like that of natural kinds, where some sort of objectivity is intuitively and common-sensically plausible; I try to work out what kind of objectivity that is and why it holds for that domain; and then I try to remove obstacles to its being extended to the legal domain, fleshing out and refining the notion of objectivity along the way.[14]

Once much of that discussion is in place, a second broad difference will emerge: my position diverges from the slogans that purport to capture realism (i.e. that truth is a matter of 'correspondence with mind-independent facts') because I accept a fundamental connection between semantic questions and social practices. I shall argue for a kind of objectivity that is consistent with the anti-realist slogan that 'meaning depends on use', and that needs no fact in virtue of which a judgment that a concept applies to a case is true, other than the ordinary theoretical support such a judgment must rely on.

To turn to Brink, while he calls his position realist, he appears to have in mind something closer to the form of objectivism defended here. Although his views have as yet been inadequately developed in connection to law, on the strength of his work on ethical realism, I should hope that he would be sympathetic to the position defended here.[15]

[13] See Michael Luntley, *Language, Logic and Experience* and Crispin Wright, *Truth and Objectivity*, for recent attempts to locate the leading issue of the realist–anti-realist debate.

[14] This is not to say that Moore himself does not make out his objectivism in a similar, domain-sensitive way, only that his embracing metaphysical realism does not help him in that central task.

[15] As far as I know, Brink's position in jurisprudence can be found in 'Legal Theory, Legal Interpretation, and Judicial Review', and 'Semantics and Legal Interpretation; (Further Thoughts)', *2 Canadian J of Law and Jurisprudence*, 181–91, which is a response to criticism of the first article. His work in ethics is *Moral Realism and the Foundations of Ethics.*

Finally, I have a less obvious ally in my attempt to defend objectivism drawing on semantics and related philosophical fields. Susan Hurley's *Natural Reasons* develops a most congenial framework, principally in connection with ethical deliberation, but also extended to the legal domain, drawing, *inter alia*, on work in the philosophy of language and mind that is used in this essay as well. I shall note my debt to her work at various points in due course.

3. STRATEGY

The strategy of this essay is as follows. First, I describe and defend the K–P framework, as it has been developed for some particular kinds of expressions (principally proper names and natural kind terms). Then I explore the possibility that the K–P framework may have more general applicability. I subsequently claim that the framework is applicable to legal concepts in particular, and I draw some preliminary implications.

Major objections to this last claim are then considered. These objections principally are: (a) K–P semantics is applicable, if at all, to expressions designating concrete objects; (b) K–P semantics is applicable, if at all, to expressions designating mind-independent objects and properties; (c) K–P semantics makes for radical indeterminacy by conceiving every aspect of a concept's content as substantive and thus open to doubt. These objections are faced by locating their common motivation—a questionable conception of mental content and its relation to objects. I then argue that what is required for the framework's applicability to law does not breach our intuitions concerning the law's dependence on the mind or social practices.

Finally, various ways of misconceiving that dependence are discussed. The themes discussed in this connection are principally law's autonomy and the distinction between applying the law and 'inventing' new law.

As the outlined strategy suggests, a large part of the discussion is philosophical: for example, the semantics of proper names and the metaphysics of ethics figure prominently in the essay. Building up a picture of legal concepts through following these philosophical debates gives occasion to trace the motivation of the philosophical prejudice that is deeply entrenched in legal theory and the consequent resistance to revisionary views. Incidentally, starting from the well-known cases and moving on to the more controversial areas also serves economy of exposition. More important, exploring the arguments in favour of objectivity in areas where objectivism is convincing, makes explicit what it is about concepts in these areas that renders them objective and sharpens what would be required for, and would explain, legal objectivity: we thus get a clear view of what we must accept in order to embrace *legal* objectivism.

Further, and perhaps more crucially, the adopted strategy makes plain that legal objectivism is a natural position. Under that strategy, the objectivity of legal content is a special case of objectivity of content in general. If the semantic arguments are sound, a presumption in favour of law's content being objective is created. The burden shifts onto non-objectivists to supply new arguments for law being an exception to the rule.[16]

The final motivation for the strategy concerns the K–P framework itself. Both supporters and critics of the authors involved often embrace or reject the framework for the wrong reasons. A full characterization of the framework and the arguments advanced within it is necessary for a serious evaluation of their merit and, ultimately, their applicability to law.

4. SYNOPSIS

This is a fairly long book. The long, detailed summary that follows may well be skipped or skimmed by readers better acquainted with the philosophy of language and mind, and with meta-ethics.

Chapter 2 sets out the alternative semantic framework. It sketches Kripke's theory of proper names, Putnam's theory of natural kinds, and Burge's theory of virtually any common noun. Both Kripke and Putnam attack what they call the traditional theory of reference. That theory holds that an expression refers to whatever fits the description with which speakers associate the expression. The relevant description has the status of analytic truth. It captures necessary properties of the referent which are knowable *a priori*, as in the case of knowing that a bachelor is an unmarried man. This cannot be true, Kripke and Putnam argue, since expressions refer to the same object in the lips of speakers who can only associate the expression with vague or mistaken descriptions. Indeed, not only individual speakers but the community as a whole can be in error about the true properties of the relevant object. One can learn that the properties one thought identified Aristotle or water are not really true of him or it. Yet on the traditional theory the preceding statement would be nonsense: Aristotle, or water, *is* what speakers, or at least the community as a whole, thinks he or it is; it makes no sense to say that the entire community is wrong on that. The important suggestion being made by Kripke and Putnam is that reference is *object-dependent*. *Which* object 'Aristotle' or 'water' refers to is not determined by the associated description, but turns instead on a matter of fact, namely which object the name-using or term-using practice is directed at.[17] So speakers' descriptions 'fix reference', in the sense

[16] By contrast, the Semantic Assumption has the curious result that objectivists have to argue for a semantic exception. I do not mean that making or rejecting the Semantic Assumption is optional for objectivists, bearing only on rhetorical effect. Rather, rejecting the Assumption will result in a different position, a position that is bound to surprise non-objectivists who are used to getting a free ride on the Assumption.

[17] Which object is in fact picked out is given by the most coherent explanation of name-or term-using practice. Note that Kripke and Putnam do not seek to explain the reference *relation* (the relation between expression and object) but the relation between sense and reference.

of indicating the relevant name- or term-using practice, but do not determine it in the sense of picking out the object that fits the description. Further, it is suggested that linguistic competence does not turn on individuals' ability to identify the relevant object, since speakers refer to objects which they cannot really identify. These suggestions are exploited by Burge, who argues that one can coherently cast doubt on commonly accepted truths about the content of ordinary nouns.

The views sketched so far (K–P semantics) work together in undermining the traditional view about the relation between thought and object, which holds that mental pictures 'correspond to' or 'represent' objects.[18] Reference is not (or not wholly) dependent on speakers' identificatory abilities: speakers' representations may be unable to discriminate between different objects, yet their thought and talk nonetheless refers to determinate objects. For example, someone who is unable to discriminate between genuine gold and good fakes (his method simply is: heavy yellow metal) may refer to gold and say something false when he says that a fake is made of gold—it's not the case that, for him, gold is any heavy yellow metal. So the traditional model does not work.

The arguments reviewed in Chapter 2 suggest a different picture of concepts:[19] a concept's content depends on the properties instances of application actually have in common. A characterization of a concept's content is a substantive attempt to specify which properties these are, which is always open to counter-instances that cannot be successfully accounted for. If stripes are proposed as a criterion of the concept of a tiger, it is always possible that some non-striped animals are discovered which we have overwhelming reasons to classify as tigers (say, crucial genetic make up); the animals we so far ignored may force us to think of striped tigers as just one breed of the species. The possibility of counter-instances, then, makes content sensitive to calls for revision and therefore *theoretical*, in the sense that substantive argument in favour of conceptual explications may be required.[20]

With that alternative in place, I provisionally assume that the model holds for legal concepts like contract or equal protection, and a sketch of the content of legal concepts is offered. Crucial evidence for the importance of the hypothesis that the model holds in law is that, if it were true, conceptual room would be made for substantive disagreement over legal concepts, as well as room for judging any understanding of a legal concept to be mistaken (including the legislative understanding). I address possible objections from the non-conventionalist camp, before turning to the major (conventionalist) objections that this account is bound to

[18] McDowell's and Davidson's views are discussed below in this connection.

[19] In Ch. 2 I argue for the proposed interpretations, as well as the compatibility, of the various views discussed.

[20] The alternate picture suggests that the analytic–synthetic distinction is blurred. Within a given structure of concepts whose standard explications go unchallenged, some part of these explications will be 'analytic', in the weak sense that speakers who can be credited with the concepts must know the relevant truths (and they will consider them as *a priori*). Yet a challenge may change that: it may cast doubt on, and call for revision of, any such truth. Note that concept explication is neither purely analytic nor purely synthetic: it concerns words as much as it concerns the world.

attract. The objections from the friendly (non-conventionalist) camp amount to the complaint that to regard semantical questions as the cornerstone of legal reasoning is to present the latter as essentially a matter of classification. The distortions allegedly entailed are that legal reasoning is made to appear mechanical, and law is 'reified', i.e. mysterious legal entities appear to be presupposed, so that controversies, say, over the application of a fairness clause turn on what 'fairness' means. This objection gives me an opportunity to clarify the account of concepts developed in Chapter 1 and preview the issues to be discussed in Chapter 3. First, it is precisely the point of the K–P framework that determining the content of a concept is not a mechanical exercise, but is a complex—theoretical—procedure shot through with evaluative judgments. Second, no commitment to mysterious entities is needed, only commitment to legal *properties*.

Chapter 3 begins discussion of the metaphysical commitments touched upon above. Claiming that K–P semantics can deal with legal concepts may be counter-intuitive. Surely, it may be objected, K–P semantics requires that the relevant expression designate concrete physical objects; it is only under that condition that one may plausibly suggest that reference remains constant across shifts in the knowledge about, and the criteria used to pick out, the referent.

I approach this objection through discussion of H. L. A. Hart's work. A central part of Hart's later writings, and indeed the starting point of his earlier expressions of his views, concerns certain semantic properties of legal concepts. Legal concepts, Hart argues, lack 'empirical counterparts', and are therefore bad candidates for the classical definitional treatment. Further, sentences using legal concepts have an all-important *performative* force. For these two, and other, independent reasons, no set of conditions of application can be given for these concepts: they are 'defeasible' (Hart's earlier formulation) or 'open-ended'.[21]

This block of objections is countered in two steps. First, I show that Hart's distinctions cut across each other. Whether an expression designates concrete or abstract objects is neutral towards the performative force of sentences using it, or its semantic open-endedness (and defeasibility). Second, I argue that Hart's semantic arguments fail and that what Hart counts as evidence for the Criterial Model is better accounted for by the K–P framework, an option that Hart fails to consider because he assumes that the only alternative to the Criterial Model is classical semantics in the definition mould (according to which a concept's application is governed by a set of necessary and sufficient conditions). Further, Hart accepts the assumptions behind the classical model to the extent that he assumes that controversy over the application of a concept is a clear sign that its content is exhausted, so that semantically unconstrained decision is required to resolve controversial cases.

A further attempt to identify the source of resistance to K–P semantics for law is made by considering the objection that K–P semantics is only appropriate for

[21] See chapter 3, section 2, for full references to Hart's work.

expressions designating *natural* objects or properties. Naturalness of the *designatum* is here conceived as 'mind-independence'. It is thought to be crucial since it provides the epistemic distance necessary for the K–P framework. The framework works, on this line of thought, because it is conceivable that discoveries may be made about natural *designata*, given that these form part of a ready-made reality whose nature may or may not be transparent to the inquiring mind. However there is clearly no scope for such discoveries in the case of *designata* that are the 'products of culture', and hence of 'the mind'. And law, *inter alia*, is such a product.

Chapter 4 takes up discussion of the alleged requirement that law should be conceived as mind-independent, in order for the K–P framework to apply. I approach the issue through discussion of ethical or simply evaluative concepts. This approach is both necessary, since in chapter 2 it is argued that substantive evaluative assumptions are involved in identifying concepts' content, and also expedient, since the considerations that ostensibly make law a bad K–P candidate are the same that have been invoked against ethical objectivism.

Chapter 4 discusses the conceptions of subjectivity and objectivity that are used in arguments for and against ethical objectivism. I discuss various forms of the subjectivity allegedly characteristic of ethical concepts (that ethical concepts are human artifacts; that they are emotive reactions to situations or events factually described; that they are mental projections on such facts), and I argue that they all face the dilemma of either rendering ethical judgment unintelligible or accepting that ethical judgment is principled. There is no clear way to distinguish the latter horn from the objectivist position, since objectivism only requires that ethical judgment be constrained, and it concludes that it is constrained by genuine properties. If the sceptic insists that mind-dependent properties cannot be genuine, despite their role as constraints, then the dispute appears to lose content. We do not know what distinguishes application of ethical concepts constrained by 'non-genuine' properties from application of natural-kind concepts constrained by 'genuine properties'. We know, of course, what distinguishes the two kinds of properties, namely that the former, unlike the latter, are conceptually connected with human responses. The challenge, however, to the subjectivist is still to explain how this connection makes ethical properties less respectable.

I argue that objectivism is consistent with dependence of ethical concepts on culture. I argue that this dependence cannot support the kind of global scepticism about ethics which subjectivists assume. This is not to say that the possibility of 'selective scepticism' is disallowed; that possibility is crucial to objectivism. Further, the epistemology of ethics requires no queer special faculties but only the combination of the usual sensory faculties with ordinary intellectual abilities to group similar things together. The absence of convergence in ethical judgment need not be explained by cultural background, in a way that would make ethical knowledge impossible, but may be explained in terms of the fact that ethical judgment, like all other judgment, may be erroneous, i.e. that ethical disagreement may be substantive. Ethical error *is* explicable in terms of cultural background in the light of certain substantive assumptions about what kind of background is bad for the acquisition of true ethical beliefs. The assumptions are themselves ethical, but no damaging circularity need arise, as long as the ethical assumptions that explain failure to acquire the right ethical beliefs are relatively independent of the content of the belief they are supposed to explain.

In Chapters 3 and 4 I try to show that very little metaphysical and epistemological commitment is necessary for objectivism in the non-natural domain. More specifically, nothing counter-intuitive need be accepted for objectivism in domains dependent on social practice, and there is no special reason to exclude law from this. Chapter 5 moves into discussion of the possibility of substantive disagreement in law. I discuss Dworkin's theory and an objection levelled against it by Joseph Raz. Raz claims that if the law's content could be the object of substantive disagreement, then the law would be radically indeterminate.[22] The dilemma underlying Raz's objection—conventional constraints or else indeterminacy—presupposes the necessity of indubitable, foundational, contents. This presupposition is distinct from the claim that there are easy cases, which is a truism. The presupposition has to do with what *makes* a case easy. It assumes that determinacy can only be the result of aprioricity, of immunity to revision. I criticize this assumption, routinely relied upon in legal theory, in the preceding Chapters, where I show it to be at least highly contentious. A version of the assumption, namely that conventional constraints are necessary, is often attributed to Wittgenstein. I discuss the ostensibly Wittgensteinian arguments, by now familiar in legal theory.[23] I argue that the Wittgensteinian considerations do not in fact support a conventionalist 'solution'—conceiving content as determined by communal agreement—but rather undermine the picture of content that creates the danger of indeterminacy and accordingly requires such a 'solution'. I interpret Wittgenstein's insistence on practices constraining concepts' application, as a rejection of external scepticism and a conception of concepts' application as grounded in substantive argument, rather than conventional arrangement.

Scepticism remains at issue in the rest of the essay. Chapter 6 continues the discussion of problems with the interdependence between practices and concepts' content, illustrating the ability of the apparatus developed in the preceding Chapters to handle well-known problems in legal theory. The discussion mostly concerns how *not* to conceive practice–concept interdependence.[24] First, Stanley Fish's efforts at a description of practices as conceptual boundaries are discussed. Fish's work is interesting by virtue of his apparent insistence on a pragmatist

[22] Raz's objection is distinguished from objections by many other theorists, which completely miss the point.

[23] No attempt at identifying what Wittgenstein actually thought is made; the discussion is confined to evaluation of arguments, variously attributed to Wittgenstein, on their merits.

[24] The general conclusion which Ch. 6 seeks to establish is already suggested in the preceding Chapters: that the interdependence has no interesting consequences, except for discouraging the image of concepts 'matching' reality.

conception of legal interpretation, despite avoiding the facile reduction of boundaries to communal agreement. It is argued that no pragmatist position is available to Fish, and indeed that his 'pragmatist' polemics are better thought of as restatements of law's dependence on social practices addressed to a type of 'realist' who ignores this dependence and conceives objectivity as 'correspondence to independent facts'. Fish's arguments provide an opportunity for sharpening the notion of practice-constraints.

Michael Moore's objection to practice-dependence is next addressed. Moore claims that such dependence results in 'discourse autonomy', i.e. immunity of claims made within each discourse from criticism coming from other discourses. Moore's paradigmatic worry is that, say, scientific progress on 'death' may be ignored by legal practice, on the strength of the alleged autonomy. In response to this objection, I argue that practices' boundaries are articulated *on the basis* of such challenges. A challenge to judicial understanding of death is *ipso facto* part of legal practice. Generally, the criterion on which a claim is judged to be internal or external is a substantive one: it is whether a claim engages and is competitive with claims that are admitted to be within the relevant domain.

A further objection (which I show to be the corollary of the autonomy objection) is that making practice-individuation a substantive matter endangers law's autonomy. The objection is sharpened by the following thought: since law may be identified, on the above suggestion, by the *concepts* it uses, rather than by the legislative or other conceptions of them, it may always be the case that the boundary between law and one's preferred morality will be eradicated. One's views may always be argued to be internal to law: to be a better interpretation of the relevant concepts. Law will then collapse to ideal law.

This objection is a form of indeterminacy objection that may survive the preceding arguments against indeterminacy. It trades on the perceived fuzziness of the distinction between concept and conception, i.e. on the inability to supply an *a priori* criterion demarcating cases of competitive conceptions of a concept from cases of discourse on different concepts. In response, it is pointed out that that very inability is a central part, rather than an unfortunate consequence, of K–P theory. It is the flip-side of arguing that the analytic–synthetic distinction is blurred.[25] K–P theory claims that the crucial distinction is *substantively* drawn, and the demand for a stipulative or analytic criterion is no new argument against the theory. I discuss different examples that illustrate how the distinction may be drawn in practice.

In sum, practice-dependence does not support 'discourse autonomy' in any alarming sense; yet that is not to say that the law's authority is breached, say, by allowing extraneous considerations to replace law proper. The boundaries between law, morality, and other discourses, and therefore the distinction between applying the law and 'inventing' new law, are fixed by substantive considerations, rather by

[25] See n. 20, and accompanying text.

an *a priori* criterion. Saying that, for example, the morality of individual responsibility bears on the law of tort, or that the medical conception of death does not so bear, are both substantive propositions about what the law is, and must be judged on their merits. To put it differently, the 'thesis' that the law is distinct from science, ethics or whatever is a truism that supplies no test for judging whether any specific claim respects the distinction. But this should be no cause for concern; the notion that respectable distinctions should only be based on *a priori* criteria is a philosophical prejudice.

Finally, I address the charge of conservatism. That objection amounts to the claim that the thesis that applications of legal concepts may be guided by past practice even where such application is controversial tends to perpetuate injustices sustained by the law in certain regimes, ignoring the opportunity for reform afforded by the discretion doctrine traditionally associated with positivism. The objection depends on the assumption that there can be no law where it is controversial what the law is. If that assumption is correct, deciding in the way most consistent with past applications will amount to choosing, for no legally compulsory reason, one among several options of deciding the case. But that assumption is what really divides the objector and his target. The thesis that the application of concepts is guided by past practice, controversy notwithstanding, entails that, in controversial cases, deciding on the basis of past practice is required by the law. If that is true, one can only be non-conservative by *pretending* there is no law, a course of action on which the thesis is neutral. So no new issue is joined here between the objector and his target: the issue still is whether there is law when it is controversial what the law is.

2

The Semantic Framework

1. INTRODUCTION

In this Chapter I shall discuss the framework within philosophy of language that I consider to be helpful in illuminating issues in the theory of legal interpretation. The rough overall claim through the entire essay is that the application of concepts is sensitive to theory. The arguments in the philosophy of language to be considered will support this overall claim, by showing that theory must explain and justify a concept's past application—its use—through substantive claims about what property the concept picks out, and how that property's nature determines further applications. For example, theory is used to explain and justify the use of 'gold' by explaining actual instances of application, e.g. claiming that they were all applied to samples of gold, as well as counterfactual cases e.g. claiming that the word would not be applied to material that simply looks like gold. Theory, therefore, guides future applications, e.g. claiming that the word should be applied to this or that instance of gold, i.e. the stuff identified by some chemical properties. 'Theory' here is meant not as a body of formal or abstract reasoning, but rather as a set of substantive claims amenable to argument. Notice that theory will be relevant *whatever* the property picked out by the concept is, whether complex and difficult to identify, or simple and identifiable by everyone.[1] What matters is that *which* property is involved is understood to be a substantive issue.

These arguments, by establishing the relevance of theory in the semantics of concepts, will make conceptual room for, and explain, error in concepts' use. Given that one of my principal aims is to undermine the view that concepts' correct application turns on conventional or stipulative conditions, I shall be emphasizing, perhaps excessively, the possibility of being both competent in, and in error about, the use of a concept.[2]

[1] For example, if the application of 'painy' is (on the best theory) governed by how a surface feels, then that theory will be claiming that what it is for something to feel so (induce pain) is determined by the unreflective activity of establishing a surface's production of the relevant tactile impression.

[2] Again, this claim should be qualified to allow for concepts whose application turns on purely phenomenological considerations where perhaps error will not be possible. See note 1.

Concepts are thought of as 'mediating between thought and the world'. The main way in which the following arguments support the relevance of theory is by highlighting the importance of (natural and social) context in the determination of content.[3] The contrast to be drawn here is not between context and the way context is represented, but rather between context and context-independent pictures or representations.

Exhaustive discussion of the issues surrounding determination of concepts' content cannot be undertaken here. Rather, this Chapter's purpose is to canvass several considerations that should at least make the philosophical framework plausible. At its weakest, the exposition should try for a tolerably clear characterization of a position which, if sound, would have the implications suggested.

I shall begin in section 2 by concentrating on Kripke's arguments on the semantics of names. The importance of Kripke's analysis is that, by attacking what he calls the classical theory of the semantics of names, he identifies some key weaknesses in the *general* (i.e. not only relating to names) classical picture. The quickest way to state Kripke's argument is that it succeeds in driving a wedge between the meaning of a name—what someone need grasp in order to understand the name—and a method of identification of the bearer. Kripke offers several types of argument against the classical picture. Among these, his modal argument is the most obscure, and widely thought to be inconclusive. Not much emphasis need be placed on that type of argument; I nonetheless sketch it since it is valuable in interpreting Kripke's misgivings with the classical view. I then proceed to his epistemic argument, and his practice-based account. The last part of section 2 considers the cases of empty names and failures of substitution of co-extensive names.

In section 3 I discuss Putnam's generalization of the argument to the domain of natural kinds, and the notion of sensitivity to substantive theory in the use of natural kind terms. I then introduce, in section 4, Burge's generalization of the argument to cases of virtually any common noun. I construe all these theories as arguing against theories of meanings that centre on (intrinsically meaningful, self-interpreting) mental configurations as the locus of conceptual content.

Section 5 directly addresses the problems involved in such theories in the light of the arguments offered so far, as well as McDowell's and Davidson's arguments against the possibility of deriving content from intrinsic mental materials. A further version of that argument, namely a Wittgensteinian type of argument to the effect that such materials cannot guard against radical indeterminacy, is postponed for a later chapter.

Section 6 discusses theoretical concepts and, in particular, the possibility of distinguishing between ascription of wrong beliefs about the same concept and

[3] I shall be using 'context' interchangeably with 'environment'. 'Context' may have a technical sense, on which it is used to demarcate indexical expressions, i.e. those whose extension varies across different circumstances of use, like 'here'. Whether the expressions with which I am concerned are such is a matter to be discussed below.

ascription of a different concept, a possibility which depends on charitable assumptions. Section 7 sketches an account of legal concepts analogous to the account of natural kinds, and introduces different objections that would purport to block the analogy. Finally, section 8 discusses a possible objection to the effect that conceiving legal questions as questions of 'classification' of events or states of affairs under legal concepts distorts the nature of legal reasoning.

2. KRIPKE ON NAMES

Kripke's *Naming and Necessity* attacks the 'classical theory' of the semantics of proper names.[4] The classical theory holds that the sense of an expression consists in a set of descriptions of properties ('set of properties', for simplicity) forming a concept grasped by a speaker; the referent of the expression is whatever uniquely satisfies, or fits best, that set of properties.[5] Hence the expression refers indirectly, via the set of properties constituting the relevant concept, which operate as criteria, i.e. identify the referent. If the classical theory is applied to the case of names, we should expect that a set of properties associated with the bearer of the name should operate as conditions of identification: the bearer will be whoever satisfies the properties. For instance, 'Aristotle' should refer to whoever was born in Stageira, went to Plato's academy, wrote the *Nicomachean Ethics*, and so forth. Given that the properties usually involve other names, we should expect that they should be further analysable and so restatable in descriptive terms which do not involve names. The end result should be general conditions.

A further point, to be taken up later, is that the properties should be specified in terms of object-independent mental materials. This requirement results from the fact that the classical picture aspires to an account of the relation of reference itself. A full picture of reference cannot but involve the bottom-line account of the relation of thought to objects; accounts not meeting this requirement will to some extent presuppose reference. The theory of names comes as an extension of the basic theory thus derived, charting its consequences in the relevant domain.

[4] Clearly 'classical theory' is a heuristic term for a cluster of ideas with wide currency. I shall not enter the debates concerning who actually held the theory thus characterized, although I shall consider variations of the theory where Kripke's arguments seem to attack a claim someone could disown. See G. Evans, *The Varieties of Reference*, for a defence of Frege as able to accommodate Kripke's critique (with an unsympathetic reading of Kripke); J. McDowell, 'On the Sense and Reference of a Proper Name', *86 Mind*, 159–85, and 'Singular Thought and the Extent of Inner Space' *in* Pettit P. and McDowell J. (eds.), *Subject, Thought, and Context*, for a similar reading of Frege while endorsing Kripke's arguments; N. Salmon, *Reference and Essence*, for distinctions within the classical camp. The last two authors clearly show that Kripke's target is real.

[5] The 'best fit' variant purports to capture the idea that the criteria do not consist in a conjunction of properties, but a 'cluster': in that case the bearer is whatever meets most of the conditions. Nothing in the argument, however, depends on the bearer's meeting all conditions: the argument purports to establish that the bearer is not identified through the criterial mechanism at all.

2.1 Modal Contexts

The best known way to state Kripke's misgivings about the classical theory is in terms of rigidity. A rigid designator is an expression which designates the same object in all possible worlds in which it exists. A flexible designator is an expression which may designate different objects in different possible worlds. 'Possible worlds' should be understood as counterfactual states of affairs. For example: in the counterfactual case in which Aristotle was born in Athens, the expression 'the great Stageirite philosopher' designates some person other than Aristotle, whereas the expression 'Aristotle' designates Aristotle. For any property which we apparently associate with 'Aristotle' we may imagine some counterfactual case in which it would yield the wrong referent: we can coherently imagine, that is, counterfactual states of affairs in which Aristotle did not have the relevant property, but someone else did, so that the property will in fact identify that other person. The point is (better) put in terms of truth conditions: the sentence

Aristotle was fond of dogs

is true if and only if (iff) Aristotle was fond of dogs, i.e. if *Aristotle* was fond of dogs in *any* —actual or counterfactual—circumstances. By contrast, the truth conditions of

the great Stageirite philosopher was fond of dogs

involve the great Stageirite philosopher (the sentence is true iff the great Stageirite philosopher was fond of dogs), which may or may not be the same conditions as those of the first sentence. They are the same in actual, yet diverge in some counterfactual, circumstances: in the case that Aristotle never went into philosophy, the second sentence's truth will depend on whether someone else (whoever was a great Stageirite philosopher except Aristotle) was fond of dogs.

Possible worlds are frequently thought of as ontologically suspect entities and consequently some objections have been entered against Kripke's notion of rigidity. I shall consider one to get it out of the way. A possible world in which Kripke would claim that Aristotle was not born in Stageira, did not go to Plato's academy etc., should really be conceived as a world which contains an individual who meets several, but not all, of the conditions actually specifying Aristotle; it is then a further question whether that man is really Aristotle, and Kripke is just assuming what he is supposed to establish.

The objection is mistaken. Possible worlds exercises are thought—experiments that help to establish how expressions behave semantically—they belong with reflecting on the way some expressions are *actually* used.[6] What contents possible

[6] This point is not new. Strawson writes in defence of his thought-experiments in *Individuals*, at 86, that '[they] are not constructed for the purpose of speculation about what would happen in certain remote contingencies. . . . They are models against which to test and strengthen our own reflective understanding of our own conceptual structure'.

worlds have depends solely on how we specify them. If we imagine a situation such that Aristotle never went to Plato's academy, we are *ipso facto* considering Aristotle not having gone to the academy: no procedure of identification is involved. By contrast, if we specify the counterfactual situation qualitatively, say, by imagining a man who has certain properties (which actually are true of Aristotle), then we do have to answer the further question: who is that person? That a question remains in the latter case in fact supports Kripke's claim that there are semantic dysanalogies between names and sets of predicates.

The dysanalogy may be sharpened through the following formula:

. . . might not have been . . . [7]

The possible world exercises concerning Aristotle above can be captured by inserting 'Aristotle' on the left-hand side and any property that could be proposed as identifying him on the right-hand side. For most properties one can think of as identifying Aristotle, the schema will be true, e.g. 'Aristotle might not have been Plato's star pupil', 'Aristotle might not have been the author of the Nicomachean Ethics', etc. This will be so irrespective of what scope we give to the contingency ('might not have been') operator. Both 'it might have not been the case that [Aristotle was Plato's star pupil]' and 'Aristotle [might have not been Plato's star pupil'] are true. On the classical theory, we should not expect this result. We should rather expect that the counterfactuals would be contradictory, since the schema should be equivalent with either:

Aristotle might have not been Aristotle

which is always false and indeed contradictory under both scope interpretations, or

p_i might have not been p_i

where p_i stands for the identifying property or properties. In fact, the latter case would yield a contradiction under one reading ('it might have not been the case that [Plato's star pupil was Plato's star pupil]'), although it may come out true by restricting the scope of the operator: 'Plato's star pupil [might not have been Plato's star pupil]'. Unlike names, then, the descriptive properties are scope-sensitive. What does the difference amount to?

Scope-sensitivity can be understood as follows: in the case of descriptive properties, the counterfactual exercises may be conceived in two ways. First, we may stipulate our domain as 'consider the author of the *Nicomachean Ethics*', and further say something about him,say, 'he was a great philosopher'. Second, we may

[7] I am using a variant of the formula proposed by Colin McGinn as a 'tidied up' version of Kripke's semantic test. See 'Rigid Designation and Semantic Value', *32 Phil. Q.*, 107–15, 108.

The spelling 'dysanalogy', rather than the more common 'disanalogy' is used deliberately, 'Dis-', whose Greek equivalent is, I believe, 'dia-', seems to me to do with standing apart, opposition, or contrast, as in 'distinction' or 'disengagement'. The Greek 'dys-', on the other hand, whose Latin equivalent is, I believe, 'mal-', is to do with ill-fitting, substandard function, and the like, as in 'malfunction' or 'malnutrition'. It seems to me that 'dysanalogy' does not stand for lack of analogy, but rather with non-perfect analogy. I do not know whether the OED includes that spelling.

stipulate our domain qualitatively, i.e. 'consider a situation in which there exists something with the property of being the author of the *Nicomachean Ethics*', and accordingly say something of him, say 'that person is a great philosopher'. In the first case, the domain is clearly stipulated as consisting of the *actual* author: the property is *indexed* to the real world. Then, given that the property succeeds in referring to its actual object (Aristotle), we may proceed to attribute whatever counterfactual property we may wish.[8] In the second case the property will refer *to the counterfactual author*, and the truth of our attribution will depend on who that is: we need to know who is identified by the property. (Note that one thing that cannot be the case is that he was not the author of the *Ethics*.)

In the case of name-involving counterfactuals, no such distinction is available: both ways of stipulating the domain will yield Aristotle in it—the name rigidly designates whoever it does. The difference identified here between names and descriptive properties is that the latter *may* be rigidified, but only through indexing to the actual world. Is the difference important?

The difference would not help Kripke refute the classical view, if he were required to prove that *no* descriptive property may be rigid, i.e. always succeed in designating its object in counterfactual situations. For we have seen that, after all, a rigidified description will manage to do just that. But the sort of rigidified (indexed) description involved here does not seem to be the kind envisaged by the classical theory. On the classical theory we should expect reference to the name's bearer to be effected *through* some conditions. We should expect that a qualitative specification should manage to pick out the bearer by itself. There are two ways in which the indexed-property solution diverges from the classical picture.

The first will be briefly discussed here, and will be taken up again at a later stage. On a rather abstract level, the requirement seems that, for the classical picture to work, the relevant properties must be such as to be available without the need to attend to objects at all; on that interpretation of the requirement, the basic question addressed by the classical theory concerns the relation of thought to objects, and the proposed solution must supply an account of how 'purely conceptual' properties relate to objects: they relate to whatever, if anything, answers to the conditions set in those 'purely conceptual' properties.[9] Empirical investigation concerning what objects there are and what they are made of is meant to come at a conceptually later stage (if at all), so that, notably, some thoughts will lack an object, without that making them any different from others (those for which the world obliges by supplying an object that complies with the relevant conditions). The 'actual F' specification in effect helps itself to objects: it uses an account of what properties someone actually has. It analyses reference as a relation between object-involving properties and objects, whereas the original task was to

[8] In that case, we may sensibly say of him counterfactually that he did not write the *Ethics*.

[9] Recall that 'purely conceptual' roughly stands for properties whose content is not in any way object-dependent: they are 'ideas' or 'representations', i.e. mental entities entirely independent of the extra-mental realm.

analyse it in terms of object-independent contents and objects. The 'actual F' model abandons the classical project, as is illustrated by the following consequence. If names designate by way of their sense conceived as indexed properties, it is hard to see how bearerless names are to be treated: either they have no sense (there is no actual F) or they acquire their sense otherwise. But it is certainly central to the classical view not only that they have sense, but that they do in the same way as the standard cases.

The second divergence of the indexed-property solution is that it picks the referent, yet the referent need not comply with the conditions. More precisely, the properties are not conditions of identity. The way the property picks out its referent is such that the properties do not attach to the bearer: the bearer need only contingently have them. Actually, the rigidity of the indexed property is brought about by leaving it open whether the object need have those properties: the actual author of the *Nicomachean Ethics* need not be (might not have been) the author of the *Nicomachean Ethics*. Hence, 'the actual author of the Nicomachean Ethics' does not mean the same as 'the author of the *Nicomachean Ethics*'. Accepting, therefore, that the rigidified description refers to whoever the name itself refers to, the referent is not conceptually tied to some particular properties. Denying that names are 'synonymous' with the description, even though the description can be used to pick out the referent, is a result more important than sometimes thought: it exactly establishes that the way reference is effected to names' bearers may well be neutral to any properties the referent may have.[10]

The thesis that reference is neutral with respect to any property may be challenged along the following lines: reference is neutral with respect to inessential properties typically employed by speakers. We can imagine those away, the objection continues, but we can surely not imagine away essential properties like 'the person issuing from this sperm and that ovum' (assuming we independently identify the content of that condition). So at most Kripke has proven the obvious: that some properties are contingent.

Again, we may distinguish between the qualitative and the indexed construals of the essential condition. In the first case, if the essential property manages to pick out Aristotle in all counterfactual situations, it will be as a result of what we consider as a matter of fact, on the strength of a particular theory: it is our views concerning the metaphysics of persons that compel us (assuming we accept the property as essential) to accept that any possible world which contains what issues from a particular sperm and ovum contains the very same individual. So counterfactually speculating that the issue of that sperm and ovum did not write the

[10] This is not to say that thinking about the object is possible without any knowledge about it, or that names do not have senses, to mention some easy misconceptions of Kirpke's argument. What sort of knowledge is necessary and sufficient will be discussed below. The point here is that an essential property need not be one a speaker must associate with the name, in order to be deemed competent.

Nicomachean Ethics is speculating that Aristotle did not write them, only assuming our theory of essentials is correct.[11] By contrast, possible worlds that are specified by means of an indexed version of the property ('consider the actual issue of that sperm and ovum') or by using the name ('consider Aristotle') contain the bearer anyway—as a matter of semantic rules—independent of any particular theory of identity. 'Consider Aristotle' is non-committal on what it is for someone to *be* Aristotle—it refers to him *whatever the right theory is.* This is why we normally permissibly say 'Aristotle might have been a cat', which we may find false, on the strength of our views on essential properties, rather than contradictory. But the very fact that we find this speculation false is proof that the name and the indexed description do refer to the bearer, albeit they attribute to him something unacceptable, in our view.

In sum, Kripke's modal arguments suggest that names necessarily refer to (rigidly designate) their bearers as a matter of semantic rules. The rules involved are such that sentences involving names refer to the bearer independent of any circumstances of evaluation: they always do. Descriptive properties also refer to their object as a matter of semantic rules, but only at the price of giving up the specified properties' status as conditions of identification (as in 'the actual author of the *Ethics*') or deriving their identificatory status by substantive theories of essentials.

Kripke's modal arguments should be best seen as registering and confirming through counterfactual thought-experiments a semantic observation, namely that reference of proper names is guaranteed independent of identifying properties. This observation suggests that using names need not be accompanied by an ability to identify bearers. If this is true, it seriously undermines the traditional theory. On this reading of Kripke's project, the modal arguments are *evidence* for the inadequacy of the traditional theory, yet evidence that could perhaps be accommodated otherwise. To evaluate the evidence, then, we need to turn to Kripke's epistemic arguments, which directly deal with what someone must know in order to use a name successfully, and argue for the crucial thesis: that ability to identify the name's bearer in the way defended by the classical theory is dispensable.

2.2 Epistemic Contexts

If the referent of a name is whoever satisfies the conditions expressed in the descriptive properties speakers associate with the name, then these properties must have the status of *a priori* truths: the conditions should have the status of stipulation. But in fact the properties normally associated have the status of *a*

[11] Suppose that there exist spiritual entities that identify a person, which may be embodied in any animal. In that case, the speculation will not necessarily be about Aristotle; we shall have to ask whether any other animals containing the crucial entity are also in the domain of consideration, in which case the person issuing from the relevant ovum and sperm will take us to the wrong individual.

posteriori empirical truths, e.g. it is a matter of empirical knowledge that Aristotle wrote the *Nicomachean Ethics.*[12]

There are further problems with what speakers need know. Firstly, speakers do not normally have descriptions which would identify the referent uniquely. 'Cicero', in Kripke's example, is usually associated with being some famous Roman orator. Even those who can list a few books by Aristotle usually run into a circularity: the books are identified as 'Aristotle's books'. Second, there may be an indeterminate number of descriptions none of which seem to have any special connection with the bearer, e.g. London is the largest city in the vicinity of Slough.[13] Rather more importantly, descriptions may be false, and in fact one is generally prepared to admit that one's information concerning the name's bearer is a misdescription of him. In all these cases, reference does not fail: *it is the name's bearer* that one has vague, trivial or mistaken beliefs about. On the classical picture, nonetheless, one should expect that the descriptions should take us to no referent or to the wrong referent. To illustrate the case of error: assuming that 'Gödel' is always associated with the property 'the prover of the incompleteness of arithmetic', there seems to be a distinct possibility expressible as 'Schmidt, not Gödel, really proved incompleteness of arithmetic'. But on the classical theory, this thought makes no sense: Gödel picks out the prover of the incompleteness of arithmetic. Then the intuitively sensible discovery seems to entail that 'Gödel' refers to Schmidt. (If arithmetic is in fact complete, 'Gödel' seems to refer to no one.) This absurdity is a consequence of the function of descriptions in the classical picture, namely to act as blueprints standing for whatever complies with the specifications contained in them.

The obvious move that promises to neutralize these objections is to socialize the picture. Under this version, individual speakers have the ability to refer to the name's bearer derivatively, even, that is, if they are themselves ignorant or mistaken. They derive that ability by relying on authoritative speakers in the community.[14]

This line of response fails. We must distinguish between two ways in which individual speakers may draw on communal criteria. The first would take the form of a chain: a speaker refers to the object that conforms to the criteria employed by whoever the speaker got the name from. The second scenario would make the speaker's ability to refer derive from other speakers who are in a position of epistemic authority, whoever these are.

In the first case, to be faithful to the idea that reference is effected through identifying descriptions, the speaker's description at any point in the chain must

[12] This problem could be possibly overcome in a socialized picture on which speakers derive the descriptions of the properties they employ from the relevant experts who enjoy epistemic authority over who the referent is. Consequently, normal speakers know the conditions by testimony and thus know *a priori* that whatever the experts tell them is true. See below for discussion of the socialized version.

[13] Cf. McCulloch, *The Game of the Name*, 274; Ch. 8 of that book makes some of the points discussed here.

[14] See n. 12.

contain reference to the source—the speaker at a higher link. This second order reference to the source of information must not be by name: it must be analysable into further chains (if chains are to be a general means of referring). We will not have gone very far if we analyse the reference of 'Aristotle' in the lips of John as 'whoever fits the criteria Fred associates with the name'; we must analyse 'Fred' in a similar way. Further, the chains involved must be such that the criteria employed do not become vague or mistaken again at any point along the chain, nor become circular by referring back to links in the opposite direction (as in 'Fred is whoever John got his information from'). It should be rather implausible to credit speakers with the vast amount of information involved in such a chain.

The second scenario looks more promising, since it does not require excessive specification of the derivation links, yet it too fails: for the experts may themselves be wrong. The following seems to be a distinct possibility: it may be discovered that Aristotle did not in fact write the *Nicomachean Ethics* (suppose this is his only achievement), but Alexander did. But if the experts' criteria for 'Aristotle' are 'the author of the *Nicomachean Ethics*', then the criteria will take us to Alexander. (We will not be able, furthermore, to state the fact that Aristotle did not write the book, since we will be contradicting ourselves.) Generally, whatever solution depends on the bearer's being whoever fits some particular identifying property will be vulnerable to this sort of objection.

Finally, apparently trivial criteria may be proposed: 'the person who is *called* Aristotle';[15] 'the person who experts *think* did such and such'. These specifications cannot be the bottom-line of reference, since they rely on some other method of referring. In the first case calling someone a name requires referring to him. The criterion may work only along the 'actual F' model, the rigidified description discussed above. In the second case, an independent criterion of identifying the bearer is required.

The most important element in the epistemic arguments concerns the role of discoveries about the referent. Such discoveries are always possible and affect the role of information possessed by speakers. Use of a name by speakers who possess incomplete or erroneous information does not result in indeterminate or erroneous reference. The referent of the name is the same as in the case of knowledgeable speakers: we want to say that the mistaken or ignorant speakers have the wrong beliefs about *Aristotle*. The knowledgeable speaker himself, nonetheless, 'stands corrected': he may find out that he did not know enough, or was in error. So even for him his information does not operate as a blueprint: it does not determine the reference of the name.[16]

[15] Note, nonetheless, that Aristotle might not have been called 'Aristotle'.

[16] Cf. Tyler Burge, 'Wherein Is Language Social', *in* George, A. (ed.), *Reflections on Chomsky*, 180.

2.3 Practice, Empty Names, Substitution

Kripke's own account involves reliance on a name-using practice which combines elements of the two socialized versions discussed above. First, it involves a chain from users to the initial persons involved in the 'act of baptism', i.e. in the introduction of the practice of using a name to refer to some individual. Yet Kripke's transmission of the name is devoid of epistemic considerations: the name refers to whoever it refers to, and users need not know anything about those from whom they acquired the name. Of course, speakers are introduced to the name-using practice by learning some facts about the bearer and forming beliefs about him. But the beliefs are useful only in connection with locating the relevant practice and are not held to express properties that necessarily figure in a set of criteria for identification of the bearer (and that holds also for the beliefs of the original users of the name): they help in 'fixing the reference' but do not supply the meaning of the name.[17]

It has been objected that Kripke's chains should be conceived as totally empty of content: they are simply causal. Hence Kripke would count one's using a name overheard in the pub as proper use.[18] But this is not necessary: we need not, as a result of the above arguments, deny that competence in the use of a name involves having beliefs about the name or being able to use the name in a way that makes sense within the community.[19] On the strength of the above arguments, the notion of 'ways of thinking' about the object is not disallowed: any minimum requirements regarding ways of thinking about the name's bearer has not been touched upon so far. In fact, Kripke allows for rather rich contents as contributing to 'reference fixing', as noted above, (while he doubts that anything more than 'that man' or something to that effect is necessary).[20] Rather, we should see the arguments as directed against the idea that the contents (thoughts, beliefs) available to competent users need amount to *methods for determining* the relevant object.[21]

[17] Note that Kripke accepts the existence of so-called 'descriptive names'—names that are introduced via identifying descriptions—as in the case of the planet Neptune whose name was introduced to refer to whatever caused the disturbances of other planets before its existence was actually confirmed. Yet Kripke insists that the properties by which the object is picked do not thereby become synonymous with the name (since new discoveries may prove them false). See *Naming and Necessity*, 96 n.

Note further that Kripke's chains are of chains of reference *transmission*; in cvontrast with the classical model, they are not supposed to explain the reference relation between the name and the bearer.

[18] Evans, *The Varieties of Reference*, 73–6. The example comes from his earlier 'The Causal Theory of Names', in *Collected Essays*, at 6–7.

[19] Cf. Kripke, *Naming and Necessity*, 96.

[20] Note that 'that man' involves ostension with a disambiguating sortal. Given that Kripke is committed to the thesis that no contents attributed to the bearer need be the right contents (that is, as a matter of semantic rules; Kripke holds that some contents need be true of the bearer as a matter of the metaphysics of identity), the sortal could possibly be the wrong one. Cf. the case of 'the morning star' for Phosphorus, where the object is actually a planet (Venus), Kripke, *Naming and Necessity*, 115 n.

[21] For a detailed defence of a reading of the type outlined here see McDowell, 'On the Sense and Reference of a Proper Name' and 'Singular Thought and the Extent of Inner Space'.

Kripke says very little about either the traditional notion of sense—except negatively, i.e. saying what it is not—or about what is required for the original determination of reference (the baptism) to work. His apparent hostility to the notion of sense, nonetheless, should be interpreted as hostility towards *a particular conception of it.*

Recall that the target of Kripke's critique is a conception of how thought relates to objects, according to which the object of thought is whatever satisfies a specification constructed out of object-independent mental materials.[22] Kripke's arguments suggest an alternative conception according to which, in McDowell's words, 'what matters is not the object's fitting some specification in the content of the thought but its standing in some suitable contextual relation to the episode of thinking'.[23] The crucial contextual relation in Kripke's picture is, as regards normal users, principally the relation to the social context, but as regards 'baptizers' it is principally the relation to the natural context.[24]

Kripke is often taken to suggest that the contextual alternative proposed is meant to deny the relevance of thought and *in its place* offer an 'external' determinant of referent in the strong sense of an 'external' picture of the reference relation itself. (Hence Rorty's protests at the 'new transcendentalism').[25] But to slide from the fact that Kripke resists the specification-fitting model of thought to a belief that he denies the relevance of the content of thought (in the area of names' reference at least) rests on the assumption that thought could be involved only by way of the specification model.

McDowell has convincingly shown that this assumption is not compulsory. A strong motivation for equating the requirement that thought be involved in names' reference to the requirement that it be involved in the form of an object-independent blueprint lies in the need to accommodate cases where there is no object at all, yet a speaker appears to have object-directed beliefs. A further motivation lies in the case of failures of substitution, where a speaker will refuse to substitute 'Phosphorus' for 'Hesperus' or 'Cicero' for 'Tully' in expressing beliefs about them.

Consider the case of a bearerless name. Here the argument seems to be the following: since we may express sensible thoughts using bearerless names, their content cannot have anything to do with objects at all (*ex hypothesi* there is no object). So, the argument goes, the content of the thought must here consist in

[22] May we extend Kripke's arguments on language to thought? *Pace* Evans, if concepts involved in thought are individuated by their meanings, then Kripke's points should cover thought as well. See McGinn, *Mental Content*, 31. Evans's objections are expressed ch. 3 of *The Varieties of Reference*.

[23] 'Singular Thought and the Extent of Inner Space', 162.

[24] 'Principally': typical users stand in a contextual relation to the natural environment indirectly, with respect to names they are deferentially using; the baptizers stand in a similar relation to the social environment by exercising essentially social conceptual capacities which are, on McDowell's picture, constitutively related to their having thoughts or even becoming acquainted with the name's bearer.

[25] See Rorty, *Philosophy and the Mirror of Nature*, ch. 6 and esp. pp. 284–95; and McDowell's critique, 'Singular Thought and the Extent of Inner Space'.

some mental blueprint; hence the object's existing is not a necessary requirement; therefore in the standard case too the thought can be conceived as self-interpreting, and it may or may not correspond to some object that meets the blueprint's specification.[26]

This reasoning fails to consider a third option: conceiving thought in the empty case as an illusion of a thought. We can insist that standing in a contextual relation to the object is a necessary feature for object-directed thought, by specifying that relation so as to allow for the possibility of error. If one is in such error (falsely believes that he stands in such a relation with some object), one will form illusory beliefs (about non-existent objects).

Of course, introducing the possibility of illusion will only recast the problem in terms of the content of perceptual experience: just as, concerning the content of object-related thought, the 'highest common factor' of both the empty and the standard case, viz. the content of the empty case, was conceived as exhausting thought, making the object's occurrence a further fact; exactly in the same way, the highest common factor of veridical and illusory experience, viz. the content of illusory experience, will be conceived as exhausting the content of perceptual experience, making veridicality a further fact. So the blueprint conception may be defended along the following lines: surely in the empty case the subject is under the illusion of being, or having been, in the presence of an object; but precisely because the question of the occurrence of the object takes us outside the subject's mind, it is irrelevant for our purposes, namely characterizing the content of thought; and the content of thought is to do only with appearances. But let us grant for the moment that illusory and veridical contents are *different types of content*, rather than content, in the first case, and content plus worldly goings-on, in the second.[27]

This move allows us the following picture. In the standard case, the right sort of situation makes the subject stand in a relation to the object, e.g. seeing it. It thereby allows the object to figure in thought, and allows the subject to think in different ways about it, form beliefs, and accordingly express thoughts. But the specification of the sort of situation that makes all that possible need not be part of the subject's thought. So the possibility that one knows which object one's thought is directed at is allowed without entailing that one need know how it is that one knows. Consequently, one may properly hold beliefs about the object—they will be beliefs *about the object*—although they may well be false beliefs (the sort of situation was such that it misled the subject) or illusory beliefs (there was no object at all, but some sort of situation capable of passing as involving an object).

Further, given that knowledge of what the sort of situation really is (the

[26] The blueprint conception is thought to be reinforced by the observation that we can refer to historical figures with whom no-one is in contact. Cf. Kripke, *Naming and Necessity*, 96 n.

[27] I shall discuss the general problem in section 5.

specification of the contextual relation) is outside what is necessary for the object to figure in one's thought, and thus also unnecessary for one to use a name competently, what is in important respects really the same situation may not strike the speaker as the same and may therefore fail to elicit the same responses.[28] Now, in the case where the two apparently different, but, in some important respects, identical situations elicit different responses systematically e.g. 'Hesperus' and 'Phosphorus', we would count someone mixing his responses (using 'Hesperus' in the morning and vice versa) as incompetent. But this is not to say that knowing more about the situation is here necessary, that one needs to know how to identify the differences between the two contexts in order to use the expressions properly. To say that one needs to respond thus in one situation and so in another is not to say that one need use a specification of the different situations to determine which one obtains. The incompetence involved here could be corrected much more easily, say by the speaker using 'Phosphorus' for Phosphorus accompanied by 'that bright star I see every morning'.

To summarize, Kripke's points (interpreted in the light of McDowell's framework sketched above) show the absurdities a blueprint model leads to: such a model would disallow saying that a speaker has false beliefs about something, and commit us to characterizing him as having true beliefs about different—or no—objects.[29] Kripke instead proposes a picture in which the object of one's thought is determined by the contextual relation that identifies the object as *figuring in* the subject's thought. The structure of the relevant context need not be part of the speaker's knowledge and thus error may be coherently ascribed. Apart from error, failure to know what the procedure of identification of the referent is does not detract from competence in general. (The importance of this point will become more evident in connection with the discussion of natural kinds below.)

An important element mentioned above is that the suitable contextual relation need not be perception, but being part of a communal practice. The baptizer's context is typically perceptual, as he normally introduces a name by ostension. Of course, it need not be: in the case of descriptive names noted above, someone may introduce a name in terms of predicates (without the predicates becoming synonymous with the name). A further non-ostensive way of becoming introduced to the use of a name is by way of participating in the relevant practice, where

[28] Cf. Kripke, 'A Puzzle About Belief', *in* Margalit, A., (ed.) *Meaning and Use*, reprinted *in* Salmon, N. and Soames, S. (eds.) *Propositions and Attitudes*; McDowell, 'On the Sense and Reference of a Proper Name', 176.

[29] Note that the classical model disallows one's having false beliefs of the *uniquely identifying* kind. The model may well allow that someone associating Aristotle with the author of the *Nicomachean Ethics*, where this property plays the role of uniquely identifying the bearer, may also falsely believe *of him* (since the reference to him is supposed to have been secured by the former belief) that he never met Plato.

again one is introduced by way of a body of information about the bearer, without that information encrusting on a name.[30]

3. PUTNAM AND NATURAL KINDS

Putnam has argued for the importance of context by focusing on natural kind terms like 'gold', 'water', 'tiger' etc.[31] He devises a thought-experiment in which a scientifically ignorant speaker uses 'water' to apply to samples of the usual stuff (H_20). In an imaginary environment—'Twin Earth'—which contains a superficially indistinguishable stuff which is not in fact H_20, a speaker identical to our original one in every 'mental' respect, in the sense of any world-independent mental properties he may have, would, by using 'water', be referring to that other stuff. The extension of 'water', and hence its meaning, would be different (it would be 'twater', rather than water). So the imaginary speaker truly says 'there is water in that glass', when twater (XYZ) is in the glass. By contrast, if the original speaker visits the imaginary place, the same utterance in his lips will be false. Therefore meaning does not turn on the purely mental materials which were supposed to be identical in both cases—'meanings are not in the head'.

Two issues are crucial to the interpretation of the argument. The first concerns what is required for linguistic competence, and Putnam's thought-experiments show that ability to identify the stuff is not involved in the possession conditions of the relevant term.[32] I shall discuss competence below. The second issue concerns the conception of the 'purely mental' materials that are assumed to remain fixed among the two speakers. Putnam often talks as if the common materials are conceptual: he says that the two speakers in the thought-experiment have the same verbalized thoughts, dispositions etc.[33] But it cannot be right to say

[30] See McDowell, 'Singular Thought and the Extent of Inner Space', 141 n. 8. Resistance to the last two varieties of 'acquaintance' may come as a result of the sharp distinction between concepts and objects, which motivates the postulation of the blueprint as the only way of their coming into contact. But Kripke's arguments directly show the failure of the blueprint model and indirectly question (as McDowell's arguments explicitly do) the cogency of the motivating distinction. I shall discuss the latter issue in section 5; I shall take up the issue of theoretical terms, which appear to be related to descriptive names, in section 6 and Ch. 4.

[31] See H. Putnam, 'The Meaning of Meaning', *Mind, Language and Reality*, 215–71.

[32] A qualification is in order: one need have *some* discriminatory abilities, in order to be credited with competence with a natural kind expression—say, one must be able to tell water apart from gold—yet one need not be able to distinguish the stuff from all possible counterfeits.

[33] See Putnam, *Reason, Truth and History*, 18. Compare his ensuing discussion, where he suggests that a 'full-blown concept' is something like concept plus ability to apply it properly, which suggests that the two speakers have different concepts only in the full-blown sense. Without the ability to apply, we are left with a concept in a reduced sense, which is supposed to be the same across the two speakers. However, that reduced concept consists in signs and representations that, as Putnam says in the same context, are not really meaningful without the ability to use them properly. Hence, it appears that we should not really call such meaningless materials concepts, even in a reduced sense. See the discussion below of Davidson's objection.

that the two subjects have the same thoughts. Since their thought involves the objects (water and twater), their thoughts are different in some respect: one's is a water-thought and the other's is a twater-thought. Identifying the thought involves appeal to something 'external', namely the environment.

Locating the individuating factor in the environment may, on one interpretation,[34] have the following implications. First, since the factor is external, it is in principle unknowable to the subject; second, the non-external part of the thought (common to both subjects) is *some sort of thought*, a sub-species (narrow, in Putnam's terms) of *content*, which is, in contrast to the external bit, completely knowable. Both points combine to yield the conclusion that, since only part of the total thought is available to the subject, he does not know, in principle, what he thinks.

Putnam explicitly wants to reject the epistemological framework that inspires this line of argument, namely that knowledge can only concern contents available intrinsically to the mind, and the ensuing scepticism about anything external. Davidson's argument in effect is that, by conceiving a part of the mind as itself 'external', the original scepticism about the external world reappears as scepticism about the contents of one's mind. Given that the epistemological assumption is not in the spirit of Putnam's arguments, the question is whether he is committed to it. A reason that he appears committed is by precisely his allowing that the intrinsic states available (and constant across the actual and the imaginary environments' speakers) are contents. Davidson is probably right in arguing that what is both constant and intrinsic across the two cases is not in any way contents; whereas what is *not* constant, and also deserves to be called contents, is not intrinsic, since it is a thought that is individuated by its object, which differs across the two cases.[35] (To say, of course, that it is not intrinsic is not to say that it is not internal.) But should the thought be in principle unknowable to the subject? Indeed it should not, as Davidson says. Each speaker has 'water' thoughts, and is in fact quite authoritative about them. They are what he thinks they are, namely thoughts about water and twater, respectively for the Earth and the Twin Earth speaker, i.e., in both cases, *the stuff each has dealt with in the past.* Of course each one's beliefs will be false if we switch his environment, but it is because they are individuated by reference to his normal environment, *as he thinks they are*, that they are false (since

[34] D. Davidson, 'Knowing One's Own Mind', *60 American Phil. Assoc. Proc. and Addresses*, 441–58.

[35] A similar complaint against Putnam (the complaint that he seems to allow for intrinsic contents) has been made by Burge, 'Other Bodies' *in* Woodfield, A. (ed.), *Thought and Object*, 97–120, at 101–106, on account of Putnam's expressing the property of natural kind terms as 'indexical', thus encouraging a picture of intrinsic contents, presumably constant across the actual and the imaginary environments, which are directed at objects only in virtue of being pointed to something. Cf. McGinn, 'Charity, Interpretation and Belief', *74 J. Phil.*, 521–35, at 531. McGinn does believe that genuine indexicals have an object-independent content, which is 'tied down' to things by the particular context in which they are expressed; e.g. 'today' has a constant content across the 1st and the 2nd of July, yet a 'complete indexical thought' is identified by further reference to the date on which it is entertained. See McGinn *The Subjective View*, 64–7 (quoted phrases ibid.). McDowell in '*De Re* Senses', *34 Phil. Q.*, 283–94, reprinted *in* Wright, C. (ed.), *Frege, Tradition and Influence*, plausibly argues that *different de re senses* can be grouped into similar sorts, thereby accommodating the constancy.

he is ignorant of the switch). What he does not know, with the result that he is rendered unable to notice the switch, is the differences in the environment—i.e. chemistry, since the only hypothetical difference is the composition of the relevant liquid—which is not something his authority should necessarily extend to. The crucial factor is not that chemistry is any more external than what properties he does have available; it's just that he doesn't know enough of it.[36] Putnam's point, then, is that there can be cases in which something is ***not known*** by the subject, rather than ***not knowable***. To equate the two types of epistemic failure would be just to ***assume*** the rejected framework, namely that only intrinsic materials are properly within subjects' cognitive reach and they are therefore the only candidates for individuating the content of thought, given that we usually know what we think.

We should reject, therefore, the idea that the Earth and Twin Earth speakers have the same thought, albeit about different objects; rather, they each have a different thought. We should also reject an implication of the same-thought view. The implication is that the contrast that makes Putnam's case plausible is between superficial qualities and micro-composition. In this mistaken interpretation of Putnam's thesis, the former make up appearances, delimiting the subject's discriminatory abilities; so that Putnam-type cases are possible where there may be systematic differences between superficial qualities, and the object's real nature.

Putnam's thought-experiment, however, is not meant to prove that the blueprint model fails where the stuff's nature depends on difficult-to-discern micro-structural properties, whereas the blueprint itself specifies only superficial qualities. Consider the case of pre-1750 and contemporary Earth. Experts' ability to discriminate gold from counterfeits has now improved, so that experts' methods of identifying gold now encompass micro-composition tests. Under the blueprint satisfaction model, modern experts' bluperints are now complete, and, for them, the contrast between superficial qualities and underlying structure is now lost—what experts now know goes beyond superficial qualities. Nowadays the chemical formula may be included in experts' blueprint, with gold being whatever satisfies the blueprint's now complete version. But this interpretation is mistaken. Putnam's point is that gold ***has always been picked out*** by 'gold', before and after the shift in experts' recognitional abilities, ***in the same way***. As Putnam says, 'gold' picks out stuff that bears a relation 'same$_L$' (i.e. same liquid) to original samples. Yet this relation is ***theoretical***—'whether something is or is not the same liquid as ***this*** may take an indeterminate amount of scientific investigation to determine'.[37] While the blueprint, in other words, may be further or closer to the stuff's appearance, the word

[36] Once we accept that there is nothing purely or intrinsically internal deserving to be called content, then there is no reason to insist calling content either internal or external. The crucial issue is whether to accept that there could be purely internal content. Recall the case of Kripke's alleged problems with the sense of bearerless names, discussed above; see text accompanying note 27. This question turns on the coherence of inner self-interpreting entities set over against external, ostensibly problematic, entities. See section 5, and Ch. 5 on indeterminacy.

[37] See his 'Meaning and Reference', *70 J. Phil.*, *in* A. W. Moore, (ed.), *Meaning and Reference*, 150–61, at 153; emphasis in the original.

refers to the stuff that is in fact the same as the samples, ***whatever the right theory for determining that relation is.*** The 'blueprint' never really acts as a blueprint, i.e. as a criterion of a term's extension, and so its status, as pertaining either to easily discriminated, superficial aspects or to 'hidden', micro-structural properties, is irrelevant.

The contrast, then, which Putnam's thought-experiment rightly interpreted brings out is the one between competence (the ability to think with a concept) and ability to discriminate its extension, and Putnam's thought-experiments show that the latter is not connected with the former in the way the blueprint model has them connected.[38]

Davidson appears to be cautious concerning what knowledge is actually necessary in order to credit the subject with different thoughts (which brings me to the issue of competence). His reservation is that it cannot be the general case that speakers may not know what they are talking about, and he thinks that this is a possibility Putnam's liberalism engenders: since we will credit the speaker with whatever meaning his words have, given his environment, without attendance to his state of knowledge, it may be the case that we will be crediting subjects whose ignorance is rather large with normal understanding. But, Davidson suggests, the imperfect understanding should be reflected in what is attributed to a speaker: if someone thinks gold is always yellow, then we should qualify our report of his state of understanding by noting this imperfection.[39] But this is surely acceptable by Putnam: what makes the speaker's assertion 'gold is always yellow' true or false turns on what gold is in his context, which is another way of saying that what the speaker means is individuated by reference to his context. The scope for error involved need not (and in fact cannot) be larger than what Davidson calls explicable error (e.g. the speaker falsely believes that gold is necessarily yellow since most people learn how to use the word in connection with jewellery, whereas we know from chemistry that the stuff is actually whitish and mixing it with other metals for purposes of hardening makes it yellow). The constraint here, namely when to attribute wrong belief or different concept, is the constraint of making most sense we can of the speaker.[40] So proper concern about the speaker's authority dictates that, in this example, we attribute wrong belief.

Putnam himself is unclear on the constraints on the attribution of content. First, he appeals to ostensive introduction to the stuff, so that 'that stuff' specifications should suffice for someone to be competent. We can agree that this is an acceptable way of being introduced to the use, although there seems to be no

[38] So what we need for Putnam-type cases is not situations in which error is easy, but only situations in which error is conceivable.

[39] I am adapting what Davidson says against Burge, yet as a way to state what he sees as a problem with both Burge and Putnam. See 'Knowing One's Own Mind', 449.

[40] I discuss this below, section 5. Note that I am here ignoring the distinctions between speaker's error and communal error. See the discussion of Burge below. I am here concerned with whether Putnam's argument has a general tendency to breach first-person authority.

reason why second-hand introduction should be excluded, given that accepting indirect *introduction* does not seem to make concessions to the blueprint model.[41] We should further recall that we are not committed to crediting with competence speakers who would fail to make any reasonable use with the word (recall Evans' example of overhearing a name in the pub, discussed in the previous section), since doing so would, successful deception apart, make a mess of our interpretation of the speaker's general behaviour. Given minimal exposure to the samples of the substance and ability to use the term in thought and action, what determines the term's correct application?

Putnam's central notion relevant here is the 'division of linguistic labour'. The idea is that speakers' intentions in using a natural kind term are to denote whatever is relevantly the same as the paradigmatic instances of the stuff, i.e. to denote the property of belonging to the kind or species. But what that property consists in is left (in virtue, always, of the speakers' intentions) for experts to decide.

This may be interpreted along the socialized version of the description theory of names discussed above: the speaker need not use his own criteria because he can always appeal to criteria held across the community, and indeed can appeal to those employed by the relevant experts. And Putnam's characterization of the practice as division of labour strongly suggests that the issue with which his thought-experiments are concerned is largely an institutional question as to who has (epistemic) authority over what.[42]

But Putnam's complaint is surely deeper (and is revealed by a variant of the thought-experiment in which pre-1750 experts are hypothetically transferred to a twater-environment). What makes it the case that water refers to water is not that the experts can tell it apart from similar stuff, but rather that this is what the environment contains. The point of the thought-experiment is to reveal the role of available information in determining the extension of the term. And what it reveals is that the term's extension is directly determined by how the term is used, namely in a world-involving way (it picks out some stuff), rather than indirectly, i.e. through a body of *anyone's* information. To repeat, this gives us no reason to suppose that anyone's, and especially the experts', information will be always wide of the mark. But there is a crucial difference between saying that the term is used to pick out things that have property X, on the one hand, and saying that the term is used so as to pick out the things that have property Y, namely that some *believe* that they have property X, on the other. Further, we should recall that it is not the case that ignorant speakers' reference is indeterminate, unless supplemented by the experts' knowledge. 'Gold' refers to *gold* in their lips (we want to say that, e.g., they believe *gold* is yellow), whereas to conceive expert knowledge as one part of the information dossier available, so that the expanded

[41] Cf. the discussion of theoretical terms in science in section 6.

[42] See Pettit and McDowell (eds.), *Subject, Thought and Context*, Introduction.

dossier would *determine* the reference, would entail that without the complete dossier reference is indeterminate.

Deference to experts, therefore, should be conceived otherwise. Speakers defer to experts to identify the object, in the sense of deferring to the best theory about what it is for something to be X (belong to the kind water), rather than deferring to some particular theory, that claims that the crucial property is such and such. The difference between the two intepretations of deference is that, on the first interpretation, correct application of a concept turns on a substantive, since genuinely theoretical, claim (the claim concerning the identity of the crucial property made within the best theory), whereas, on the second interpretation, correct application turns on a claim that has the status of a degenerate truth: there is no question in the second case whether the relevant theory correctly identifies the property involved, since by hypothesis whatever that theory claims *will be* the property. (If we apply the second reading to the pre-1750 example, since water will *be* whatever the favoured theory then said it is, the meaning of water will have undergone a change in the meantime, since current experts identify water differently.)[43]

In sum, Putnam's arguments should be understood as supporting a semantics of natural kind terms, which claims that their correct application is governed by the properties that in fact collect paradigms together, which is a matter for theory to establish.[44] His thought-experiments are meant to show that use of the terms is world-involving, so that the role of theory should be conceived along the lines of the first—non-reductive—model suggested above. Such theory is substantive and purports to characterize the property that collects together instances (paradigms) of the kind, and has to account for competitive theories, as well as simpler, normal speakers', beliefs.

4. BURGE AND THE SOCIAL CONTEXT

Tyler Burge's thought-experiments deal more directly with the impact of the environment.[45] He considers the question: what is the relation between mental contents and (primarily) the social environment? His thought-experiments have the following structure: assuming that all states of a person described non-intentionally and individualistically, i.e. independent of the relations to the natural (social and physical) environment, are constant, his propositional contents will vary

[43] See S. Hurley, *Natural Reasons*, 194, for a similar distinction between two types of deference to theory claims, in terms of the differences in the scopes of the existential and the modal quantifiers.

[44] Obviously, some of the stereotypes may be revealed to have been incorrectly classified as stereotypes—some fool's gold may have been considered one of the paradigms.

[45] See 'Individualism and the Mental', *4 Midwest Studies in Philosophy*, 73–121; 'Other Bodies' op. cit.; 'Two Thought Experments Discussed', *23 Notre Dame J. of Formal Logic*, 284–93; 'Individualism and Psychology', *45 Phil. Rev.*, 3–45; 'Cartesian Error and the Objectivity of Perception', *in* Pettit P. and McDowell J., (eds), *Subject, Thought, and Context*.

with variations in the environment. For instance, a speaker believing that his arthritis has spread to his thigh will have a false belief, yet if we counterfactually suppose that in the community 'arthritis' is not used exclusively for inflammation of the joints but also for limb complaints, he will have a true belief; hence the social environment is individuative of propositional content.

Burge's initial exclusive emphasis on the social environment, and his frequent use of non-natural kind terms (arthritis, sofa, contract, brisket) may lead to the following misunderstanding: just as Putnam's thought-experiments reveal nature as determining extension of natural kinds, Burge's own reveal the community having that role for non-natural kinds. But this misses the point. First, Burge's thought-experiments differ from Putnam's in that they directly consider the individuation of propositional attitudes, rather than simply terms' reference. Secondly, Burge shifts the emphasis to questions at a conceptually prior stage to that of most of Putnam's thought-experiments: what is important for the counterfactual situation is that the relevant expression be used in the counterfactual community so that one application or another will be correct. It can be left as yet unclear what correctness turns on, and the thesis should therefore be neutral towards the actual standards of correctness.[46] Thus the thesis has general application: it addresses expressions designating both natural and social objects. The standards are constrained by what the community does, but there is no short-cut from there to conceiving constraints as conventional. Such a short-cut would be, for instance, to claim that in Burge's case it is actual experts that count, even if in Putnam's case the actual experts are unimportant.[47]

The interpretation proposed above is not perhaps within the letter of Burge's early arguments. But it is supported by his more recent arguments.[48] There he makes it clear that the constraint imposed by the claim that meaning and propositional attitudes are determined by the social environment is not to be equated with their *reduction* to what most of the community or some within it (the experts) claim proper use consists in. Further, there is no way to respect the anti-individualistic thesis while construing the individuating factors conventionally (i.e. in terms of what most or some members of the community think the case is). It seems that, if Burge's anti-individualism is granted, such an interpretation would launch us on a regress. If we are to re-interpret 'X' as 'what most people think of as X', then we need to specify 'X' *in* the re-interpretation.[49]

This is an important point: it may be misleading to call Burge's thesis 'anti-individualistic', since so calling it may suggest that his positive proposal is that

[46] This is not in contrast to what Putnam claims; his Twin Earth experiments support the particular hypothesis that water's real nature in fact determines the extension of 'water'.

[47] See Introduction to Pettit and McDowell (eds.), *Subject, Thought, and Context*, for a possibly different reading.

[48] See 'Intellectual Norms and Foundations of Mind', *83 J. Phil.*, 697–720; 'Wherein Is Language Social' op. cit.

[49] I argue that it does launch us on a regress in Ch. 4, section 11; a similar argument is deployed in Ch. 5, in connection with discussing Wittgensteinian arguments.

mental content is fixed by the social environment in the above, reductively 'collectivistic', sense of what all, or most, members of the community think. To repeat the point from a slightly different angle, Burge's central argument is that the relevant reduction cannot go through: if the content of a concept is determined by the social environment, and that is conceived as 'what most people think that concept means', then we should need an independent way to individuate the concept as it figures in people's thoughts. We cannot fall back on the social determinants of content, since these are what we set out to analyse as 'what most people think . . . '. Burge's point is that we cannot avoid falling back to the social determinants, albeit in a different way: individual content is not intrinsically meaningful, but is rather fixed by the social environment; yet the latter should not be further analysed in terms of how people think the concept should be used, as this will lead us back to individual understanding and so we will end up in a circle. Rather, it should be specified as the way the community has been *in fact* using the relevant concept. Burge's thesis is not captured in the contrast between one and many people's conceptions; rather, it is captured in the contrast between intrinsically meaningful mental states and the practice of applying concepts.

Reading Burge as proposing the 'social' solution, in the reductive sense rejected above, is motivated by taking his thought-experiments as simply pointing to differences between individual misconceptions and communal standards of correctness.[50] But Burge's purpose is more comprehensive, and his recent arguments support the more ambitious thesis: in his recent thought-experiments, a subject holding a non-standard belief about sofas is not supposed to suffer from any misconception. On the contrary, he fully appreciates what the 'conventional' characterization of sofas is, yet doubts that it is the correct one. The subject is best thought of as holding a non-standard theory, arguing that the *community is in error*, and that current understanding should be revised.

Burge supports his conclusions through consideration of what he calls the dialectic by which actual experts correct idiolectic mistakes. He argues that the success of experts' arguments, and ultimately what it is to be an expert, turns on the ability to defend a conception against challenges, especially in the form of counterexamples: crucially, meaning-giving characterizations, purporting to guide practice (e.g. apply 'chair' only to. . .), are responsible to examples. For instance, characterizing the meaning of 'chair' as 'four-legged piece of furniture meant to be sat on' fails in view of chairs without legs. Given the interdependence of examples and characterizations, attempts to arrive at a correct characterization of the communal norm have the status of substantive claims, amenable to argument, and this leaves room for reflection to correct and thereby change the conventional characterization of the norm involved. This in turn may result in a request for

[50] See Pettit and McDowell (eds.), *Subject, Thought, and Context*, 9–13.

changes in the actual practice, to the extent that it does not conform to the norm to which it should actually conform.[51]

To see that there is a distinction between conventional understanding and the meaning of a concept we do not need to invoke actual cases of revisionary conceptions calling for revision of practice; much less do we need to invoke successful such calls for revision. We only need see that hypothetical such challenges are conceptually possible. In Burge's own example, someone doubting that sofas are meant for sitting on is clearly not doubting that sofas are sofas.[52] If conventional understanding were the ultimate constraint on meaning, the distinction would collapse: such doubts would make no sense.

The thrust, then, of Burge's arguments is clearly against the notion of criteria: his rejection of individualism is not exhausted in the claim that we would normally credit subjects with propositional attitudes they imperfectly understand, as when we credit someone with arthritis-beliefs on the strength of the communal meaning of arthritis, rather than on the strength of his own definition. On the contrary, the fact that we may credit someone with a conception of *arthritis* (diverging from the best conception available), rather than dismiss him as having a different concept, is the by-product of an argument: the by-product is rejection of the principle that understanding involves grasping indubitable truths, whereas the argument's conclusion is that the model of individualistic individuation of thought is unworkable: no content could be ascribed independent of the normative communal structure. (Recall that what that structure is, is a substantive matter, and so a matter over which anyone stands corrected.) The by-product comes about in virtue of rejecting, together with individualism, its chief motivation, the project of connecting thought and reality via indubitable mental contents.[53]

Before turning to discussion of the motivation behind such 'mentalistic' theories, let me elaborate on Burge's anti-criterial points. Burge's thesis is that conventional norms, in the sense of conditions for correct application of a concept implicit in widely acceptable meaning-giving characterizations, are not the ultimate constraints on meaning—hence they do not operate as criteria. This is not to say that vulnerability of such norms does not come in degrees. This is quite beside the point. The point is that challenges are conceptually possible, while it is precisely a *substantive* issue whether a particular challenge is plausible or not. Surely many concepts' conventional content is especially firm and difficult to challenge. (This is a substantive claim itself: it amounts to an attempt to think of some plausible challenges and failure to come up with any.) It is difficult to think of a plausible challenge to the standard meaning of 'red' (as applied to a traffic light), or

[51] See Burge, 'Intellectual Norms and Foundations of Mind'.

[52] Recall that his doubt need not rest on imperfect understanding: the challenger may admit that the explication he is challenging enjoys consensual status, yet offer reasons for explaining how the community was led astray, and suggest tests for his claim. Compare: 'there are no cats; martians have induced massive cat-hallucinations'. Not plausible, but stateable.

[53] Cf. Burge, 'Cartesian Error and the Objectivity of Perception', 119.

'Mayday'. It is nevertheless possible that some such challenge will be offered. So some concepts *could* in fact be treated as quasi-criteria. The point is that criteria cannot be the general constraint; nor can they be the ultimate constraint.

Further, it is intuitively plausible that complexity is crucial: the more a concept's content is connected to other concepts and practices, the more likely it is that challenges may get off the ground. Concepts' complexity nonetheless is itself a matter to be established substantively. In chapters 5 and 6, I shall discuss problems associated with challenging conventional understanding of concepts. But I should note here that rejecting conventional constraints does not undermine determinacy of conceptual content; instead, by making content a matter of substantive argument, it makes content more stable.

5. THE REAL TARGET OF THE THEORIES

All three views attack in somewhat similar ways a theory of meaning that would make meaning depend on a method of identification of the referent of the expression and ultimately of the thought expressed.[54] I construed the three views as having that as their target, rather than the more superficial aim of denying that an individual's criteria work, and opting instead for someone else's criteria (e.g. the experts) or for the world as imposing an 'external' constraint on individuals' reference. The ambitious target, then, is the view that speakers' characterizations of the relevant object do at all operate like criteria. In contrast to that view, the three sets of arguments converge on a picture of reference being effected through (direct or indirect) transactions with the relevant object, with speakers' beliefs about it being *about it* by virtue of the transactions, rather than by virtue of the further fact that the object conforms to some object-independent specification contained in the beliefs. Consequently, the beliefs may or may not be true; they have the character of cognitive efforts amenable to substantive correction.[55]

This interpretation depends on there not being room for any individualistically individuated beliefs or other attitudes. In all three theories discussed it seemed perhaps possible that, despite the relevant arguments, there could be a position which preserved a role for individualistic contents. In Kripke's case, uses of bearerless names and cases of failure of substitution could suggest that there is a role for individualistic content which is there irrespective of the environment, so that the general case is a combination of such content plus external constraint. In Putnam's case, the two subjects in the thought-experiment could perhaps be

[54] K-P semantics (after Kripke and Putnam), my name for the theory of concepts discussed in this Chapter, is chosen for simplicity. It is now evident that the account owes much to Burge, as well as McDowell and Davidson. This caveat applies to uses of the abbreviation throughout the entire text.

[55] Recall that fallibility of belief presents a difficulty to the classical view only in connection with ostensibly *identifying* beliefs; a classicist could hold that various ancillary beliefs may be false of the referent. Cf. note 29, above.

construed as having some common contents, on which natural facts superimpose. And in Burge's case, individualistic contents could perhaps be those that may or may not match conventional contents. In all three cases, I argued that a purely non-individualistic interpretation is available. But perhaps more need be said in favour of anti-individualism.

Putnam and Burge make explicit that their target is an epistemology that is Cartesian in spirit, and that this is the key to the coherence of the view they attack. That epistemology is guided by the special status which it attributes to introspective knowledge, and is made possible by the idea of special mental objects. Let me briefly discuss these notions, in order to clarify the argument against the availability of individualistic contents, and discuss the issue of the normative constraint on the individuation of contents so far suppressed.

Individualism is motivated by a particular picture of the mind, and an epistemological prejudice. The prejudice is that only indubitable truths are capable of grounding knowledge. The picture is essentially one in which the mind is an autonomous realm, reached by the 'world's doings' after they have been suitably translated into some or other sort of 'representation'. Two species of indubitable truths result: analytic truths, i.e. sentences true by virtue of meaning alone, and so thought to involve solely the mental side of the divide; and sentences concerning representations of the environment (traditionally, sense-data reports, upon which more complex—but in themselves fallible—hypotheses were built), i.e. sentences which involve the mental side's supposed transactions with the environment.

Analytic truths should not be that important, ever since Quine's famous critique of the analytic–synthetic distinction, in 'Two Dogmas of Empiricism'.[56] Analytic truths were thought to be immune from revision since they express truths 'by definition', and therefore necessary truths—how can it not be the case that all bachelors are unmarried? Further, these truths could not coherently be doubted, since they should be known *a priori*: understanding the relevant expression should entail realizing they are true.[57] The tacit assumption here is that meaning depends on the range of empirical confirmation. Now since analytic truths are true by definition, in the sense of stipulation, the range of confirmation is universal: they are unrevisable, they must be held true, come what may.[58] Quine's criticism is that

[56] In Moser, P., (ed.) *A Priori Knowledge*; see also W. v. O. Quine, *Word and Object*. Rorty relies on Quine's critique for rejecting foundationalism: cf. *Philosophy and the Mirror of Nature*, esp. ch. 4. Quine also attacked the kind of indubitable truths involving sense-data, but I am ignoring this part of his critique since Quine's own view appears to run into some empiricist difficulties I cannot discuss here.

[57] Cf. Burge, 'Intellectual Norms and Foundations of Mind', 699.

[58] See Putman's distinction between a purely linguistic version of analyticity as based on synonymy, and a conception of analyticity as unrevisable truth: see his '"Two Dogmas" Revisited' and 'Apriority and Analyticity; Beyond Wittgenstein and Quine', in *Realism and Reason*. Putnam is there making a complaint similar to Kripke's, namely that aprioricity (what Kripke calls epistemic necessity) and necessity (in the sense of metaphysical necessity) do not always go together; necessary truths may be discovered *a posteriori*, and contingent truths may be picked out *a priori* (by stipulation). Both truths may serve, in different cases, as the basis of meaning. Cf. Kripke, *Naming and Necessity*.

no such truths exist, because 'drastic enough changes in the system' may accommodate them.[59]

Despite the apparent demise of the analytic–synthetic distinction, the picture of the mind behind it still informs the classical conception of the relation between thought and object. The mind, by virtue of its autonomy, is thought to have direct access only to its own doings, i.e. the representations. Concerning those, perceivers must be infallible. The epistemological problem is therefore defined as the question whether the representations 'match' reality. The problem of meaning is defined along similar lines, that is, as the question of the relation of thought to objects.

Conceiving the mental as autonomous makes radical scepticism inescapable. This is because the mind engages only with 'ideas' or 'representations'; consequently, whether these 'match' what exists beyond them is always precisely beyond the mind's reach. (This is the well known problem of the 'veil of ideas' or 'veil of perception').[60] The logical possibility of illusion, in the case of perception, is thought to reinforce this line of thought: since illusion is experientially indistinguishable from veridical perception, the veridicality of the latter case is a 'further fact', inaccessible to experience.[61]

Classical foundationalism sought to render the contents of experience indubitable; but, given the autonomy of the mental, what it could relatively easily secure was the indubitability of representations, although it was establishing an inference to what lies beyond the mental that was called for. That this project should be doomed is rather obvious.[62] On the foundationalist conception, we only know what *appears* to be the case, and hence every reason that we might think of for its actually being the case is part of how it appears to us, and must therefore already presuppose the link to reality which it strives to establish.

The inevitable scepticism sketched above is in a sense shallow: it assumes that some contents *are* available, and questions whether they are veridical. The assumption seems justified if we focus on the 'argument from illusion'. That argument claims that illusory experience is indistinguishable from veridical experience, in order to prove that veridicality turns on some 'external' fact; the argument keeps

[59] I deal in the text only with the conception of analyticity as aprioricity. The 'linguistic' version of analyticity fails as a foundation because it must be defined in terms of synonymy, definition, interchangeability or necessity, either in a way that the latter, defining notions are constrained so as to presuppose analyticity (as Quine shows in 'Two Dogmas'), or else by leaving the possibility open for those notions to be dependent upon substantive, hence vulnerable, truths.

[60] See J. Bennett, *Locke, Berkeley, Hume*, 68 ff; Rorty, *Philosophy and the Mirror of Nature*, 140. The 'veil of perception' is the result of the autonomy of the mental in connection with perceptual knowledge, whereas the 'veil of ideas' is the form of the problem with respect to the connection between thought and reality in general.

[61] Recall the discussion of bearerless names and their connection with the argument from illusion in section 2.3. And note that the possibility of deception in the domain of knowledge of other minds (coupled with the autonomy picture) generates the relevant sort of scepticism there.

[62] See, *inter alia*, Davidson, 'A Coherence Theory of Truth and Knowledge', *in* LePore, E. (ed.), *Truth and Interpretation*.

mental autonomy in the background. But mental autonomy attracts a deeper sort of scepticism, namely whether any contents at all are available to the mind. Autonomy requires that what is available to the mind be completely specifiable independently of whatever lies outside it. Now even constructing appearances while respecting this restriction should be impossible, since the individuation of appearance involves that which appearance is an appearance of.[63]

A related point is made by Davidson. He notes that the structure that makes scepticism inescapable is the mind–world division conceived so as to make them independent of each other, so that their matching must always be a 'further fact' to the representations. The shallow form of the problem is that however we strive to connect them we shall end up with more of the mental entities we started off with.[64] The deeper form is that, once the division is set, the relation of representation itself will collapse: it is impossible to construct the 'uninterpreted reality', over against which concepts are supposed to be set, without recourse to our familiar concepts which supposedly belong with the 'mental', and, by the same token, it is impossible to give content to the notion that mental contents are 'representations' of anything.[65]

The broad alternative approach to the mental is to conceive it as 'world-laden',[66] i.e. to conceive mental content *as* worldly goings-on. This conception disallows scepticism, at least as far as scepticism takes the form of doubting whether 'representations' match 'reality'. It weakens, then, the motivation behind the criterial view, for the following reason: the latter view needs the possibility of radical scepticism, i.e. it is based on effectively admitting that whether X is the case is bound to be beyond our reach; criteria then function as 'proxies' for what the case is.[67] (Further, it is doubtful whether criteria can actually work, once the possibility of scepticism has been granted. First, in being 'proxies' for what is the case, they do not really yield what they are supposed to, namely knowledge that

[63] This way of putting the problem is McDowell's distinctive way: see 'Singular Thought and the Extent of Inner Space'.

[64] See 'A Coherence Theory of Truth and Knowledge'.

[65] See Davidson, 'On the Very Idea of a Conceptual Scheme', in *Inquiries Into Truth and Interpretation*, esp. 192; 'The Structure and Content of Truth', *87 J. Phil.*, 279–328, esp. 302–4.

[66] Susan Hurley's term in *Natural Reasons*, 92 ff. John McDowell's 1991 John Locke Lectures, recently published as *Mind and World*, are the best presentation of this approach. See also Putnam's recent adoption of this approach—which he dubs, after James, 'natural realism'—in his 1994 Dewey Lectures, published as 'Sense, Nonsense and the Senses: an Inquiry into the Powers of the Human Mind', *91 J. Phil.*, 445–517.

[67] See McDowell, 'Criteria, Defeasibilty and Knowledge', *68 Proc. Brit. Acad.*, 455–79; and the extended version of the same paper *in* J. Dancy, (ed.), *Perceptual Knowledge*, for the conception of criteria as proxies. Cf. W. Lycan: '[A]ntirealism in most of its forms comes from *morbid fear of scepticism*. Scratch almost any antirealist argument or 'argument', and you find a premise that is really a lemma; lurking behind it is an assumed conditional to the effect that if the premise were not true, then reality would be forever hidden from us, and we would never have any good reason to trust our senses, and so forth. Such background conditionals are rarely argued for, since they are rarely made explicit, nor in my experience can support be readily supplied once the conditionals are brought into the open.' (*Judgement and Justification*, 195–6).

the world around is thus, that S is in pain, etc.[68] Secondly—and more interestingly for my purposes—if criteria are supposed to ground content, where do *they* get content? I shall discuss criteria, in connection with scepticism about concepts rather than perception, in Chapter 5.)

On the approach recommended here (by contrast to the criterial view), what is the case, is a matter of fact accessible in principle, yet substantively established. Take mental contents in the particular case of classical 'ideas', or, as we would now say, thoughts, beliefs, intentions, and other propositional attitudes.[69] Those contents are objectively determined in the following sense: thought is individuated by its object. Yet this way of putting the relation is obviously too crude: first, to distinguish the object of thought finely enough, the subject's purposes and actions should be taken into consideration; and secondly, objective factors affecting his relation with the environment have to be accounted for as well. Hence, what thought will be attributed depends on the most coherent story available concerning the subject, taking into account his environment, his other thoughts, desires, beliefs etc., as well as other constraints in his capacity to deal with that environment (e.g. sensory defects). Each propositional attitude is identified only by reference to such a story about the agent and his relations to his environment.[70]

The story thus construed is theoretical, i.e. a substantive account which can be refined, altered or abandoned in the light of new findings. What is *a priori*, in other words, is that content is determined via such a theory, by reference to the relations between subject and environment (subject to the constraints discussed below), *not* that any particular content-ascribing theory is true. As a theory, it is constrained by the 'data' it has to account for (the subject's linguistic and general behaviour etc.); but a different sort of constraint is necessary by virtue of the interrelation of its 'data'. Since the attribution of, say, a belief, depends on the attribution of other attitudes, the characterization of the subject's actions, and so forth, and also on the meaning of the language used, while that meaning itself depends on the relevant propositional attitudes, there must be a way to avoid the apparently inevitable 'bootstrapping'.

This latter constraint is supplied by the principle of *charity*. Charity requires that

[68] See McDowell, ibid. Note that Crispin Wright has withdrawn his confidence in the anti-sceptical power of criteria in 'Second Thoughts about Criteria', *58 Synthèse*, 383–405. His earlier paper is 'Anti-Realist Semantics: the Role of Criteria' *in* Vesey, G. (ed.), *Idealism: Past and Present*.

[69] See McDowell, ibid., Davidson, 'A Coherence Theory of Truth and Knowledge', and Burge, 'Cartesian Error and the Objectivity of Perception', for the framework discussed in connection with perceptual representation.

[70] A further innocuous way in which the object-individuation thesis is too crude is that it supposes that one's environment need contain whatever object one may successfully think about. Yet quite obviously one may acquire, say, the concept of 'mud', without one's environment containing any, as long as one has the concepts of 'water' and 'dirt'. See McGinn, *Mental Content*, 35. A further qualification discussed above is that one need not have objects in one's *immediate* environment, and may acquire the corresponding concepts through theoretical description chains (while the latter are of course revisable and hence not the ultimate constraint on reference). See sections 2.1 and 3 above, on ways of acquiring competence in the use of names and natural kind terms, respectively.

the speaker be rational. Rationality certainly involves consistency; yet any (linguistic and general) action may be made consistent, by suitably reinterpreting the features of the relevant situation. Consequently, charitable constraints must be substantive. The speaker must mostly believe in truths, have sensible desires, use language properly etc. In other words, charity requires that natural contents be attributed to him, i.e. that he be ascribed attitudes we deem reasonable. Without that constraint, attribution of contents becomes intractable: not only might we end up attributing more or less unintelligible contents (say, beliefs about rabbit-slices, rather than rabbits); worse, we would find ourselves unable to view the subject *as a subject*, viz. as a thinker, believer etc.[71] Charity then enables us to attribute some, and indeed 'eligible', contents.

In order to sharpen the notion of charity I shall briefly consider two related widespread misunderstandings of it. First, it is not the case that charity amounts to the requirement that we endorse any old belief, say about unicorns, as true. This thought actually flies in the face of the notion of charity, since it supposes that there is some other, non-charitably constrained, way to identify belief, which is then declared true on the strength of charity. Rather, charity is what enables us to ascribe beliefs: it is a *constitutive, non-optional* constraint. This is not to say, secondly, that only true beliefs will manage to get ascribed (so that no unicorn-beliefs will ever be identified). Charitable ascription does allow for, indeed requires, the possibility of error.[72] This is done through what Davidson calls 'two interpretive devices'. The first is the evaluation of how well-placed and equipped the speaker is

[71] See Davidson, 'On the Very Idea of a Conceptual Scheme' and 'A Coherence Theory of Truth and Knowledge'; D. Lewis, 'New Work for the Theory of Universals', 61 *Australasian J. Phil.*, 343–77, esp. 375–7. Both sometimes are taken to write as if some contents, albeit not the right ones, could be always attributed. But the total failure of attribution is the absence of charity is elsewhere stressed by both. The total failure is a variant of McDowell's notion of 'darkness of inner space' on the dualist conception. Note that I am here ignoring subtle complaints against Davidson recently expressed by McDowell in his *Mind and World.*

[72] The complaint that charitable interpretation has difficulty in distinguishing between what is believed true and what is true is part of what McGinn suggests in 'Radical Interpretation and epistemology', *in* LePore, E. (ed.), *Truth and Interpretation.* He argues that if belief is individuated by reference to its objects, then someone hooked up to a machine inducing him to hallucinate that he is being chased by a tiger, and moving his legs in a 'running' fashion, must be construed as having beliefs about electrodes, and thus his action will be rendered irrational. This is, in effect, to ignore the need for an attribution of intelligible attitudes including desire and intention together with the attribution of belief. Clearly, the most coherent story we have available about how the world is, the story constraining and making possible the attribution of belief etc., is the one in which parts of the world—electrodes—induce hallucinations. The illusion-producing mechanism is then part of the objective, external story. Under that story, the agent is not well placed to have true beliefs, and so the story allows us to attribute (explicable) error. So we may say that the subject has beliefs about electrodes—although we may also say that he has no beliefs at all—*and the illusion of beliefs about tigers.* (Of course, that story may not be available, but I do not think that McGinn wants to make a point about epistemic difficulties; rather, he seems to be making a point about the theoretical commitments of the thesis that beliefs' individuation is object-dependent.)

Note the affinities between McGinn's objection and the 'argument form illusion', discussed above viz. that illusory experience must be experientially indistinguishable from veridical.

to observe aspects of his environment. The second is the evaluation of the connections among the beliefs attributed to the speaker, with special emphasis on the speaker's epistemic beliefs, i.e. beliefs in sentences whose truth the speaker counts as supporting the truth of others.[73] Note that the two 'devices' are not in fact an adulteration of the notion of charity. Rather, they are essential aspects of it, insofar as charity requires that we make as much sense as possible of the subject under interpretation, given the subject's relations with the environment; and *explicable* error actually enhances our understanding of a subject's speech and action.

Let me summarize the discussion so far. I have argued that K–P arguments amount, in effect, to a theory of the relation between thought and object that diverges from the classical conception. K–P theory argues that the content of thought is individuated by the object at which it is directed. Resistance to this picture derives from a probably incoherent, and in any case not compulsory, metaphysics of the mind and from some epistemological prejudice.

According to K–P theory, identifying the meaning of an expression requires reflection on the character of the objects on which it is applied. Such reflection is necessarily constrained by evaluative assumptions. I shall postpone until Chapters 5 and 6 sharpening the necessity and the character of such assumptions, as well as further discussing how, given such assumptions, we may still end up attributing error or irrationality to the subject, but I shall give in the next section a preliminary discussion of the issues involved through a consideration of the problems associated with the reference of theoretical terms.

6. THEORETICAL TERMS AND THE DISTINCTION BETWEEN DIFFERENT BELIEF–DIFFERENT CONCEPT

Theoretical terms offer an opportunity to illustrate how normative constraints allow for the distinction between ascription of the wrong conception of a concept and ascription of a different concept (and ultimately, the ascription of any concept at all). This discussion will give a preview of the discussion of substantive and conceptual disagreement to be developed in Chapter 5. It will also introduce a line of argument that is meant to defuse a general objection against the application of the semantic arguments canvassed in this chapter to legal concepts, an argument that will be fully developed in Chapters 3 and 4.

Theoretical terms are different from natural kind terms (and from names also), one may claim, since they are meant to stand for whatever, if anything, conforms to the conditions set out in their introduction. Therefore they seem to have at least a larger 'conceptual' element than natural kind terms, so that their reference is partly determined in the opposite direction: from condition to an object that complies with the relevant conditions.

[73] See Davidson, 'The Structure and Content of Truth', 321.

The quick way to deal with this argument is to point out, with Kripke, that the properties described in the introduction of such terms are not in fact conditions, but tentative reference-fixing devices, liable to be amended as more information is made available concerning the physical property they are really meant to capture. But, it will be objected, this is not always true, and this is revealed by considering cases like 'phlogiston'. Kripke's move, the objection continues, should in effect entail that 'phlogiston' beliefs were awkward reference-fixing attempts directed at oxygen; or else there seems to be a legitimate category of genuine descriptive introduction, which just happened to fail to find a worldly referent. Perhaps then all theoretical terms work like that, and the world just happens to oblige. So the argument is really a variant of the case of the bearerless name.

The argument depends on the idea that, in order to be able to characterize some belief as the wrong belief directed at some object, there should be enough common ground between the wrong belief and the correct specification of the object's properties. The common ground then, on which the differences can be located, must be conceptual, so that whether we ascribe wrong belief about the same thing is ultimately judged on conceptual grounds. 'Conceptual' here is opposed to object-dependent. If we insist on object-dependence, we must end up with the absurd result of saying that phlogiston beliefs are really dependent on oxygen, since no other object is available here. By contrast, if we allow for object-independence of concepts, we avoid the absurdity: 'phlogiston' has nothing to do with oxygen, since there is no (conceptual) common ground between the concept 'phlogiston' and the concept 'oxygen'.[74] But this is fallacious.

Phlogiston-beliefs are object-dependent, or rather environment-dependent, not by taking oxygen, but by taking combustion, as their object. More precisely, phlogiston theorists should be understood as having false beliefs about combustion, part of which are beliefs about a non-existent element (phlogiston). Of course, combustion could yield any sort of belief. Aspects of the environment that constrain the attribution of belief include facts about 'how well placed the subject is', e.g. the availability of instruments capable of checking for the occurrence of combustion in the absence of oxygen, other theories held true at the time, etc. Consequently, we make best sense of the phlogiston-believers in attributing phlogiston-beliefs.

It should not be thought that we cannot, by virtue of upholding object-dependence, accept that it is 'cognitive value' or significance that anchors phlogiston- and oxygen-beliefs in combustion. We only need deny that these cases give us reason to suppose that cognitive value is an exercise of 'pure conceptual capacities', where these are conceived as individualistic mental goings-on, i.e. as

[74] Of course this line of thought would have the well-known difficulty in accounting for cases where we *want* to say that two 'concepts' are about the same thing: we want to say that classical and modern 'atom' explications are about the same thing—they are in fact *conceptions* of the same concept—whereas the above line of thought would have to treat them as two different concepts (their specifications do not agree). But I shall ignore that here.

self-interpreting mental objects. Once this point is granted, we may say that 'theory carries the burden of reference', not only in those cases but in the general case as well.[75] In fact, considerations of theoretical terms reveal that contact with the environment need not be pictured on the basic model of perception, but on any kind of cognitive access. Theoretical terms must then be seen as more theory-sensitive than normal empirical terms, in that their application is usually governed by more complex considerations concerning their relations to the environment.

7. INTERIM PARALLELS WITH LAW

A rough analogy with legal concepts could be construed as follows: attention to the way legal concepts are used reveals that their use is governed by theoretical considerations. The application of a legal concept is governed by substantive claims concerning the property that collects together what counts as paradigmatic applications of the relevant concept. These claims are substantive—insofar as they are typically defended by invoking actual as well as counterfactual applications of the relevant concept—or at least are submitted as defensible in that way and therefore sensitive to the possibility of future challenge. The best explanation, then, of legal practice shows that lawyers treat legal properties as genuine properties over which not only lawyers in general but the original 'reference-fixers' (the legislators) may be in substantive error. In terms of intention, legislators (crucially) intend that the *property* a concept stands for, rather than their own attempt at capturing its nature, be respected in the law. The identification of the property is therefore a matter of theory.

Theories of the properties picked out by legal concepts are constrained by a body of 'data' which includes archetypical applications as well as claims about the nature of the relevant property made in the course of defending these applications—typically, judicial decisions. The latter operate as constraints insofar as any errors in the attempts to capture the property, which may be attributed by the theory, must be explicable. A correction of conventional wisdom must be such as to make best sense of its object, namely the thoughts and actions of practitioners dealing with the relevant concept. Given that the business of explaining the meaning of such concepts in this way cannot be carried out unless such charitable assumptions are made, substantive assumptions about the values by which legislators and interpreters are apt to be guided are essential. The general constraint of making the best sense of the practice guarantees that the interpreter cannot 'impose' his own values on the practice, on pain of making the practice inconsistent. For example (an example further discussed in Chapter 6), although it may be the case that one's favourite ethical theory dictates that fetuses are fully-

[75] Cf. F. Kroon, 'Theoretical Terms and the Causal View of Reference', *63 Australasian J. Phil.*, 143–66.

fledged persons and should therefore be afforded equal protection of the law, interpreting the Fourteenth Amendment so as to yield that conclusion would make a mess of a consistent practice of discounting aborted fetuses for purposes of succession, permitting abortifacient contraceptives, and so forth.

The above sketch involves the claim that legal practice is such that it takes substantive theories to identify the content of the properties involved in legal concepts. The claim is supported in part by the argumentative character of legal practice, the fact that practitioners engage in substantive debate over the application of legal concepts. The account could be resisted along the lines of an error theory: although practitioners' self-understanding of the practice is well captured by the sketch, practitioners are in error, for there is no substance to the properties involved. The content of legal concepts is fully specifiable by a non-revisable set of conditions, or by the set of communally accepted criteria associated with the introduction of the concept.

This response is essentially a claim to the effect that best sense of legal practice is made by discounting as mistaken lawyers' efforts at capturing something substantial (the properties that 'really' correspond to legal concepts). If these properties are not in fact 'real', and hence no discoveries may be made about them, as the objector would claim, we respect practitioners' desire to be rational by exposing the error. Therefore the objection, if successful, would entail that the appropriate method for determining the content of legal concepts is not substantive theoretical inquiry but perhaps only elucidation of individual aberrations: individual lawyers can be misled about the content of legal concepts, but the business of theory is only to identify the communal standards against which correctness of application should be measured.

This line of argument is also important since it may be (and has been) levelled against ethical concepts. Law, on that variant, cannot involve genuine properties since it is nothing but institutional enactment of ethical rules of conduct. But these are nothing but conventional arrangements, whose content can only be clarified by conceptual analysis.

Another (weaker) route towards disallowing substantive theory is to claim that legal concepts are not related to genuine properties because there is 'nothing in the world of fact' to which they correspond legal concepts do not designate things or stuffs, and so their application cannot be guided by theories of the nature of their referents. This thought may make the start of an argument for a conventionalist account, on which the content of law is identified by the criteria operative in legislators' minds or current during the introduction of a piece of legislation.

These two objections are addressed in the next two Chapters, in reverse order. I first deal with the second objection, on which Hart launched his theory of the semantics of law; I argue that the objection trades on the notion of 'purely conceptual' entities, or on some defective conception of the 'mind-dependence' of legal properties. The claim that legal concepts lack theoretical depth rests on the supposition that legal concepts do not pick out properties common among facts and events, but rather *make* a class of facts and events legally significant. The essentially arbitrary character of those concepts is central to the first objection, which I proceed to consider in Chapter 4, where I argue that, far from making better sense of ethical and legal practices, the error theory can make no sense of them at all. Chapter 5 addresses the objection of indeterminacy, namely that, in the absence of conventional constraints, no constraints at all are available to a theoretical account of the content of legal concepts. I argue there that the threat of indeterminacy in fact disallows the conventionalist approach. In Chapter 6, I principally argue that the dependence of the law's content on social practices supports, rather than undermines, the objectivity of legal content, provided that practices are not conceived conventionally. Further, I argue that rejecting conventionalist distinctions between different practices does not amount to confusion of different practices, and so does not collapse law to what an interpreter would like it to be.

8. CLASSIFICATION?

There is a different sort of objection that must be addressed before turning to the ones sketched above. That objection runs as follows: transposing to law a framework of analysis developed in connection with concrete, perceptually salient, objects requires a 'reification' of law in several ways. First, the transposition assumes that there are legal entities, just like the physical entities discussed by Putnam and Kripke. Secondly, it presents legal reasoning as a problem of classification, i.e. a problem of collecting such legal entities under the appropriate head, so that, armed with the correct classification, we may easily conclude on the legally required result (e.g. once we have identified event X as a contract, or A and B as contract parties, we straightforwardly deduce that A is obliged to perform).

The picture resulting from applying K–P semantics to law, continues the objection, distorts the true nature of legal reasoning: the form legal questions really have is 'should the plaintiff win?' or perhaps 'does the plaintiff have a right to win?' And that sort of question requires reflection on past normative practice, namely who has won in what circumstances, and indeed reflection guided by ethical and political considerations (who *should* win under what circumstances). It is not the case, therefore, that legal judgment turns on a subsumption exercise, with the legal consequences (the requirement that some course of action be taken backed by potential use of state coercion) being attached at a conceptually distinct stage; rather, when and why state coercion should be used is *the* question that is being asked in asking whether the plaintiff should win.[76]

Let me first comment on how this objection differs from the ones considered in

[76] I intend, in part, that my imagined objector argue that a Dworkin-type conception of legal reasoning is incompatible with the account defended here.

the previous section. The latter did not doubt that legal reasoning consists, largely at least, in a classification problem, but claimed that correct classification turns on the satisfaction of certain criteria, by some state of affairs; whereas the present objection doubts whether classification is the right picture of legal reasoning at all. The present objection then *a fortiori* casts doubt on the thesis that criteria are crucial to correct classification, but this is not an issue between the present objector and the account I defend in this essay. On my account, to give a list of criteria for a contract's validity is not necessarily to give an answer to whether a particular contract is in fact valid: theoretical reflection on, say, unconscionability, may distinguish between two cases both of which apparently satisfy the criteria. Similarly, from the standpoint of legal disputes, disputants are not arguing about definitional or criterial issues; they may well agree on a list of criteria for tortious liability yet disagree on whether a certain defendant should be held liable. The account defended here, therefore, is compatible with the present objector's own account on that score, so that, unless the present objector has an independent argument that shows that only *he* is entitled to reject the importance of shared criteria (perhaps because the account defended here fails), no issue should be joined.

The present objection does have a point of contact with the objections to be discussed in the next Chapters, namely the complaint that analysing legal reasoning in terms of classification questions supposes that there exist mysterious legal entities. But this should not be a problem. All that is necessary for the account proposed is that there be (irreducible) legal *properties*. The ontic commitment we must make is simply that there are properties that collect together some states of affairs or events such that no non-legal allegedly equivalent property can collect together the same class in a principled way. We only need maintain, in other words, that, say, 'negligence' collects together certain actions, and that no analysis of 'negligence' in non-legal terms (e.g., 'behaviour that fails to be guided by adherence to . . . ') would be able to collect the same class of actions except by circularly depending on 'negligence' or, at least, on other legal properties. Of course a question may arise concerning the *status* of such properties: it may be argued that such properties are different from the 'real' properties which are plausibly involved in natural kinds in that they are, say, 'mind-dependent'. But this is a question to be pursued (it is in fact pursued in the next two Chapters) only after the prior question has been answered, namely whether we are indeed committed to the existence of such properties. The ontological status of such properties, therefore, is an in-house dispute among different conceptions of adjudication as actually involving classification, and can for the moment be left open in order to concentrate on the present objector's insistence that any classification-based picture distorts legal reasoning.

One worry expressed by the objector is that legal reasoning is essentially guided by ethical and political assumptions, whereas conceiving it as a matter of classification makes it appear a matter of pure empirical investigation, in the course of which events or states of affairs are identified and classified under the relevant head, provided they meet the conditions of membership set out by the concept. But clearly this picture of classification is precisely the *target* of the K–P account as set out here. In the first place, it has been repeatedly stressed that concepts should not be thought of as abbreviating sets of conditions on which membership depends; rather, membership claims turn on substantive theories of archetypical applications of the concept. Consequently, meaning-giving characterizations are substantive theories of the concept's use, whose aim is to supply norms for future applications, and as such are subject to revision in the face of theoretical challenge.[77] In the second place, as I argued in section 5, such theories of concepts' use are constrained by substantive evaluative assumptions. Reflection on communal use needs assumptions on how the community *should* be using a concept in the relevant context. Explicable error aside, 'thunder' should be applied to the relevant phenomenon sometimes occurring during storms, its correct application being governed by what thunder really is (here some meteorological theory is relevant, relating facts about pressure systems and atmospheric electrical charges to phenomena perceptible at the earth's surface); 'courtesy' should be governed by what courtesy really is (here some ethical–social theory would be relevant, whose scope would include an account of the role of courtesy in society that would explain why one should be courteous); and 'law' should be governed by the relevant theory which would include an account of the law's role, where ethical and political considerations would be relevant. Again, although extending the analogy to law might be questioned, if it were allowed, the resulting account would be ethically and politically loaded, rather than neutral, and this is the important point in connection with the present objection.

A further worry may be that 'classification' suggests that a neat carving up of states of affairs and events is possible, so that in principle at least all cases can be antecedently classified. Here again, K–P semantics rejects such a possibility, as was made plain in connection with Burge's arguments above. Since classification turns on substantive theory, challenge and revision is always possible. Further, the complexity of the relevant concepts reinforces the open-endedness of the picture. (As an example of concepts' complexity, liability, intentional action, and responsibility are plausibly interdependent, and different conceptions of each are bound to affect conceptions of the others.) Since many concepts are plausibly interdependent, new material putting pressure on our understanding of our classifications may come from a variety of sources. Legal concepts are typically complex, their complexity involving not only other legal concepts, but political, ethical, and even scientific concepts as well. For instance, biological discovery that fetuses have brains from the first week after conception is bound to influence the

[77] Cf. the discussion of the unconscionability example, above and generally sections 2–4.

standards for correct application of 'murder', 'equality', etc., at least on some theories of personhood.[78]

Finally, there is perhaps a phenomenological worry. Legal judgment is plausibly arrived at through rather unstructured reflection on the parties' claims, guided by the evaluative question (should the plaintiff win?), rather than the taxonomical one (does the plaintiff have a valid contract?). Hence, it is argued, even an evaluatively constrained theory of classification misplaces the emphasis, as far as the phenomenology of legal reasoning is concerned. But this is not entirely true. Although often the judgment that the plaintiff should win is available before his claim is neatly classified under the relevant heads, the latter stage—the *justification* of the judgment—is crucially important: the judgment may always be challenged, and this is where the importance of classification issues becomes apparent. Within the context of an adversarial procedure, challenges *are* thrown up, and in fact take a 'classificatory' form: the defendant may tacitly accept the claim that there is *prima facie* a contract, yet object that he has no liability since the circumstances fall under an exception head; or he may dispute whether he has entered into a contract at all, since the circumstances are relevantly different and should therefore be distinguished; or he may question the principle under which he would appear liable by citing actual or hypothetical counterexamples.[79] The dialectic of legal argument is often actually, and always potentially, based on such 'classificatory' arguments.[80]

In conclusion, the K–P account of concepts should allow for the old 'subsumption' picture of legal reasoning, purged of the illusion of concepts as abbreviating sets of conditions of membership, and the concomitant illusion of 'mechanically' matching events or states of affairs to those conditions.

[78] Dworkin's example, in conversation. These considerations support a substantive, hence vulnerable, taxonomy of fields of enquiry, thereby undercutting ostensible cases for or against so-called discourse autonomy. This is not to say that law's autonomy is impugned. I shall discuss this issue in Ch. 6.

[79] See Hurley, 'Coherence, Hypothetical Cases, and Precedent', *10 OJLS*, 221–51, for discussion of hypothetical counterexamples.

[80] A different challenge to this account of legal reasoning is found in Stanley Fish's arguments, who not only claims that judges 'just see' how the case should be decided, but also that any justification offered in support of their judgments is an effort at 'dressing up' the judgment to make it more presentable to those who believe in the myth of substantive justification. This challenge is discussed in Ch. 6.

3

Empirical Counterparts and Hart's Semantics

1. INTRODUCTION

In this Chapter I shall discuss an ontological objection that purports to block K–P semantics in the legal domain. According to that objection, K–P semantics is plausible for expressions referring to concrete empirical objects; but legal expressions do not refer to any such objects, and should therefore be treated differently.

The absence of empirical 'counterparts' is among the fundamental semantic characteristics of legal concepts on the basis of which H. L. A. Hart launched his own *sui generis* legal semantics. This Chapter's further aim is to review Hart's own semantic framework and explore the question whether K–P semantics could account for what Hart perceived as important semantic aspects of legal concepts. I shall argue that K–P semantics better accounts for those aspects.

I shall begin by considering Hart's arguments. I shall then try to locate the general motivation underlying the view that K–P analysis should be restricted to expressions designating empirical objects. In section 2, I discuss Hart's key semantic theses: primarily that legal statements carry normative force, and that legal concepts are open-ended. I shall argue that Hart's account is marred by philosophical error: namely, by a bad conception of evaluation, and a prejudice to the effect that concepts' application can be governed only by incontrovertible, non-substantive conditions. I shall argue that Hart's semantics is unconnected with whether or not 'counterparts' to legal concepts exist. In section 3, I discuss the major target of Hart's semantic arguments—reductionism—and argue that K–P semantics is a far better anti-reductionist framework. In section 4, I shall try to explain the thought that the non-concrete nature of the objects of legal concepts makes them semantically special. I shall argue that that thought is confused, and I shall reconstruct it as the thought that mind-dependence of legal *designata* is semantically crucial.

2. HART'S SEMANTICS

In discussing Hart's semantics, I accept Gordon Baker's point that a consistent line can be traced through Hart's early and later work;[1] thus I shall comment, sometimes extensively, on claims Hart later modified or abandoned. I am not especially interested in showing the continuity of Hart's thought. However, his early work represents a line of thought many would still find important and in the right direction, and therefore deserves comment.

Hart accepts that much of understanding legal concepts consists in questions of classification.[2] He also thinks that the content of legal concepts is, like other concepts, roughly conveyed either by means of explicit definitions or ostension.[3] So far, no substantial thesis on the semantics of legal concepts is derived. Rather, Hart introduces some further premises that promise to yield important results; some of them are meant to have quite general applicability, while others are argued to be required by the specifically legal nature of Hart's object.

The major general premise is that concepts' semantics must start with attention to how an expression is *used*. This premise directs attention to actual instances of application, and consequently to sentences like 'X has right Y', rather than to single words in abstraction from such judgments of application. The requirement that the explication of concepts focus on such sentences entails that the social practices within which such judgments are produced are relevant to the understanding of the concepts themselves.[4] This is Hart's major *methodological* premise.

A further premise, whose importance I shall dispute, is that legal concepts lack 'empirical counterparts'. They 'do not have the straightforward connection with counterparts in the world of fact which most ordinary words have and to which we appeal in our definitions of ordinary words'.[5] This is Hart's *ontological* premise. One immediate problem must be mentioned here, and taken up later: it may be the case that the importance of social context, Hart's methodological premise, only comes about because of the ontological one. In other words, it may be because legal concepts are non-empirical that context is considered important by Hart. Alternatively, by taking context as the general constraint, Hart's ontological premise will result from attending to how words are used: it will be as an outcome of our investigation of the context of use that we find out that legal concepts do not have empirical counterparts.

On the basis of the premises just set out, Hart derives two broad theses

[1] 'Defeasibility and Meaning', *in* Hacker, P. and Raz, J. (eds.), *Law, Morality and Society* (hereinafter 'Defeasibility').

[2] Cf. *The Concept of Law* (hereinafter *CL*), 121–2.

[3] In *CL* he points out that ostension is not much different from introduction by definition with respect to determinacy of application: he points out that 'all men must take off their hat upon entering a church' and 'all men must do this' (followed by a demonstration of the required behaviour) both need to be constrained by certain assumptions about the context in which the instructions are set. See *CL*, 122–3.

[4] See, *inter alia*, *CL*, v; and 'Definition and Theory in Jurisprudence', *in Essays in Jurisprudence and Philosophy* (hereinafter 'Definition').

[5] 'Definition', 23.

concerning the semantics of legal concepts. The first is to do with the *force* of judgments of application of concepts to cases, and the second with the *open-endedness* of legal concepts. The first thesis has two versions. In its first version, the thesis is that use of legal concepts is primarily not descriptive but ascriptive. For instance 'X has a right to compensation' does not describe a state of affairs, but rather *creates* a state of affairs. This emphasis on the so-called performative character of legal utterances is central to Hart's early view but was later phased out.[6] The second version shifts emphasis to the so-called 'internal' aspect of rules. The internal aspect is that of treating rules as carrying normative force, i.e. as standards of appraisal of agents' conduct, and in fact as standards endorsed by the user of the relevant rule. Hence, in the central case, sentences using legal concepts have a non-descriptive element, namely normative force, since they are uttered from the internal point of view.

The open-endedness of concepts also comes in two versions, defeasibility and open texture. Defeasibility is the key notion in Hart's first attempt to capture the fact that no closed set of conditions can determine the application of a legal concept. For instance, although we can normally give a list of conditions for correctly applying 'contract', this list will only be rough: there is an indefinite number of conditions defeating the application. Hart initially thought that this fact entails that sentences using legal concepts do not have truth value (they only create legal consequences, e.g. ascribe certain rights or responsibilities, as mentioned above).[7] The notion of open texture appears in Hart's further attempt to capture essentially the same phenomenon: the conditions of application available will inevitably run short of determining a concept's applicability in every situation.[8]

Let me turn to a closer examination of the various theses.

2.1 *Use*

Hart's methodological premise is not problematic as far as the semantics defended here is concerned. In fact, it is a central thesis of K–P semantics, as set out in Chapter 2, that a concept's content is determined by its use, and so by attendance to sentences applying it; and further that specification of conceptual content is only possible in the light of assumptions about the context of the social practices within which the relevant concept is being employed. It is of course part of K–P semantics that accounts of concepts' use may be complex and revisable, i.e. that it may take substantive theory to establish the way in which use of a concept determines its conditions of application. Hart has no argument to the effect

[6] See 'Ascription of Responsibility and Rights', *49 Proc. Arist. Soc.*, 171–94, hereinafter 'Ascription' (later disowned) and; 'Definition'. In *CL* the theme has disappeared, but cf. 'Jhering's Heaven of Concepts and Modern Analytical Jurisprudence', (hereinafter 'Jhering') in *Essays in Jurisprudence and Philosophy* at 275–7, (published after *CL*). See G. Baker, 'Defeasibility' and Neil MacCormick, *H.L.A. Hart*, (hereinafter *Hart*) for the connections of Hart's views to speech-acts theory.

[7] See 'Ascription'. [8] See *CL*, 120 ff.

that how a concept is actually used is necessarily transparent to practitioners (although he does appear to assume, as will emerge, that no substantive theories may be involved in specifying conditions of application). It seems therefore that Hart's admonition about attending to use of the language in its relevant context may be respected, as it should, without yielding Hart's own semantics.[9]

2.2 Force

The force considerations adduced by Hart are notoriously problematic. Hart's initial emphasis on the performative character of legal sentences results in several difficulties. The performative force is brought about by the speaker's capacity: it is only on a judge's lips, rather than a layman's or even lawyer's, that the sentence 'X has a right to compensation' brings about a change in a state of affairs. The identity of the speaker is then supposed to take the full semantic burden of rendering the sentences non-truth-conditional.[10] But then the question arises whether a sentence uttered by a speaker divested of judicial competence has different content than the apparently identical one uttered in the course of adjudication. Further, the same question arises with respect to the relevant sentence embedding in questions, conditionals, etc.[11] In such cases it seems that the content of the sentence 'X has a contract' does admit of truth value, and indeed its truth conditions seem to involve the conditions for correct application of the relevant concept, independent of the identity of the speaker; these cases might be argued to be parasitic on the focal case of judicial utterance by supposing that they constitute a prediction of the all-important judicial utterance, so that their truth conditions would be derived by some suitable reduction. But this seems hardly plausible, and Hart has said much against such reductions. Further, Hart later made clear that one's judicial capacity adds *finality* to a sentence, which he had, it seems, originally conflated with

[9] Note that Hart restricts his attention to *actual* instances of use, and indeed does so in the context of expressing his hostility against the abstract reasoning favoured by jurists attracted by the 'heaven of concepts'. This may seem in tension with attendance to *hypothetical* instances which were admitted as relevant in Ch. 2. Hypothetical cases, however, are employed in order to shed light on *actual* use. For instance, they may act as counterexamples to erroneous specifications of the conditions of application supposedly derived from actual use. They are used in arguments to the effect that some specification of a concept's content actually misrepresents actual use. They are thus part and parcel of the theoretical character of the specification of content, i.e. a result of the fact that such specifications turn on reflection and substantive argument. But it is certainly theory directed at, and attempting to characterize, actual use, rather than abstract heaven-of-concept type theory, that is called to play the content-specifying role. So the issue turns on whether theory is barred from playing that role, a question on which Hart's arguments are not decisive.

[10] As Baker says, the special consequences arising out of the speaker's judicial status are a matter of institutional framework. Hart later explained that they are due to further rules (those that Hart called secondary rules which bestow authority on judges to resolve disputes, so that the resolutions thus produced become, under the right circumstances, unchallengeable). The rules that pertain to judicial authority should therefore be sharply distinguished from the rules that pertain to, e.g., contracts.

[11] Cf. Baker, 'Defeasibility', 30.

infallibility, so that he had thought that the relevant sentence's semantic properties were altered in virtue of the utterer's capacity.[12]

More generally, although there seems to be some truth captured in the claim that judicial utterances have some kind of performative character, this character cannot be the dominant semantic feature. The reason is that judicial ascriptions are constrained: there are right and wrong ascriptions of legal rights. A lawyer may correctly say that 'X has a contract', whereas a judge may say so incorrectly. In fact, Hart has himself provided in 'Ascription of Responsibility and Rights' an account of such conditions, namely the normal, if defeasible, conditions for a contract's obtaining.[13] Now to say that ascription is constrained by a set of conditions, even an open-ended one, is to say that it is *properties* that are ascribed—say, the property of having a contract. In the central cases at least, it is sometimes true that X has entered into a contract, and therefore a judge may correctly ascribe that property by characterizing the facts as a contract—by applying, in other words, the concept of a contract. Whereas in other cases the same statement is false, and a judge who applies the concept does so incorrectly.

While it may be that Hart originally thought that the very fact that conditions are not of the kind expected, viz. closed exhaustive sets, is intimately connected with considerations of force, to insist on force as rendering sentences incapable of bearing truth value commits one to a curious legal emotivist position and the attendant problems of emotivism.[14] The emotivist seems faced with a dilemma. *Either* there is a genuine property that is getting ascribed whenever a concept is applied, and hence ascription is constrained by the conditions of correct application of the relevant concept (namely, whether the corresponding property is instantiated), in which case the performative element will be peripheral to the question whether X had a contract (though it may be relevant to the question whether the utterer was in fact in a suitable position of authority for legal consequences to follow, namely questions pertaining to the conditions of being a judge, which are separable from the original issue of whether X had a contract). *Or* there is no genuine property, and therefore no constraints to the ascription. In the latter case we will have a full reduction—contract obtains whenever judges say so, *which is to say that there is no real content to 'contract'*; for a judge, there is no distinction between correctly and incorrectly applying the concept of contract.[15]

[12] See 'Definition', 29; *CL*, 138 ff.

[13] MacCormick notes that ascription is rule-bound (*Hart*, 17). Baker points out the inconsistency between Hart's attempt to explain content solely in terms of force, and his own account of defeasible conditions ('Defeasibility', 35). Hart accepted both that judges may be wrong and that there are truth conditions for sentences applying legal concepts ('Definition', pp. 29 and 33, respectively; and *CL* 138–40). I attempt to explain Hart's endorsement of the apparent inconsistency below.

[14] The parallel case of emotivism in ethics is discussed in the next Chapter.

[15] The move from conditions to properties may be questioned. Perhaps the conditions pertain only to the speaker's being in some state of affairs, e.g. being a judge. Then those conditions could obtain both in cases which we would normally characterize, as, say, contractual liability as well as cases we would characterize as tortious liability. Hence there would be no real distinction between these two. (Compare Hart's 'scorer's discretion', in which to be out is for the umpire to say so, which Hart rightly

But this conclusion is severely counterintuitive: an error theory is required, explaining how it is that certain states of affairs appear to be collected together in a principled way by the property of having a contract, and does not seem forthcoming.[16] Note further that the fully reductive exercise should be carried out globally, if the analysis purports to cover law in general.

I do not mean to say that Hart was at any point committed to such reductions—quite the opposite. But, before attempting to diagnose the motivations of the problematic claims, it is interesting to note the difficulties he ran into by introducing force considerations into the analysis of law.

Further difficulties appear in Hart's later attempt at characterizing the force of legal sentences, based on rules' internal aspect. That aspect figures in Hart's theory in rules' conditions of existence. For something to be a social rule, people must take a 'critical reflective attitude' towards the behaviour that figures in the rule's content. That attitude consists in treating the behaviour as required, and criticizing others for failure to behave accordingly.[17]

The internal standpoint, on the other hand, seems to figure in rules' conditions of identification. Hart seems to claim that someone who did not regard the behaviour that figures in a rule's content as required, and supporting criticism, he would be missing some important part of the rule. From his external standpoint, all that would be visible would be a regularity of behaviour correlated to some circumstances (as well as hostile reactions correlated to failure to behave in the way identified under the same circumstances), rather than behaviour in *conformity* to a rule. At most, Hart seems to say, an external observer may be able to describe how people who take the internal point of view try to act in order

comments is a different game from cricket: *CL*, 139. As Hart says, cricket's rule for being out is not for the umpire to say so; if it were, the umpire would have no rule to follow.) However, there is in fact a distinction between these two cases, and consequently it appears that there exist two distinct properties—say, one's being liable in contract and one's being liable in tort—picked out by the relevant concepts. Indeed, to the extent that conditions of application are fine enough to individuate different concepts, then it must be the case that an equal number of properties are being picked out. I am not concerned with where these properties are located, as it were. They might well be 'subjective' properties. For example, to the extent that there are conditions individuating and distinguishing between different colours, then there must be an equal number of colour properties, which include essential reference to how things appear to the subject. I shall return to the question of ontic commitment below.

[16] Note that a reduction of the concept of having a contract, say with the help of some sceptical social theory, to some independent concept may still be subject to the same constraint of explaining what collects together what appears to be the extension of contract. It may succeed in doing so (we may in other words get a concept of, say, contract-ideology that is coextensive with our original concept of contract), while the performative element will still be irrelevant: the judges, under that scenario, are after all constrained in their ascriptions by a *property*, (albeit the newly discovered one, whose nature is different from what we thought; for example, contracts would turn out to obtain whenever the pressures of the market led the weaker party to despair, rather than whenever a party exercised his freedom to agree with another to mutual benefit). If, on the other hand, the constraint is not met (why should it?—maybe some properties are after all fictions of the ruling class), then it falls on the reductive theory to explain away contract practices. At any rate, only under the second, fully sceptical, scenario may it be the case that the performative element will be central, i.e. where it is discovered that there has never been any constraint on judges' application of the concept of a contract.

[17] *CL*, 54–6.

to conform. But then he may only say things *about* them. The implication seems to be that from that (non-extreme) external standpoint one will not be able to reason with the rule, and derive its requirements, in the way participants who take the internal standpoint can.[18]

Neil MacCormick has objected that there is a non-extreme external standpoint—what he calls hermeneutic—that is richer than Hart thinks. One can avoid taking the internal standpoint and still be able to make statements *of* the rule, not about it.[19] One may apply the rules of vegetarianism and warn a vegetarian that a dish ought not to be eaten, without taking the internal standpoint towards vegetarianism. What is the feature of the internal standpoint that is not part of the hermeneutic standpoint? MacCormick says it is *commitment*. The holder of the hermeneutic standpoint need not approve of the rule, but only appreciate that it operates as a standard, i.e. that it seeks conformity. The hermeneutic standpoint, then, presupposes the internal, but is different from it.

MacCormick explains the availability of the hermeneutic standpoint in terms of a distinction between cognitive and volitional capacities. The former make available a rule as a pattern of behaviour, allowing for judgments as to what behaviour is or is not in conformity with the pattern—how the pattern extends. The latter pertain to one's preferring, or not, that the pattern be conformed with as a standard. From the hermeneutic standpoint, one need share the cognitive element of participants' understanding, but only need appreciate the volitional element.

The point that one may apply a rule, i.e. use it as a standard and state what it requires, without a desire that it be a standard, is beyond dispute. But MacCormick's explanation illuminates a difficulty in Hart's internal aspect of rules, as well as statements made from the internal standpoint, both of which, MacCormick accepts, are presupposed by the hermeneutic standpoint.

Hart considers the internal aspect to be constitutive of a rule. According to MacCormick's formulation, the internal aspect consists in a preference. But what is the object of the preference? It cannot be a preference that people conform to the rule, on pain of circularity: preference, if it is a constitutive condition for something's being a rule, must turn something into one. MacCormick takes *patterns* to be the object of preference.[20] It may appear, then, that the desire that it be treated as a standard, can turn a mere pattern of behaviour into a rule.

I shall suggest that this is an illusion: different patterns of behaviour either are or are not in accordance with a rule. Preference comes analytically too late to make

[18] *CL*, 86–8. See ibid., 99, for the connection between internality and ability to apply the rule.

[19] *Hart*, 34–40. Hart later accepted (see *Essays on Bentham*, 154) a similar point formulated by Raz (see *The Authority of Law*, 153–7).

[20] The same is true of Hart's own formulation. The critical reflective attitude must be held towards something other than rules. It cannot be constitutive of a rule that it is used in criticism of others, although criticism can be a *consequence* of having a rule. *Given* a rule, one may use it in criticism of others. (I am indebted to Mark Greenberg here.) But Hart needs people's using something else in criticism of others to *constitute* a rule.

any difference; and where it appears to make some difference, the difference is explicable otherwise.

Consider the practice of cars stopping at red lights. This description should be adequate for picking out the kind of thing over which Hart's internal aspect may range: we may identify a pattern of behaviour, and we know what it takes to conform. Now suppose we make the volitional move and treat it as a (desirable) standard. Has it turned into a rule? The answer does not seem clear; not until the description of the pattern is glossed with more assumptions.

Consider two scenarios. Under the first, red lights are part of a more general traffic practice, they play a role within traffic management, namely they allow for the safe alternation of vehicle movement from different directions and pedestrian crossing etc. Under the second, they play no such role. Traffic is exclusively regulated by roundabouts. In fact, they play no role at all. People just stop there.

Applying a volitional layer in the first scenario will come too late. The first scenario describes a rule already—the rule that people ought to stop at red lights—since it describes all that could matter to a rule, namely the rule's *point* within a scheme of social practices. Whatever normative power stopping at the lights may carry derives from that point, not from the extra layer of volition we imagined to apply. It will be no objection to claim that the scenario describes a rule only because a volitional layer has already turned it into one. If that is the case, then *that* volitional layer must have applied to a different, simpler scenario. If the scenario as it stands already contains the (ostensibly) rule-constituting layer, then it must be a reduced scenario over which the volition was originally exercised. As long as the scenario contains a point capable of justifying conformity, the volitional layer will be superfluous. But what if it does not?

This is our second scenario: no point has been specified, and so, in this case, desiring that stopping at lights be treated as a standard must be able to do the job. But what kind of a rule will we have turned the practice into by virtue of this desire? How does that rule handle cases like ambulances or bicycles? We will not know, unless the point of conforming is revealed.

Of course, there are cases in which it appears that the volitional layer by itself turns a pattern into a fully-fledged rule. For example, if the sovereign supplies the volitional layer, by expressing a wish that cars stop at red lights, then surely out of the practice of stopping at red lights, under the second scenario in which they perform no function whatsoever, a perfectly intelligible rule is created. But even in that case, normative power is conferred by a point, namely the point of doing as the sovereign wishes. That point individuates a different rule: not the rule that one ought to stop at red lights, but the rule that one ought to obey the sovereign, which trivially contains the former. The scenario would now be covertly changed, since it would include the specification of an entirely different background of practices that include sovereigns, subjects, and political arrangements. Under that variant, a normative structure different than those described in the original two scenarios will have been created by the sovereign's wishes, in the same way that Hart's 'scorer's discretion' is different from cricket.

Hart's model was not intended to capture the sovereign scenario. If anything, his project was to explain rules' normativity without the help of sovereign commands.[21] Nor did he intend to claim that patterns of behaviour isolated from the background framework of social functions and purposes can be turned into rules by virtue of volitional layers. Rather, his thought seems to have been that the volitional (or attitudinal, if we want to keep closer to his own formulation) layer ranges over practices considered against the background of functions and purposes—together with their points, in other words; but he thought that the evaluative element characteristic of rules, or judgments that use rules, could only be conferred by some such attitudinal or subjective-preference states.[22] In the next Chapter I shall argue against that conception of evaluation: I shall argue that one cannot really detach the evaluative component from evaluative classifications without losing sight of the relevant pattern. By contrast, to conceive evaluation in terms of an attitude or a stance towards non-evaluative materials is to be committed to the possibility of neat detachment of value from pattern. But, I shall argue, if one really has the pattern in sight, i.e. if one can correctly apply the relevant rule, then no attitude is needed.

Hart's insight, then, is that rules are constitutively connected with an evaluative

[21] Recall, moreover, that Hart's internal–external distinction is supposed to capture any kind of rule. As MacCormick observes in 'The Normativity of Law: Comment', *in* Gavison R. (ed.), *Issues in Contemporary Legal Philosophy*, law can confer mormativity on anything, but moral rules must be accounted for by grounds that justify their content, not the demand for conformity to them.

[22] I am not confident in this interpretation: perhaps Hart took the stronger view that attitudinal states could *add up* to rules' purposes or points. I criticize that idea together with the one described in the text, in Ch. 4, section 4, in the context of non-cognitivism in ethics.

Consider yet another interpretation of Hart's argument: in talking about the internal aspect, Hart is describing how a rule becomes *operative* in a society. The critical reflective attitude does not generate rules, but adopts rules, whose content is conceptually independent of that attitude, in the regulation of social behaviour. The attitude then is necessary for a rule to take hold in a society, and in this sense it is part of the explanation of the rule's operation within it: unless many people use a rule in criticism of others, the rule will remain a potentiality. Under that interpretation, the critical attitude plays a very weak role. It does not make up a rule's point, nor does it confer value on a rule whose point is attitude-independent. Rather, it just adds a rule to a society's repertoire of norms.

Whatever the right interpretation of Hart's internal aspect and its relation to rules' normativity, we may better regard Hart's point as a point of 'natural history'. That is, Hart may be trying to explain how rules in general come about, or how a pattern of behaviour acquires normative significance, or how a rule is adopted and starts to be applied in a society. Irrespective of the merits of such an explanation, it may be that Hart did not intend it as a point about how rules are *applied*. If that is so, then the historical explanation would be independent of questions arising within the practice of applying a rule. The explanation would be *about* rules, wheras questions of application require thinking *with* them, reflecting on what they require. That kind of reflection may not involve having an attitude towards patterns of behaviour, but must involve grasp of the rule's point or purpose, in the light of which behaviour may be judged as in accordance with, or falling foul of, the relevant rule. Under the historical interpretation of the internal aspect argument, Hart would not be committed to attitudes' figuring in rules' conditions of identification. His 'natural history' account would seek to explain the genealogy of normative systems, but could be neutral with respect to questions arising within normative systems, provided it were recognized that such questions are evaluative. He might allow, therefore, for different conceptions of the *practice* of evaluation, and so could allow for a cognitivist conception of rules' application.

aspect allowing them to figure in normative discourse, and in the absence of that aspect rules are distorted. This insight is correct and valuable, but is spoiled by Hart's conception of evaluation. Critical attitudes cannot explain norms, because they range over norms. Further, Hart's suggestion that judgments about what a rule requires must necessarily take into account the rule's evaluative aspect is also correct. But, having identified the evaluative aspect with attitudes, Hart is naturally inclined to think that one must share those attitudes in order to be able to make judgments of application (or at least to make them 'from a point of view'). Instead, he should be saying that one must take into account a rule's point or value.

By substituting a cognitivist view of evaluation for Hart's projectivism, Hart's original intuition that values are essentially involved in rules' application is preserved, while the temptation to think that one must endorse the rule in order to apply it is avoided.[23] The view sketched in the preceding chapter (and further defended in Chapters 5 and 6), viz. that one must assign a value or point to a practice in order to determine what it requires (or in order to determine a rule's extension), is consistent with Hart's insight that values are essentially connected with rules' application; it is also consistent with MacCormick's point that application of a rule may be a purely cognitive matter, that volitional states need not figure in reasoning with rules. Against the background of some general practice individuated by its value, one may identify aberrations or local mistakes. For example, I may consider tiddlywinks a silly game, but, provided that I have a view on the point of games in general that includes thoughtless amusement as a major justification, I may occupy something like MacCormick's hermeneutic standpoint and explain its requirements to someone, in the light of my 'game theory'. Analogously, provided that I have a theory that justifies treating any decision taken at Westminster as law, I may determine, in the light of that theory, how absurd or wicked statutory provisions must apply.[24]

[23] I defend evaluative cognitivism in the next Chapter.

[24] Note that the precise picture is one of interdependence between assigned value and agents' behaviour. Tiddlywinks, conceived in terms of behavioural facts neutral towards two competing conceptions of the point of games, act as a constraint for these theories. The one that can better account for that behaviour, e.g. thanks to the greater weight it assigns to thoughtless amusement as part of games' background justification, may be preferred over one in the light of which the behavioural facts would be mysterious. In order to agree that the behavioural facts are a game, one may have to change one's more austere theory of games' justification to allow for silly games. In Ch. 2, section 4, I illustrated the same point in terms of Burge's arguments about the interdependence of concepts and examples. In Ch. 5, section 5, I shall further discuss the interdependence of concepts and paradigms in the context of Dworkin's view on substantive disagreement in law. And in Ch. 6, section 4, I shall discuss the point in connection with different examples of constitutional and statutory interpretation.

There is no difficulty in accommodating apparently global scepticism within the picture of interdependence of assigned value and examples. An anarchist may not share the view that law is justified coercion, because his views address a more abstract issue, that of the relations between community and individual. For him, law, conceived in terms neutral to the dispute he has with non-anarchists, is a set of

2.3 Open-Endedness

As mentioned above, Hart's open-endedness claim is essentially a negative thesis. It is meant to deny that there could be definitions, i.e. sets of individually necessary and jointly sufficient conditions such that every putative application of a legal concept will have a determinate truth-value depending on whether the conditions are satisfied. The early formulation was that there is an indefinite number of circumstances in which, despite the fact that the accepted sets of conditions obtain, the relevant concept's application is defeated.

Whether defeasibility correctly characterizes concepts' application turns on how to conceive defeat. In some circumstances, what count as conditions of application obtain, yet application of the relevant concept is inappropriate. The crucial question is how to characterize, in those circumstances, the putative conditions. The defeasibility thesis takes conditions to maintain their status as conditions of application: they are satisfied, but special circumstances give us an independent reason not to apply the concept.

This conclusion is counterintuitive. The natural thing to say is that the circumstances *show* that what we took to be conditions of correct application are not really such—that, in the light of these circumstances, the satisfied conditions lose their status as conditions of application of the relevant concept.[25] The circumstances involved, by giving us reasons to withhold application, make plain that what we counted as individuative conditions are in fact unacceptable as they stand, and should be qualified to take into account the relevant circumstances; i.e. they should be revised so as to accommodate the fact that the newly encountered circumstances are relevant to the concept's content and are hence *related* to the original conditions. (Why are the 'further' circumstances important, if they are not related to the concept? Rather, the very defeating power of these circumstances is testimony to their relevance to the concept, which is to say that our original conditions failed to capture something important about the concept.)

For example, suppose that it is thought that the principal condition for correctly sustaining an objection of provocation so as to reduce a charge of murder to that of manslaughter is that the deceased person's behaviour is such that it brings about loss of control in the defendant. Now consider a case in which this condition

data to be accounted for. He must explain those data, and will probably do so by conceiving law's purpose in terms of abuses of man's liberty or some similar idea. Whether he can successfully account for that, as well as other sets of data, on the basis of conceiving order as aberration of a more fundamental human value, will count for or against his political theory. Cf. Ch. 2, section 6; Ch. 6, section 3.

[25] McDowell argues, in connection with Wittgenstein's notion of criteria, that, in the case of further circumstances being unfavourable, it is not the case that the ostensible criteria are satisfied anyway, and yet the support they afford is defeated: it is not the case that 'some condition, specified in terms that are applicable independently of establishing a claim, is a criterion for the claim anyway, though whether it warrants the claim depends on further circumstances, but . . . whether such a condition is a criterion or not depends on the circumstances'; 'Criteria, Defeasibility and Knowledge', *68 Proc. British Academy*, 455–79, at 463. My discussion of defeasibility owes much to that article.

obtains, but the provocation involved was long-term and the defendant had therefore the chance to 'cool off' between the acts of provocation and the criminal act. Assuming that the opportunity to 'cool off' makes the objection unsustainable, then our conditions stand in need for revision: it is not required that the act be done under loss of control *simpliciter*, but that loss of control must be, say, sudden and temporary, rather than involving a gradual weakening of judgment. By contrast, the defeasibility thesis is, in effect, to regard the conditions that are fulfilled as warranting the application of the relevant concept, its defeat being brought about by the novel consideration. But surely in this case the circumstances are occasion for *revision* of the conditions (and thus for denying that they are warrants as they stand), for sharpening, in other words, the concept's content.

Consider a further example. Suppose that provocation is thought to turn on sudden and temporary loss of control, thus perhaps making a condition of temporal proximity between the ostensibly provoking act and the killing, as in the previous case. Now suppose that someone is subjected to deeply offensive behaviour, goes away, and, returning after two hours with a gun, proceeds to kill the offender. Suppose further that we feel compelled, upon evaluating the circumstances, to grant a provocation claim. In that case, we should conclude that the temporal proximity condition is not right; *not* that the claim fails a necessary condition, but should still be sustained, rather that temporal proximity is not really a condition of provocation.

What explains the circumstances' role in compelling us to apply, or withhold application of, a concept despite our original list of conditions? Any intuitionist overtone here should be rejected. Circumstances 'defeat' because condition lists are conclusions of a *theory*. Temporal proximity was considered as a condition, in the last example, in view of a theory that explained and justified why provocation should count in mitigation at all, a theory that placed provocation within a conception of responsibility and agency. The pressure to grant provocation despite the lack of proximity is again *theoretical*: it comes from the appreciation that even someone who reacted to abuse two hours later may have still been unable to control his behaviour rationally. If that is true, then distinguishing in terms of temporal proximity is shown to be unprincipled, in the light of the point of granting provocation objections—namely assumptions about the relation of criminal responsibility and one's having the opportunity to deliberate upon one's appropriate behaviour calmly.

The theoretical role of circumstances, as grounds for revising conditions, does not only arise (although it is made obvious) in special cases. Judgments of application are always substantive, i.e. require evaluation of circumstances and their possible relation to the relevant concept. 'Normal' conditions are themselves context-dependent (they try to account for 'normal' context). In fact, the responsibility of conceptions to examples discussed in the previous chapter is implied by the contextual nature of the specifications derived from paradigms: the 'normal' conditions are nothing but specifications attempting to capture what is essential about the paradigms (the property that collects them together) and are therefore responsible to counterexamples, i.e. cases who do not match the conditions, yet are arguably instances of the same property.[26]

On the above suggestion, the correct way to render the intuition captured in the claim that concepts are irreducibly defeasible is to say that concepts' conditions of application are context-dependent and in principle revisable: correct application depends on theory and is therefore sensitive to circumstances. To offer a list of conditions of provocation is to claim that this list explains and justifies use of the relevant concept in the central cases (the stereotypes), and thus in the circumstances relevant to those central cases. In the light of different circumstances, the list is liable to be affected, and be substituted by an enhanced list that can better account for the original, as well as novel, cases.

The doctrine of defeasibility is based on the correct observation that no final formula can be supplied, which could govern a concept's application in every possible set of circumstances. However, that is to say that there can be no *unrevisable* formula; not that there can be no defensible, theoretical formula that explains and justifies novel cases' resemblances with the paradigms.

It may be objected that this emendation rescues the notion of conditions by trivializing it: conditions cannot be what one would have thought, namely conditions that support a judgment of application independent of circumstances. The ideal, after all, according to this objection, was that we should be able, armed with grasp of the conditions, to know that conditions should support a judgment just in case they obtained. We should not be further required to evaluate the conditions' correctness itself, and perhaps even change the conditions, before we can conclude that the judgment is warranted.[27]

Indeed, this ideal is misguided, and should be rejected. But why should it be the case that conditions work only by way of the rejected ideal? The defeasibility thesis, posing as a rejection of the ideal, turns out in fact to endorse it tacitly. Conditions *are* conceived, by the defeasibility theorist, along the suspect lines: they are pictured as yielding support independent of circumstances, the latter being a further source of possible support which could in principle go against the original support. Judgments of application are then conceived as consisting of two tiers: the first involves context-independent conditions, and the second contextual, and therefore *condition-independent*, considerations. For a defeasibility theorist, in an 'easy case'

[26] Cf. Ch. 5, section 5.1, on easy cases.

[27] Notice a different triviality. Suppose one proposes, on accepting that novel circumstances may be relevant and lead to changes in the conditions, to offer the following as the conditions of X: the disjunction of the conditions governing application in the past, present, and the future (and further assume that this takes the form of a disjunctive condition, rather than a disjunction of conditions, and that disjunctive conditions are acceptable). This *would* be a trivial property, since the condition does not determine application in a principled way. Note that failure to determine it in a principled way is not the result of the fact that the property is complex, rather of the fact that nothing can be offered by way of explaining the relations between the disjuncts; complexity itself should not be a problem, as long as it is *explicable* in a principled way. I cannot address the question of disjunctive properties in particular here.

where only the conditions' obtaining is known, presumably the relevant judgment is correct in the way the definition model would have it.[28]

Accepting the definition model's context-independent conception of conditions, instead of correcting it in view of its failure, leads to further tensions in the defeasibility model. Special circumstances show that conditions cannot *entail* support for the judgment of application. But it is not questioned whether the relation need have been one of entailment. Worse, it is accepted that conditions do entail support, albeit not definitively so, instead of realizing that whether support is afforded at all is a matter of theory, rather than logic. Further, when conditions seem incompatible, the assumption that they should still count as conditions that govern application independent of context leads to the conclusion that all incompatible considerations yield conflicting support, instead of the position that whether each really yields any support depends on theoretical evaluation in the circumstances.[29]

Hart's notion of open texture shares the same prejudices with the definition model as the defeasibility thesis, and thus constitutes an inadequate response to it. Specifically, Hart fails to see that the considerations adduced against the definition model point towards a conception of conditions as revisable.

Open texture is argued to be the result of certain considerations regarding the relation between rules and situations. First, the rule cannot 'step forward to claim its own instances', nor do the latter 'wait for us clearly labelled'. Hence, only clear, paradigmatic cases are certainly captured by a rule, so that its application is 'automatic', whereas in other cases 'no firm convention or general agreement dictates its use'. So, in the absence of convention, application is not 'subsumption and syllogism', but turns on resemblances defensibly relevant and close. Second, our 'relative ignorance of fact and relative indeterminacy of aim' entail that we shall not be able to foresee every circumstance, and hence that we cannot effectively take a position as legislators on whether or not we wish a rule to be applied in such unforeseen circumstances.[30]

Strictly speaking, Hart takes open texture to refer only to language's inherent defects at expressing requirements, whereas the human shortcomings are proposed as a further defect. But, as Baker argues, the notion of open texture is built on the premise of the impossibility of framing rules so as to cover every possible case without scope for discretion. Thus the linguistic defect is not really independent from the human.[31] Consequently, the two considerations collapse into one, namely the possibility of unforeseen circumstances.

[28] A difference with the definition model would be that, for a defeasibility theorist, the abstract possibility of defeat should have alerted us to say that *assertibility*, rather than truth, of the judgment is supported. But the notion of assertibility is premised on defeat's being the right way to conceive the possibility of unfavourable circumstances, and cannot be appealed to at this stage. Both the definition theorist and the defeasibility theorist would agree that the concept is applicable, in the circumstances described, and that its application is warranted by context-independent considerations.

[29] See McDowell, 'Criteria, Defeasibility and Knowledge', 464.

[30] See *CL*, 123–7.

[31] 'Defeasibility', 37.

Here, the prejudiced conception of how conditions should work is even clearer. It is assumed that conditions should be able to warrant judgments 'automatically', by simple syllogism, so that application could be incontrovertible. Further, they should not call for evaluation of the relevant circumstances. So Hart ignores the conception of conditions as substantive, non-automatic, and potentially controversial judgments sensitive to circumstances. In a revealing passage the content of which was mentioned above, Hart writes that novel circumstances cannot be dealt with by the definition model, since, in making a judgment of application, one 'chooses to add to a line of cases a new case *because of resemblances which can reasonably be defended as both legally relevant and sufficiently close*'.[32] Defensible similarity is contrasted with conditions. Hart's response to the failure of the definition model is *to retain it only partly*. He accepts that the rule's content is, in effect, the definition. The defensible judgment, in the passage quoted, is not considered to be part of the rule; it is an exercise of discretion, of a choice concerning how to extend the rule beyond its boundaries, rather than a judgment concerning what *is* the extension of the rule. The prejudice that the content of a concept should be captured in incontrovertible conditions rendering application 'automatic' is not challenged. 'Contract', *sensu stricto*, is what the definition says it is.

Regarding the legislative predicament, Hart appears to give a different reason for characterizing the substantive, ostensibly discretionary, judgments as falling outside the law's boundaries. There must be cases, he argues, which legislators never thought of. *Ergo*, they have been left unregulated. But this argument trades on an ambiguity. What is it for a case to have been thought of by the legislature? It seems that the idea is that legislators have actually envisaged certain cases, and that it is those to which they intended the law to apply. For instance, they envisaged a motorcycle or a car going through the park, while enacting the law that no vehicles are allowed in park. Now, given Hart's view that the content of the law is exhausted in what they envisaged, one option is to say that only these cases are actually covered. That is, only in the specific circumstances actually envisaged does the law apply. Another option is to say that the content of the law is *responsible* to those circumstances. The first option could be very restrictive. Why not say, on that option, that only the particular cars or motorcycles envisaged, pictured in the legislative mind's eye, so to speak, are covered? What makes it the case that, say, new models not in production at the time of enactment are also covered? The only apparent answer is to say that they are relevantly similar.[33] So one either has to take

[32] *CL*, 124; emphasis added.

[33] The argument can be repeated, *mutatis mutandis*, if one takes the view that conventional meaning, rather than that in the legislative mind's eye, governs application. What is the convention relevant to copyright law? The convention extant at the time the law was enacted, which may not include, e.g., computer programs? Or the convention extant at the time questions of application arise? Hart's argument underlying the distinction between core and penumbra is that applications of the core of a concept have been authorized by the legislature. That justification has some bite if application is restricted to cases actually envisaged, but the restriction results in the absurdities described in the text. The justification for applying a statute on the basis of conventions must be different: it must be

the line that the minutest difference from the actually envisaged case makes for discretion, and thus trivialize discretion (as well as make it difficult to see what a general concept is); or one has to accept that the specific, as well as similar cases, are covered by legislative intent. That is, the content of the law extends to similar cases as well; therefore, adding new cases carries a responsibility to defend their being similar to the legislative paradigms.

So the only consideration that I can see distinguishing, for Hart, an 'envisaged' from an 'unforeseen' case is not that it was actually 'in the mind' of the legislature, but that it is not controversially similar to paradigmatic cases. Thus, the Hartian constraint to the content of law is really the one discussed before, namely that the answer to the question whether a case is covered by the law should be uncontroversial. The considerations of legislative intent, combined with the prejudice that only non-controversial content merits that status, reformulate this as the claim that, since only some cases of application may be non-controversially attributed to the legislature, those cases exhaust the law's content.[34]

Related to Hart's assumption that rules may be said to govern application only insofar as their guidance is incontrovertible is his assumption that the application must be 'automatic'. What sets cases ostensibly calling for discretion apart is the fact that some degree of creativity must be exercised to establish the judgment. The judge must exercise some choice. Hart clearly thinks that this choice is not free: he writes that the judgment involved must be defensible. The implicit contrast must be that the central cases do not call for such defence. But again there is an ambiguity Hart fails to consider. To say that a case does not require defence is not to say that it is correctly decided irrespective of defence, that it is not *amenable* to defence. The latter would hold only if the 'easy' judgments of application were not judgments in a strong sense, i.e. if they expressed stipulations

part of a theory that claims that judges are justified to apply a statute according to what it means. To preserve Hart's argument about the special authority concerning application of the 'core' of a statute, one would have to speculate that legislatures intended, *as a matter of historical fact*, that conventions be used. That speculation is implausible, especially if future conventions, rather than those current during enactment, must be justified as the basis of application. If, on the other hand, legislatures are attributed the intention that conventions be used as a *philosophical* matter, i.e. on the basis of a thesis about the use of language, Hart's argument about the legislative predicament will have been abandoned, and we will have moved back to the discussion about language in general. The new argument must be that speakers' use of concepts should be interpreted on the basis of what the concepts mean, rather than what speakers think they mean, and that concepts' meaning is given by conventions. Against the new argument, we may insist that what underlies continuity between old and new conventions is defensible similarities among objects picked out under the different conventions. Such similarities may only be defended in the context of a theory about the kind of thing that falls under the concept, whereas the insistence that conventions govern application must stem from a prejudice that concepts' extension must be specifiable *a priori*.

Compare the conventionalist conception of Putnam's deference to experts, discussed in Ch. 2. See further Ch. 5 on Wittgensteinian arguments.

[34] So the claim that I attribute to Hart is not that the legislature actually intended to cover the particular subset of cases that are not controversial, but that the attribution of a particular set of cases to legislative intention should not be controversial. See further Ch. 4 on controversy as a constraint to the content of law.

and were therefore degenerate truths. In taking the substantive nature of 'hard' judgments as setting them apart from the easy ones, Hart in effect assumes that the only way a rule could determine an application is by way of such a stipulative, 'conventional' relation between the rule and the relevant case.

Hart takes it as a premise that the rule 'cannot step forward to claim its own applications', nor do the latter 'wait for us clearly marked'.[35] Instead of concluding that application turns on substantive and vulnerable judgments, he retreats into a position in which the rule does step forward, only not far enough.

2.4 Counterparts

It should be obvious from the discussion so far that the lack of counterparts does no real work for Hart's semantics. Consider the force arguments. Hart thought that the primary use of legal concepts is that in which some legal state of affairs is created, and in 'Definition' he connected this to the concepts' lack of empirical counterparts. As noted above, the force of some legal utterances depends on the institutional context: depends on further rules conferring special authority on judicial statements. We may accept that a legal system's being in place has the consequence that judicial decisions have a special status. But then this status will cover whatever content such decisions have, whether it relates to specifically legal notions like 'contract' or 'tort', or to commonplace empirical expressions like 'vehicle', '£1,000' etc. Conversely, the special force is absent in case a layman uses legal expressions. So the distinction based on the utterer's identity cuts across the distinction between expressions with or without 'counterparts'.

One could pursue Hart's argument further, by claiming that the non-empirical character of these power-conferring rules, or perhaps of the master rule (the Rule of Recognition), makes an important semantic difference. But I will not pursue this line, for two reasons.

First, that line would concede that the ground level legal concepts like 'contract' have whatever semantic peculiarity they do, not by virtue of *their* non-empirical nature, but by virtue of that of the secondary or the master rules. Second, in *CL* Hart has launched his major semantic claims on a different basis, that of open texture.[36] And open texture is clearly independent of an expression's empirical, or

[35] Similarly, in 'Jhering', 269, Hart says that the juristic conceptual heaven myth supposes that 'the meaning of all legal rules is fixed and predetermined before any concrete [*scil.* question] of their application arises'. He then proceeds to talk about the legislative predicament, implicitly taking the line that the questions of application that *were* in fact envisaged by the legislature do fix that meaning.

[36] Of course the internal point of view makes some semantic difference in Hart's scheme: it is a condition of adequacy for any semantic theory to capture the normative nature of legal concepts, both on Hart's view and the one defended here. What is important for my argument here, however, is that Hart's mature view comprises both the internal aspect and open texture independent of type of expression. In terms more congenial to the framework defended here, Hart's twin constraints are to give an account of concepts' content that accounts both for the possibility of surprise and their normative significance.

other, nature. Hart's example illustrating open texture is 'vehicle' in *CL*, and 'gold' in 'Jhering'.[37] Open texture, like the earlier defeasibility thesis, is based on the claim that circumstances may affect use of a concept; they are related to a potential for surprise, for situations not neatly captured by the standard explications of conceptual content. Such potential does not turn on the concepts having 'counterparts'. Hart writes that 'there can be no final and exhaustive definitions of concepts, even in science'.[38] In fact, there are interesting questions concerning the relative conceptual openness among different types of expressions; that is, the relative possibility of further circumstances having an effect on the application of various types of concepts. But it is clear that normal empirical concepts do have such potential, and therefore counterpart considerations do no work in establishing Hart's semantic thesis.

Why did Hart think that counterparts are that important? I have discussed what he originally thought *lack* of counterparts implied, namely lack of truth conditions. *E contrario*, he must have thought that ordinary empirical concepts do have such conditions. Yet the open texture arguments seem to cover empirical notions as well. If it is the case, for example, that open texture entails that concepts' content is to be given in terms of assertibility conditions, then empirical concepts' content will also be thus given.

In the preceding sections, I argued that Hart's conclusions depend on some unquestioned assumptions concerning how an account that treated legal concepts as standing for legal properties should work, so that, by giving up these assumptions, all of Hart's observations can be accounted for. One might want to resist this move along the following lines: that, *given* Hart's conclusions, there is no reason to distinguish between different types of concepts. But if one wants to reject Hart's conclusions, and account for his arguments otherwise (as I have proposed to do), the distinction will reappear. That is, the move back to an objective account like the one I have been defending may only be sustained, if at all, for empirical concepts, whereas legal concepts at least will resist the move; for these, Hart's account is closer to the truth.

I shall argue that such an objection relies on a different argument for the supposed failure of my objectivist account in the domain of legal concepts. The objection does not rely on lack of counterparts, but some notion of mind-dependence. To show this, I must further examine possible motivations for resisting the objectivist account. In the next section, I shall consider Hart's major target: reductionism.

3. HART'S TARGET: REDUCTIONISM

Baker plausibly argues that Hart's desideratum is twin: to reject both reductionism and 'realism', two apparently incompatible desiderata. Roughly, anti-reductionism

[37] At *CL* 125 and 'Jhering' 275, respectively. [38] 'Jhering', 275.

must be a thesis that there are no non-legal concepts such that each is coextensive with each legal concept. For instance, there is no concept coextensive with the concept of law.[39] If so, the apparent result is that law is primitive: if irreducible, it must be inexplicable (the 'realist' implication). But reduction is a large topic and more must be said to sharpen these questions.

Reductive claims are motivated by hostility towards some types of concepts. Using certain concepts appears to involve commitment to a corresponding type of property that appears mysterious or otherwise objectionable. The reductionist wants to demystify that type of property or otherwise restructure ontic commitment. The way to achieve this is by claiming that he can *redescribe* the offending domain, that he can express anything that is expressed in that domain without using any of the concepts characteristic to it. Although reductionist and anti-reductionist claims involve concepts or statements, it is questions about properties or entities that make the debates important.

There seems to be an intuitive distinction between eliminative reductionism and identity reductionism. The first sort amounts to the claim that something does not really exist, i.e. that the property to which an expression is supposed to correspond is never instantiated. It is the unicorn type of reductionism. Unicorns do not really exist, claims the reductionist, and proceeds to give an account of what the surface unicorn phenomena really consist in, e.g. perceptual illusions accompanied by undue confidence in the wrong sort of information, which in the right context can combine to produce unicorn-beliefs. That is, eliminative reductionism must be accompanied by an error theory. An identity reductionist does not deny that his target class of entities or properties exists (that his target concepts have instantiated properties), but claims that that is 'nothing but' another, reducing, class. For instance, to say that beliefs are 'nothing but' neurochemical episodes is not to say that beliefs do not exist (that they are figments of our imagination), but that they are identical to a class of such episodes.

It is difficult to make the distinction sharp. Common between the two apparent kinds of reductionism is ontological conservatism. Both types reduce total ontic commitment. In the first case, unicorns are deleted from our inventory, and in the second the same entry into the inventory, so to speak, comes under alternative heads.

There are two strategies against both types of reductionism. The first is to claim that the two sets of concepts involved (the reducing and the ostensibly reduced) are not coextensive. G.E. Moore's move against definitions of the predicate 'good' represents such a strategy. That is, for any property X, captured in an ostensive definition, something may be good and not X. The second strategy accepts that

[39] Even more loosely, anti-reductionism can be expressed by the claim that statements in one 'discourse', i.e. employing one class of concepts, are not equivalent to statements in another, i.e. employing a different class. But, since what kind of equivalence is involved here may be controversial (semantic? logical?), I prefer to express the thesis in terms of concepts' extensions.

the reducing set of concepts is coextensive, but denies that it is necessarily so. The necessity involved must be either nomological or metaphysical.[40]

For coextensiveness to be nomological, there must be a law correlating the properties corresponding to two set of concepts expressible *in those terms*, i.e. describing one class of properties by the concepts of the reducing set and correlating that to the other class of properties described by the concepts of the set to be reduced, and justifying the claim that the correlation expresses a law of nature.[41] *Mutatis mutandis* for reductions based on claims of metaphysical necessity.

The anti-reductionist now may deny, in the first case, that there is any law of the kind described above expressible in terms of the two sets of concepts, so that the concepts are coextensive, if at all, accidentally. Or, in the second case, he may claim that although the concepts are coextensive in fact, they are not counterfactually so; it is possible that a property corresponding to the ostensibly reducible concept could be instantiated without its instance possessing the ostensible reducing property.

Identity and nomologicity may cut across each other,[42] so that four positions issue: properties F and G are identical, and there are laws expressible in terms of concepts of Fs and concepts of Gs correlating them; Fs and Gs are not identical, but there are laws as above correlating them; Fs and Gs are not identical, and there are no laws of the appropriate kind correlating them; Fs and Gs are identical but there are no laws of the appropriate kind correlating them. On the present account, Donald Davidson's claim that there are no psychophysical laws correlating mental and physical events is an example of anti-reductionism on the ground of failure of nomologicity, while the fact that he considers mental events to be physical events, since all events are physical events, makes his position a kind of 'anomalous monism' (the last of the four disjuncts above).[43] Functionalist theories of mind argue that, since functional states could be realized in many different ways, the actual correlation between mental and brain states is not metaphysically necessary and hence cannot warrant reduction of the former into the latter.

Further, a general defence against reductionism involves questioning the reducing class. A successful reduction must be such that the class to be reduced is identifiable in a way that does not presuppose the object of reduction. More precisely, it must be possible to pick out a genuine reducing property by a concept that is independent of concepts in the target area. For instance, reduction of

[40] Cf. D.-H. Ruben, *The Metaphysics of the Social World*, ch. 1.

[41] I am focusing on properties for simplicity, but clearly entities or events may be the object of reduction.

[42] Identity is to do with entities, properties or events, whereas laws depend on the concepts in which they are expressed. I do not believe that this point is controversial, but it does not affect my purposes anyway.

[43] See 'Mental Events', *in Essays on Actions and Events*. Davidson argues that any attempt at law-like generalizations connecting mental and physical events will be circular to the extent that mental-level constraints will always be necessary; and that the generalizations will be rough and thus not strictly law-like.

France to a group of individuals, in the context of metaphysical individualism, even if that group is specified so that not only present, but past and future French individuals are included, must involve a property that collects together these individuals and does not itself depend on the property of being French. Ignoring the past and future constraint for the moment, it is possible to identify all native French citizens in a France-neutral way (say, by specifying their parents), so that the ensuing complex property will manage to pick out all of them; yet there is nothing in common between these persons other than the fact that they are *French*. The reduction is then unsuccessful, since the property of being French presupposes the existence of France.[44]

In law, the reducibility issue concerns properties. That is, the question is whether legal concepts can be reduced to concepts that carry no commitment to legal properties, so that either legal properties are eliminated; or they are shown to be the same as some non-legal properties, i.e. the legal and the reducing concepts both pick out the same class of things, events, etc., necessarily or nomologically.

American Legal Realism is a kind of reductionism. It (or its vulgar form) amounts to the claim that the law can be reduced to what the 'judges say it is'; it can be construed as the claim that the sentence 'the law requires X' can be translated into 'judges are likely to decide that X'. In its most obvious form, the reductive claim is eliminative, in the sense characterized above. It amounts to denying that there is any genuine legal property, in the sense that claims of the form 'law requires X' do involve commitment to the existence of legal properties, but the commitment is misguided. I will ignore this form, since it involves discussion of possible error theories explaining the surface judicial behaviour. I shall concentrate on a reductive identification version, under which legal facts are 'nothing but' facts about judicial behaviour.

We may see Hart's response to the effect that judges' behaviour is itself constrained by legal requirement as posing a dilemma to a Realist. *Either* the reducing concepts fail to be coextensive with the legal ones, for judges may go wrong in their decision (so the class of judicial decisions about contracts will not be the same as the class of litigated contracts); *or* the concepts will be coextensive, yet only by accepting the further condition of judicial decisions' following, i.e. correctly applying, the legal rules. The second horn implies that the proposed analysis would be circular: the law is analysed in terms of judicial application of the law. Moreover, the analysans—judicial behaviour—will be only contingently related to the analysandum: judicial behaviour will be connected to the law only in so far as judges happen to correctly apply the law.

Condition theorists (in the sense that Hart attacks, viz. proponents of the view that legal concepts can be analysed into sets of necessary and sufficient conditions)

[44] See Ruben, op cit. Cf. McDowell, 'Non-Cognitivism and Rule-Following' *in* Holtzman, S.H. and Leich, C.M. (eds.), *Wittgenstein: to Follow a Rule*, for a similar move in the context of reduction of ethical to non-ethical properties.

may also be considered reductionists, in a limited sense. Reductionism usually carries a view that the object of reduction involves some non-respectable metaphysical commitments. A condition theorist of the classical definition school may be a reductionist in the milder sense that he may claim that legal concepts can be fully analysed through conditions expressible in terms of non-legal facts. For instance, he may claim that we may analyse 'contract' in terms of a perhaps complex non-legal condition (or, if the immediate reduction is itself in legal terms, e.g. offer, acceptance, consideration etc. viewed as legal terms, then he may claim that these terms are ultimately reducible to non-legal ones).

Hart's open texture argument may be thought of as a coextensiveness-based defence. The definition theorist's complex condition may pick out events or states of affairs that are not contracts, or may leave some contracts out. If the definition theorist extends his condition to cover difficult cases, say by adding the constraint '. . . and whatever other situations judges will find sufficiently close and defensibly resembling the central cases', then coextensiveness will have been secured at the price of trivializing the condition: the augmented condition would not capture a genuine property, since it does not rely on an underlying principle uniting the various components of the condition, something that all its compliants have in common, other than their being contracts.[45]

Anti-reductionist moves are powerless against K–P analysis, because K–P claims that purport to give the content of a concept need not pose as reductions. First, claims that for something to be a contract is for something to be X (where X stands for non-legal properties) are *theoretical*, rather than *definitional*, and so K–P semantics disallows reductive moves of the classical, necessary and sufficient conditions, type. Secondly, K–P semantics is not committed to simplifying statements about legal concepts by reducing them to statements about judicial behaviour or statements about any other non-legal facts or events. It may support the autonomy of legal concepts and thus block theoretical versions of reductive moves, e.g., in the Americal Legal Realist style.

The theoretical nature of legal claims implies that they are substantive attempts to capture what collects certain states of affairs together as, say, contracts. A claim that purports to explicate the term 'contract' does not postulate a non-legal property that may be substituted for contract, but is aimed at elucidating what it is that groups together novel cases and paradigms, i.e. what the relevant similarities

[45] Compare n. 27, and accompanying text, above. Notice that Hart believes that there does not seem to be a 'single quality' shared by all cases, capable of being captured in a definition; see *CL*, 15 and long note of 234. Notice further that his view that, in hard cases, something's being a contract is determined in a special way—that in such cases conditions are defeated, rather than shown mistaken—suggests that he should grant that the relevant definition does individuate contracts *sensu stricto*, yet misses cases that ought to be characterized as contracts (or includes others that ought not to be so characterized), albeit in some attenuated sense. Hence, he would not be quite entitled to use his open texture argument as a 'failure of coextensiveness' argument against the definition theorist. The peculiarity of Hart's conception of the function of the 'defeat' of conditions posing as necessary and sufficient is discussed in section 2.3, above.

are (perhaps in the light of relations with other concepts). Commitment to legal properties is not questioned. A legal property *characterizes* a group of ordinary, non-legal entities (or events etc.), so that pluralism occurs only at the level of properties.

The theoretical relation between legal and non-legal facts bears a resemblance to the definitional relation. The theoretical relation requires that if there is a difference in legal facts, non-legal facts do not remain unchanged. This is parallel to a general theoretical responsibility: if there is a difference in theory, there must be a difference in the data.[46]

The theoretical relation differs from the definition relation, in many ways. First, a theoretical claim does not express a conceptual necessity but, at most, a 'synthetic' identity.[47] As Kripke and Putnam have shown, necessity and synonymy (in the classical sense of analyticity) need not go together. Consequently, claims about what it takes for something to be a contract do not pose as analytic truths, i.e. truths that must be held unrevisable come what may.[48] Rather, revisability (and the concomitant accountability to criticism and counterexamples) is essential.

Further, the theoretical nature of the claims implies that novel cases are handled in a different way. If a case arises which is a contract but is not X, where 'X' stands for the feature presented as individuative of contracts by the theory, failure of coextensiveness will not count against the theory's alleged reductivist claims, for the theory need not make such claims: such a case will imply that the theory is *wrong*, and is to be revised, so that it accounts for both past and novel cases in a principled way (or that, if it fails to do so, it is to be rejected in favour of a different theory).[49] In the latter case, its failure to capture the novel case is to be understood as a failure to capture something important about 'contract'.

Recall that novel cases are not essentially different from settled cases as far as the relevant theory is concerned. Characterizing a state of affairs as a 'contract' involves a defensible claim, viz. that it bears the required resemblances to the

[46] This formulation expresses the relation of supervenience. See Hurley, *Natural Reasons*, 295–303 and 'Coherence, Hypothetical Cases and Precedent', *10 OJLS* 221–51 at 233–4, for a defence of the possibility of supervenience without reducibility. Dworkin has recently endorsed the view that legal facts supervene on non-legal facts. See 'On Gaps in the Law', *in* Amselek, P., and MacCormick, D.N., (eds.), *Controversies About Law's Ontology*, 85. Cf. Ch. 4, section 7 on problems allegedly arising out of the supervenient character of ethical properties.

[47] Note that this point is about differences between K-P and definitional claims. A synthetic identity claim *could* be reductive. For example, the claim that temperature is mean kinetic molecular energy is both theoretical and reductive. However, the looser relation of supervenience may hold among other *relata* (Fs may *be* Gs), without there being a way of to reduce statements about Fs, expressible in those terms, to statements expressible in terms of Gs. Recall Davidson's supervenience claim discussed above, according to which mental events are physical events, while there are no psychophysical laws capable of supporting reduction of statements in mental terms to statements in physical terms.

[48] Cf. the discussion in the previous Chapter. David Brink makes the parallel point about taking synonymy as what he calls the 'semantic test' of identity or constitution in order to block naturalism in ethics, *in Moral Realism and the Foundations of Ethics*, 162.

[49] Note that the meta-theoretical claim that the content of 'contract' is given by the best theory is not reductivist: it does not amount to the claim that the content is whatever some particular theory claims it is, but rather that there is some best theory such that contract shall be what that theory, whichever it is, says. See Hurley, *Natural Reasons*, 295–303.

paradigmatic cases, in both easy and hard cases. A theoretical account supplies, but does not rely upon, a general characterization of conditions of something's being a contract. That characterization has no criterial status: it is only a synopsis of the theory's substantive claims. The unimportance of these characterizations stems from the theoretical nature of conceptual explications, an important aspect of which is what Burge calls 'responsibility of characterizations to examples', discussed in the preceding Chapter.

The responsibility of characterizations to examples further blocks any objection based on the lack of 'a single quality' necessary for, say, contracts. It is essential to the theoretical account that conceptual pressures on a characterization may come from an indefinite number of sources. Cases may reveal interrelations between concepts which have not previously been noticed and thus have not previously been allowed any role in determining a concept's correct application. If such a case obtains, the theory must change accordingly. The requirement is that application in such cases be defensible as principled, i.e. that there be good arguments for classifying such cases together with the paradigms, which is just the requirement that the relations between the various concepts be defensible. Note further that it is not possible, on the present account, to delimit in advance possible sources of challenge, since that would be tantamount to delimiting in advance the concept itself: to the extent that challenge may come about by virtue of hitherto unnoticed connections with other concepts, the judgment that, say, the application of 'contract' cannot be influenced by considerations of civil rights is a substantive judgment turning on claims about the content of the concepts involved and is therefore liable to be undermined.

Moreover, the theoretical approach accounts both for non-entailment between non-legal and legal facts, and for the fact that judicial behaviour is constrained by what legal concepts require. On the first score, non-legal facts are connected by theory to, and therefore do not entail, legal facts, just as data do not entail theory in science.[50] On the second, theoretical accounts insist on, rather than deny, judicial constraints: judges' behaviour is constrained by conditions of correct application of legal concepts, so that any attempted reduction of a concept's content to judicial behaviour is bound to be circular. In fact, such constraints are, on this account, operative in exactly the same way in settled and novel cases. Consequently, Hart's difficulties, i.e. the tension between holding that only in easy cases do such constraints strictly operate and insisting that some constraints in a relaxed sense are also at work in the 'penumbra', are avoided on a theoretical account.

In sum, it appears that a theoretical account respects, and makes better sense of, all of Hart's constraints (though certainly not in the way Hart thought they should be respected): namely, what I called the possibility of surprise, the non-passive and

[50] See Hurley, *Natural Reasons*, 295–303. Cf. Brink, *Moral Realism and the Foundations of Ethics*, 164 ff and 174 ff, who argues that unless theoretical, rather than logical, relations were allowed between concepts, scientific identifications e.g. between 'heat' and 'kinetic molecular energy', would be ruled out, since they involve substantive 'bridging' generalizations.

yet constrained character of judgments of application (and the concomitant absence of entailment among non-legal and legal facts), and generally the intuition that although legal concepts can be elucidated, they cannot be reductively identified with any behavioural or other empirical facts. As I noted, despite his anti-reductionism, Hart takes the ontologically conservative line of refusing to countenance legal properties as such. Part of the explanation for this is surely his unquestioned assumption that conceiving concepts as designated by predicates expressing properties entails the classical model of definition, single qualities, and reduction. But there may be an independent motivation for his ontological conservatism, a motivation that survives satisfaction of the other motivations by the account proposed here.

The K–P account takes care (or so I have argued) of Hart's motivations, by essentially depending on the notion of *discovery* about conceptual content. But perhaps discovery cannot make sense in contexts like law. Hart's independent motivation could amount to something like this: scepticism or reductionism about legal properties cannot be right, yet neither can realism about them. Despite the existence of constraints on judgments of application of legal concepts, these constraints cannot consist in some properties' real nature. A property *sensu stricto* can only be something intrinsic about some object or event, which constrains cognitive efforts in a way independent of us. But law is essentially something we 'make up as we go along'; we make it up bearing in mind how others before us (especially legislatures) have themselves made it up, although the degree of freedom available with legal concepts is certainly greater than with expressions designating normal empirical objects. Further, conceiving the law as involving properties with a discoverable nature may even fall foul of a specific Hartian consideration, namely the fallacy of conceiving law as extending itself into an infinite range of situations, 'unfolding what is already there'.[51]

Gerald Postema has expressed a related, yet different thought about the supposedly special relation between cognitive efforts and their object in law:

> Participant theories [unlike observer theories of natural phenomena] do not have the distance from the phenomena they try to account [f]or that observer theories sometimes enjoy. Thus, while different and mutually incompatible observer theories may be possible without the coherence and orderliness of the phenomena being compromised, this is not true for participant theories of social practices.[52]

[51] See 'Jhering', 269.

[52] 'The Normativity of Law', *in* Gavison, R. (ed.), *Issues in Contemporary Legal Philosophy*, at 103. I do not know where Postema stands on the question of ontic commitment, but the cited point seems to echo a view as conservative as Hart's.

4. ANTI-REALISM AND ONTIC COMMITMENT

This line of thought—focusing on an allegedly special relation between inquiry and its object in the legal domain—rests on a motivation independent of all of Hart's semantic arguments, I have claimed. Let me further support this claim. It is not the case that countenancing genuine properties by itself entails commitment to realism, K–P semantics or anything else.

First, let us accept that K–P semantics competes with some form of anti-realism. Now anti-realism is distinct from ontic conservatism: it is a thesis about how to understand declarative sentences—*inter alia*, sentences like 'there are Fs'—rather than about the question whether Fs really exist. Anti-realism proper is distinct from domain anti-realism, a species of domain scepticism.[53] An anti-realist wants to deny that all sentences involving F have a determinate truth-value; he insists that only those which are effectively decidable, i.e. whose content can be backed by a body of warranting information linking them to experience, have some such value (described in terms of assertibility, rather than truth).[54] *Prima facie*, then, an anti-realist can be ontologically liberal, i.e. accept that any entities to which we appear be committed to are part of 'reality', adding his decidability caveat about how to understand reality.

4.1 *Ontological Liberalism*

An anti-realist need not confine his ontology to observable, or perceptually salient, objects, provided some links to experience are available for any type of object.[55]

[53] Crispin Wright distinguishes three brands of anti-realism. The first, whose development is attributed to Michael Dummett, is to do with understanding declarative sentences in a discourse, and amounts to the idea sketched in the text viz. that one needs to be able to use the sentence in conditions whose obtaining cannot be evidence-transcendent. The second is what I call in the text domain-scepticism, whose typical exponents are, as Wright notes, John Mackie on ethical discourse and Hartry Field on mathematics. These theorists accuse participants in each of these discourses of committing an error in metaphysics—contrary to the discourse's surface structure, there is nothing out there making ethical and mathematical sentences, respectively, true or false. The third is what is known as expressivism, and consists in the thesis that apparently declarative sentences in a discourse are in fact mere expressions of attitudes. See Wright, *Truth and Objectivity*, 3–7.

In looking for a motivation for objecting to the applicability of K-P semantics to law, we must look to the last two of these brands of anti-realism. Although Wright gives the contrary impression in setting up his tripartite distinction, only these two really concern particular domains. Although the first, Dummettian, anti-realism can surely be expressed in terms of what holds for a particular domain or discourse, it is driven by views on the concepts of understanding and truth in general, and should in principle apply to *any* discourse. Wright appears to accept that, ibid., 7 ff.

[54] Note that anti-realism may not allow for the possibility of discovery about concepts' extensions, since such a possibility may imply that some sentences have a determinate truth value despite our not being in a position to establish it. In that way, anti-realism may deny in principle that an entire community may be in error about the extension of a concept. Again, this will hold for any concept, independent of legal concepts' ostensible peculiarities.

[55] See Michael Luntley's detailed defence of ontologically liberal anti-realism, *Language, Logic and Experience*, esp. ch. 9.

The link to experience in the case of theoretical entities is plausibly argued by Michael Luntley to be *perceptual skills* making non-salient objects cognitively available. For example, anti-realists may treat observations that depend heavily on theory—such as observations of events taking place in cloud chambers—as empirical: they may treat the entities involved as available to experience, where experience is taken to include the special kind of awareness that results from scientific training. Legal training could well serve as such a skill, if legal concepts were to be treated as theoretical terms (though presumably an anti-realist could reject the K–P thesis that hard cases make for *discovery* of concepts' content). In any case, nothing seems to turn on acceptance of non-empirical properties itself.[56]

Second, assuming that the supposed non-empirical nature of legal *designata* is equivalent to their lack of perceptual salience, it would be a strange move for a K–P opponent to base his attack on a property's non-empirical status. Expressions designating perceptually salient objects (call them empirical concepts) are, if anything, less readily accounted for by K–P semantics—they are precisely more suited for *empiricist* semantics (conversely, it is non-empirical entities that empiricist semantics has trouble with). Empirical objects (still in the sense assumed above) make for more stable concepts: challenges against the commonly accepted content of an empirical concept usually have to be backed by claims about perceptual error, illusion, and the like.[57] Baker cites an example of what passes as a dog falling apart and revealing a clockwork mechanism; and Hart imagines samples of what passes as gold by all chemical tests to be revealed to fail to emit the right sort of radiation.[58] In such cases, the anti-realist resistance to theoretical intrusion is more plausible: it is relatively difficult to argue that such cases justify revision of the content of 'gold' or 'dog', and it is far easier to say that these cases fail the criteria, or, at least, that the question whether they should be classified under the familiar concepts admits of an arbitrary answer. By contrast, notions whose content depends on various assumptions about facts not readily perceptible and which are (relatively more) intricately connected to other theoretical notions are cut out for K–P claims: it is easier to claim that there are grounds for revision of our conception of 'electricity' than our conception of 'light-bulb'.

So the distinction backing the claim that K–P semantics are more suitable in empirical, than in legal, discourse cannot be the distinction between observability (or perceptual salience) and theoretical character that I have been discussing. It seems that the distinction in question relates to objects' naturalness. The objector seems to have in mind the world-view according to which the natural world exists

[56] Recall that Hart's semantics purports to be generally applicable: first, he certainly intends that it should be able to treat empirical predicates like 'vehicle' and 'gold', as mentioned above. Secondly, he says that his semantic claims concerning law derive from general developments in the philosophy of language, and the issue of language–thought relations more particularly, without qualification of domain. See 'Jhering'.

[57] See Burge, 'Intellectual Norms and Foundations of Mind', *83 J. Phil.*, 697–720 at 716.

[58] 'Defeasibility', 48, and 'Jhering', 275, respectively.

in some strong sense (say, independent of us). By contrast, whatever is not part of the natural world can only be said to exist in some weaker sense. This thought would go some way towards accounting for reluctance to countenance suspect properties. The extension of legal concepts should not be identified with a class of instances of a legal property, the objector would say, because this would imply that there is something that the instances share that is mind-independent, which is not the case.

It is still difficult to see how one could combine refusal to accept legal properties and resistance to both reductionism and scepticism about law. The mind-dependence criterion is again neutral on ontic commitment. The intuition which the objection set out in the preceding paragraph purports to capture does not concern existence of properties, but *direction of individuation.* McGinn writes:

> [I]f colours or moral values, say, are taken to be projected onto the world by the mind, then there can be no explaining the relevant distinctions of mental content by reference to prior worldly distinctions. . . . What the mind projects cannot also introject. What it spreads cannot also be spread on it. If we took natural kind taxonomy to be a (mere) projection of the mind, not determined antecedently to the operations of the mind, then we could not *also* suppose that our system of natural kind concepts is structured by what natural kinds the world we live in actually and objectively contains.[59]

The question, McGinn argues, is focused by asking how concepts' extensions and properties' classes of instances match. K–P semantics is taken to return an answer concerning natural kinds according to which the concept is determined by the property. By contrast, projectivism claims that it is the other way around: concepts determine properties.[60]

I believe that McGinn's distinction in terms of direction of individuation is the real basis of the objection to K–P semantics' applicability to legal concepts. In the remainder of this chapter, I shall make a preliminary exploration of the objection construed in the light of that distinction.

If that is the distinction we are after, then the objector argues for a mixed view: natural objects are such that their properties determine the relevant concepts, whereas the opposite holds for law. The difference is motivated by some intuition concerning the different concepts and properties. Postema, in the passage cited in the previous section, formulates the intuition in terms of 'distance'. McGinn puts it thus:

> Fundamentally, it is the epistemic distance between the essence of a kind and the way we represent it that determines whether strong externalism [viz. the natural-kind direction of individuation] will be true of it (for us). Projected essences will lie at no distance from our conceptions of them.[61]

[59] *Mental Content*, 11; emphasis in the original. [60] Ibid., 12.

[61] Ibid., 51 n. 67. Nothing here depends on McGinn's distinction between strong and weak externalism.

Of course, if the contrast were drawn simply on the basis of *direction* of individuation, then no question of 'distance' between property and concept would arise in either case. In both cases one is individuated by the other. But the required asymmetry arises thus: there can be, in the case of natural kinds, some slack between *conceptions* and properties (and, hence, the corresponding concepts). But no such slack is available in the case of concepts individuating properties. If something's being red were something's seeming red, then no epistemic distance would ensue. The mind-dependent, as I call them, properties are epistemically transparent. A difficult case, not quite matching the representation, is *eo ipso* not part of the concept's extension. By contrast, the slack available between the property of being gold and representations of gold things, on the other hand, allows for us to be in error, and by the same token allows for doubt and revision.

This line of thought is questionable. In Chapter 2 I argued that the semantic character of natural kind concepts does not arise out of the distinction discussed here, viz. kinds' appearance and their essence, but rather out of *semantic* considerations, namely whether use of such concepts is such that their conceptions carry a responsibility of substantive defence, or openness to doubt (when henceforth I write in terms of doubt, I shall also have in mind theoretical character).

The present formulation makes openness to doubt turn on the simple criterion of whether one can go wrong about the content of a concept. Although concepts are not specially privileged, since they may sometimes be 'externally' individuated, *conceptions* play the privileged role: they consist in mental content accessible in a transparent way. So the contrast is between cases in which conceptions may differ from concept, and cases where no such difference may obtain, i.e. in which conceptions and concepts are identical.

Although we need not deny that cases of the latter type may occur, it is far from clear that only 'natural' predicates constitute exceptions to it. That is, concepts other than those picked out by natural kind terms may be theoretical. Again, the crucial consideration is this: concepts such that their conceptions cannot fail to be identical with them are those for which doubt cannot coherently be accommodated. Doubting whether 'painy' is correctly applicable to things capable of producing pain, for instance, may be doubting whether 'painy' is applicable to painy things (it may be failure to grasp the concept). We may insist, nonetheless, that doubting whether 'sofa' applies to pieces of furniture made for sitting is not doubting that 'sofa' applies to sofas, but is rather doubting whether sofas are what they are thought to be.

4.2 Epistemic Distance and Doubt

Drawing the distinction in terms of 'distance' or 'slack' encourages the following line of thought. Concerning natural kinds, one can express doubt about the relevant concepts' content because one can refer to the kind without having to employ the concept. One can pick out the kind in terms of a 'physicalistic' description, and then proceed to ask whether that class is really X, where X stands for the accepted specification of the concept's content. For instance, one may pick out water by H_2O, and then proceed to ask whether it need be liquid (assuming that that is a property commonly ascribed to water). By contrast, no such description may be available in other cases to anchor doubt: there is no property one may use to pick out contracts other than those contained in the conventional explication. (Although intermediate cases like 'sofa' may arise, the objection continues, where someone may use sofas' perceptual properties to pick them out and then proceed to ascribe to them his favourite property, no such possibility exists in the case of law, where no property other than the abstract legal one is available to pick out the relevant class.)

On this objection, the doubter is pictured as not thinking with the concept he appears to be criticizing, but with a 'reduced' version of it. So he is not doubting whether water need be liquid, but whether H_2O need be liquid. His thought 'water need not be liquid' contains the referent of water, but does not employ the concept 'water'.

The 'reduced' concept move is not convincing. The doubter need not have any alternative way of identifying the extension of water; he may not have even *any* way to identify the referents—he may rely on others for that.[62] The most straightforward interpretation of 'water is not liquid' is that something is said about the concept water, as much as about the stuff.[63] And the point of appealing to semantic intuitions in the natural kind cases is exactly that doubts concerning the relevant concepts are expressible.

Further, there are other ways in which doubt about conventional meaning may be raised. The doubter may concentrate on what he considers a counterexample. He may draw attention to something on whose description, in terms neutral to the crucial concept, everyone agrees. For example, that it is a solid substance at room temperature and has various other characteristics. Then, he may proceed to claim that it is a sample of water. In this example, it is even clearer that the availability of the neutral description is of no help to our 'reduced-concept' objector. The doubter expresses a doubt about the concept of water, a doubt that can only be adjudicated by considering competing views on what it takes for something to be water.

An analogue in law for that kind of doubt can be framed. The doubter picks out an event in terms neutral to the conception of 'contract' he is about to attack, and proceeds to claim that it is a contract, despite everyone's agreeing that one of the conventional conditions does not obtain. His doubt is about the concept's correct application.

The 'reduced' concept move aside, the mixed view we are considering does not

[62] Identification is not important: the doubter may not have any other concept capable of picking out the class, and still express non-standard thoughts about it.

[63] See Burge, 'Intellectual Norms and Foundations of Mind', 711–12.

deny that *some* concepts are such as to admit of doubt about their content. So the issue turns on whether concepts like contract are such. To exclude such concepts from doubt, one needs convincingly to argue against the intuition that when one is doubting that contracts need consideration, one is not doubting whether contracts need be contracts.

In sum, I have traced resistance to accepting K–P semantics to law to considerations of mind-dependence, and specifically the idea that, for mind-dependent properties, conceptions individuate concepts. I have argued that such considerations cut across observability or even naturalness of the domain. Rather, they turn on whether the relevant conception is such that it is *responsible* to the properties of its extension, or whether it *individuates* such properties and hence determines the relevant concepts' extension.

It is beyond question that legal concepts *are* different from natural kind concepts. But mind-dependence is too loose a notion to determine legal concepts' semantic properties. In the Chapters that follow, I shall argue that the difference is better conceived in terms of the fact that theories of legal concepts have human practices as their object, and are therefore in that sense mind-dependent. That dependence, however, does not necessarily imply that what individuals, or even communities, think is the extension of legal concepts, is decisive (or so I shall argue). Rather, the dependence on practices implies that what people *do* is decisive—even though, especially for law, what they think may also become important through precedent. I shall argue that dependence on practices, properly conceived, leaves room for doubt and supports the theoretical character of concepts' application.

The most plausible case for legal conceptions individuating concepts may be some sort of projectivism. Projectivism would support a model of legal reasoning as constrained, yet not by mind-independent properties. The combination involved may yield a picture of application that is constrained, without by that token turning into a picture on which application is a matter of fact.[64] In the next Chapter I shall discuss whether that represents a coherent, and better, alternative to K–P analysis. More specifically, I shall examine whether a satisfactory conception of constraints can be had within a projectivist model, and I shall argue for an objectivist model that makes no bizarre metaphysical commitments.

[64] So the intuition, misconceptions of which are the ideas that law is non-empirical or non-natural, is that law's content is non-factual (its application is not governed by a matter of fact).

4

Mind-Dependence and Cognitivism

1. INTRODUCTION

The question I am examining is whether K–P semantics may be applicable in the analysis of law. K–P semantics consists (in a nutshell) in the claim that some concepts have semantic depth, i.e. that the meaning of some concepts turns on a substantive theory that best accounts for the nature of paradigmatic instances of the property which they designate, or paradigmatic objects falling into their extension, so that the correct application of those concepts is sensitive to that theory. An objection bound to be raised in this connection is that K–P semantics is appropriate, if at all, only for concrete, perceptually salient entities, and not for abstract properties like the ones that legal concepts may be said to designate. This objection was deflected in Chapter 3, and reconstructed as the objection that law is an inappropriate domain not because of lack of perceptual salience, but because of mind-dependence. Mind-dependence, it will be objected, makes legal concepts inappropriate for K–P semantics, since that analysis requires that its objects be in the 'external world'.

In section 2, I shall explore the objection from mind-dependence, and connect it with similar objections raised in ethics. In the subsequent sections I shall discuss non-cognitivism concerning values, which is supposed to be a consequence of the mind-dependence of evaluative properties. In section 3, I shall discuss subjectivism about values and its relation to non-cognitivism. In sections 4 to 6 I shall discuss the conceptions of subjectivity and objectivity implicit in non-cognitivism. I shall argue that both conceptions are wrong. Further, I shall argue that no reduction of value to 'subjective' properties, on the conception of 'subjective' under criticism, is possible, and that the way the distinction between subjectivity and objectivity is drawn by non-cognitivists makes for serious problems in every—not only the evaluative—domain. In section 7, I shall discuss the alleged queerness of evaluative properties. I shall argue that evaluative properties are natural properties, and I shall defend their metaphysical and epistemological respectability *vis à vis* objections of explanatory irrelevance. In section 8, I shall discuss what is the right sort of scepticism in ethics. I shall argue that no global scepticism succeeds, while selective scepticism is possible and in fact militates for the objectivity of evaluative judgment. In sections 9 and 10, I shall discuss respectively objections from the failure of convergence of ethical opinion, and the alleged unworkability of attribution of substantive error on ethical discourse. In section 11, I shall suggest how disarming the non-cognitivist objection in ethics succeeds in disarming it in law as well. This Chapter as a whole continues discussion of the metaphysical and epistemological commitments necessary for legal objectivism. It should further support the claim that very little indeed is required by way of such commitments for the law's content to be objective.

2. MIND-DEPENDENCE

A general idea that lies behind arguing from mind-dependence to failure of the K–P framework is this: legal properties are products of the human mind; consequently legal concepts cannot have semantic depth, since semantic depth requires that there be a difference between what we think the properties are, and what they in fact are. Such a difference could only hold true on the supposition that there is a fact of the matter concerning legal properties, and this is an ***absurdum***: only ready-made ('mind-independent') things possess fact-of-the-matter natures.

The objection just sketched needs much sharpening in order to be evaluated, but its broad motivation would suggest an argument familiar in many areas, notably ethics. I shall discuss the issues involved, but in connection with the nature of ethical properties, judgments, etc. The reason for this is the following: law, according to a view with considerable currency, is just the domain of institutionally endorsed morality. If morality is essentially inappropriate for K–P treatment, then, on that view, no hope would exist for the law. (Of course, having established that ethics *are* K–P-appropriate does not waive the burden to argue that law in particular is K–P-appropriate as well; I shall leave that question for the end of this Chapter.) Further, the view I am taking concerning the way in which the content of legal expressions is established, while short of identifying law with morality or ethics, does imply that ethical judgment is necessary in order to identify the content of the law.[1]

Both considerations make it crucial to counter the objection from mind-dependence in the context of evaluative judgment. But let me first try to elaborate the rationale of the objection in general. What is being denied to mind-dependent properties is a conception of objectivity: it is not the case, the objection goes, that what such properties consist in turns on some 'fact of the matter', or at least some deep such fact, so that there could be a sensible distinction between correct and incorrect applications of the relevant concepts (where experts, at least, are concerned). The crucial consideration is that such properties, being mind's

[1] This version of the necessary connection thesis has been described in the preceding Chapters and is further characterized in the next two Chapters. Briefly, substantive ethical theory is necessary in order to identify the law, but the latter's content may or may not coincide with the substance of that theory.

creations, cannot be properties of a 'ready-made' world, of things 'in themselves'. Even at this unclear stage, the metaphors seem to suggest that the plausibility of claims to objectivity (on which claims of semantic depth depend) turns on the world being thus and so independent of the mind's cognitive efforts (or even its presence). Things, on this picture, divide into those essentially within, and those without, the mind. The objectivity characteristic of that second sort of things is then explained somewhat along these lines: nature, by virtue of the fact that it exists (and is thus and so) anyway, *impinges* on us; by the same token, it may always keep surprising us, since our efforts at knowing how it is may always be to a greater or lesser extent misguided.[2] But the rest (i.e. non-natural things) cannot have this capacity for surprise: either they are immediately (and incorrigibly) available to the mind or at worse they are indirectly so accessible, by virtue of their being, as it were, 'designed' by us.

'Mind', according to this objection, should be conceived as some kind of collective or 'communal' mind. How exactly to specify that will be left open for the time being. But clearly the objector need not claim that no one can be surprised or go wrong about mind-dependent properties; he only need claim that competent or expert speakers, or at least the community as a whole (conceived on the basis of its specification being left open), cannot go wrong.[3] This caveat should be borne in mind in the ensuing discussion.

A form which the notion of mind-dependence takes is conceiving mind-dependent entities or properties as 'artifacts'. K–P type claims cannot be made in those cases, it is argued, because the truth about such properties' or entities' essence cannot plausibly be said to transcend even what the appropriate experts have to say about it (which seems to be another way of saying that there is no scope for discovery and surprise). Unlike natural kinds, artifacts' nature is not picked out by locating exemplars and inquiring after their distinctive nature; we do not stumble across a clock, and set out to work out what it is made of. Rather, their nature is given: a clock is any time-keeping device, and it does not matter what forms it takes as long as it fulfils that purpose. Artifacts then seem to be the perfect candidates for the traditional approach, viz. capable of being captured in definitions (usually specifying their function).[4]

[2] Recall that the explanation of natural properties' capacity to surprise us is supposed to be that what is subjective resides within the mind and is therefore epistemically accessible, whereas what is objective may or may not match the content of mind's cognitive efforts. See Ch. 3, section 4.

[3] How to specify the 'communal' mind is of course extremely important. I have already argued in Ch. 2 against individualism as characterized by Burge, and I have claimed that, once that is rejected, the content of both individual and 'communal' minds is determined by external constraints, and therefore appeal to communities will not make the difference the present objector imagines. I shall reconsider the issue in the light of the mind-dependence objection below. In Ch. 5, another—Wittgensteinian—formulation of the problem is discussed.

[4] Cf. D. Wiggins, *Sameness and Substance*, 87–9. In *Problems from Locke* (hereinafter *PFL*), 88–93, John Mackie attributes to Locke the thought that expressions designating artifacts, *inter alia*, have only nominal essence, i.e. their extension is whatever fulfils an *a priori* specification. Mackie corrects Locke with respect to the *explanation* of this semantic property: see discussion below.

Putnam has argued that artifacts are well within the ambit of his semantic claims. We can imagine a case in which every instance of what pass as pencils turns out to be a living organism (perhaps sent by Martians to spy on us); or a different case, in which Twin-Earth pencils are superficially indistinguishable from actual pencils, but are in fact organisms, whereas actual pencils are manufactured. In the first case, Putnam says, we should say that pencils are in fact living organisms whereas in the second we should say that Twin-Earth 'pencils' are not really pencils. What is the appropriate description in each case turns on what the things we call 'pencils' on Earth really are, rather than whether a thing (actual or counterfactual) answers to a definition current among users of the term.[5]

Putnam's argument here splits into two points. In the first place, even in the case of expressions like 'pencil', 'chair' etc., competent users' dossier of information used to pick out a term's extension does not determine that extension. In the case where Earth contains artifactual pencils and Twin-Earth contains living 'pencils', both Earth and Twin-Earth speakers have identical information dossiers, incapable of discriminating between the two kinds of objects. Rather, the difference in the objects' nature dictates that the English and Twenglish expressions have different extensions. In English, Twin-Earth does not really contain pencils, but only their 'epistemic counterparts', pencil lookalikes. So extension is not determined by the extant criteria.

Of course, one might say, the extension is determined by the 'underlying' nature of the examples, but that nature is 'functional'. Whatever serves a purpose or function—say, sea-travel—belongs to the extension of 'ship'. There are different ways to fulfil that purpose or perform that function and, given the interaction of these functions with the environment, new such ways may be discovered. But the functional essence itself is, in the case of artifacts, given. No discoveries may be made concerning *that*: a ship is whatever serves for travel on water. So, the argument continues, the lack of depth of artifact terms *is* explained by the fact that they involve some sort of invention; yet, as Mackie points out, that does not mean that there are no transactions between the mind that invents the term and associates some 'ideas' with it, on the one hand, and the environment, on the other. Adultery, Mackie says, need not be a purely imaginary category. Rather, what matters is that some terms are invented in order to designate whatever fulfils the associated descriptions (in contrast to natural kind terms, that are invented to designate a stuff 'whatever properties and constitution it may turn out to have').[6] So the compliants of artifact terms are answerable to the definition, rather than the other way around.

Putnam need not resist that line, and in fact this is the second part of the point

[5] 'The Meaning of Meaning', *Mind, Language and Reality*, 242–4.

[6] Mackie, *PFL*, 93.

he is making: we *may* conclude that certain expressions do designate functional kinds, so that their extension is determined by the specification of the relevant function; and we may further conclude that such a function is entirely specifiable *a priori*, so that no discoveries are possible about it. Yet to establish that some case is such, we need to test intuitions by devising counterfactual tests like the ones concerning pencils above. It may thus be the case that even if all local examples of what passes as a pencil turn out to be living organisms, we would stop calling them pencils—we might say that we could still *make* a pencil on the basis of the functional specification.[7] Our intuitions may go either way for each case, i.e. towards an 'artifactual' or 'natural kind' treatment, but it is those intuitions that determine an expression's semantic properties, and just what they are is not part of the expression's sense—it is not analytic. Hence an expression's being associated with what appears as a stipulation does not suffice to render it a non-deep expression: *lack of depth is not on an expression's surface.*

A further source of resistance to assimilating non-naturalness of an expression's *designatum* with criterial content is found in Burge's work: if the content of expressions standing for artifacts is given in genuine stipulations, then no one who understands the expression can coherently doubt the stipulation. Yet someone doubting that sofas are meant for sitting on is expressing a coherent doubt that is either true or false, rather than talking nonsense.[8]

But even ignoring such reservations, the crucial observation is that the objection from artifacts involves commitment to the view that the content of artifact terms is captured in definitions, and this is a strange result. Evaluative properties, for one thing, are extremely implausible candidates for such analysis, unless we conceive ethical concepts as stipulative, and accordingly explain away all disagreement as only apparent, brought about by insufficient grasp of the definition (or perhaps failure to appreciate that the same expression is answerable to different definitions in different cultures, if inter-cultural disagreement is at issue). Law, on the other hand, is even more readily understood as a social product, yet it seems particularly difficult to attempt to reinstate the method of definition in its analysis, especially after Hart's classic discussion.[9]

This implausibility arises from collapsing introduction by description to lack of semantic depth (i.e. to the *stipulative* status of the introducing description). The background motivation for this lies in a picture of conceptual freedom, which, in

[7] Adrian Moore suggested this point. Note that I here suppose that 'being manufactured' is included in the *a priori* specification of a pencil's function. See Moore's introduction to A. W. Moore (ed.), *Meaning and Reference*, especially sections VIII and IX.

[8] See 'Intellectual Norms and Foundations of Mind', *83 J.Phil.* 697–720. See Ch. 2, section 4.

[9] I do not mean that the criterial move is not available to someone who deploys the artifact argument and yet finds the defintiion model embarrassing. But, as I argued in the preceding Chapter, the motivation of the criterial model is independent of the motivation of the artifact argument. The former is a global thesis about concepts, whereas the latter relies on some property (mind-dependence) characteristic of some expressions. I am here concerned with the implications of that property.

turn, results in further implausibilities. Mackie cites Locke's version of this picture, in connection with concepts like 'murder' or 'incest':

> these abstract *ideas* being the workmanship of the mind and not referred to the real existence of things, there is no supposition of anything more signified by that name, but barely that complex *idea* the mind itself has formed . . . and [this] is that on which all the properties of the *species* depend, and from which alone they all flow; and so in these the *real* and *nominal essence* is the same[10]

Although such concepts *are* taken to be related to real things, the 'ideas' determine which of the things fall under the relevant heads, unlike 'substances', whose relation with 'ideas' is the opposite: regarding the latter, we have to learn through observation what things *ought* to be classified under the relevant expressions. The cited passage sets up a simple test—we may call it the Lockean test: if a category is invented by the mind, rather than found already there in nature, then it is necessarily immune to discovery and revision.

As mentioned in the previous Chapter, this way of thinking would have the unfortunate implication that theoretical terms would be treated as stipulations (their 'nominal essence' should determine their compliants). Only macroscopic natural entities would escape such treatment. Yet theoretical terms do not seem to admit such treatment; by contrast, they seem paradigmatically deep in that there seems to be scope for discovery about their real content. They seem *targeted*, in other words, on nature in the way Locke envisages in the case of concepts whose content we are to be taught 'through experience, rather than reason'.

The crucial consideration, then, seems to be the targeting: whether or not concepts have semantic depth depends not on whether they are introduced by way of an apparent stipulation, but on whether the introducing 'definition' captures some properties about which discoveries and corrections may be made.[11] Consequently, concepts like 'incest' or 'murder' *may* have such depth: they may be used to pick out properties we could learn something about. Once we abandon the simple Lockean test, it is no longer obvious that these concepts should not have any depth.

[10] Cited in Mackie, *PFL*, 89.

[11] Mackie accepts that the crucial distinction turns on how concepts are intended. He also argues that Locke saw the distinction himself, but thought that such linguistic intentions were misguided. See *PFL*, 93–100. 'How the concepts are intended', however, is ambiguous. Intentions surely count in determining what kind of object 'introducers' of the concept, if there have been any, thought their concept refers to, but may still fail to determine fully the extension. What intentions to ascribe is a theoretical matter, that is bound to be influenced by the nature of a putative object of intention. For example, whether it is intended that 'gold' stand for the stuff, or for superficial properties, will be partly decided on the basis of whether there is any deep nature to paradigmatic instances. Now if the objects have discoverable natures, the introducers' criteria may fail to identify the object uniquely, or determine the extension, and may have to be revised. Cf. the discussion of Kripke's and Putnam's arguments on introduction-intentions, Ch. 2.

Cf. C. McGinn, *Mental Content*, 59 ff, who seems to take the view that *theoretical* considerations about the objects' nature are important, and argues, for example, that observational concepts are in fact necessarily such that their extension is determined by their intension, i.e. the properties associated with the relevant concepts, since they are essentially phenomenal (they turn on how things *seem*).

So whether the kind of mind-dependence important here is true of an expression is to be settled through reflection on its use. This question may cut across the distinction between mind-dependence and mind-independence *simpliciter*: it is surely the case that adultery, unlike rocks, would not exist in the absence of minds, yet this does not entail that the content of 'adultery' cannot fail to be transparent to minds' efforts. The artifact argument appears to slide from a causal to other senses of mind-dependence. As David Brink argues, no one doubts that artifacts, for example, are causally dependent on human minds in the sense that they depend on their designers' beliefs and desires. Yet the kind of dependence that the artifact argument needs is different: it is a form of *constitutive* dependence. The objector needs to show that artifacts' nature, and the content of artifact terms, are constituted by the relevant beliefs of artifacts' designers or terms' inventors. He needs some kind of dependence that guarantees epistemic transparency of such objects' nature, so that it cannot fail to be what we think it is.[12]

The interesting kind of dependence is not established by the artifact argument, and therefore that argument gives us no reason to doubt that the question of semantic depth is, in principle, to be answered through reflection on concepts' use. In fact, testing whether ethical and legal concepts have semantic depth, i.e. involve the intention that they pick out properties about which discoveries may be made, seems to yield positive results: typical use of ethical concepts involves *substantive* defence of claims about their content; and diverging views on their content attract accusations of *substantive* error. But perhaps, it might be argued, this is not the case (i.e. ethical concepts are not really used in this way); or, even if they are so used, the use is misguided—they *cannot* have the depth speakers seem to assume they do. This last move directs the charge of error to speakers at large: in believing they are dealing with semantically deep expressions, they are committing a higher-level error (their semantic beliefs are mistaken).

3. NON-COGNITIVISM AND SUBJECTIVISM

We saw that there is no quick way from mind-dependence to lack of semantic depth. The notion of mind-dependence may be fleshed out, however, in different ways that may seem to make a case against semantic depth. That is, an account of the nature of ethics may identify a characteristic that explains ethical concepts' alleged lack of depth. The standard such metaphysical account is built around a conception of ethical properties as consisting in *subjective responses* to ethically

[12] See D. Brink, 'Semantics and Legal Interpretation; (Further Thoughts)', *2 Canadian Journal of Law and Jurisprudence*, 181–91, at 183–4. Notice that the converse causal dependence is also neutral towards constitutive dependence: sensations are no doubt causally dependent on the environment, but most philosophers think that they are constitutively dependent on the subject's mind.

neutral facts. Usually, the responses are thought to depend upon attitudinal or affective dispositions, rather than the exercise of conceptual capacities.[13]

There are two strategies to connect the response account to lack of depth. The first claims that ethical concepts have no depth since they are not used to describe anything, but only to express some attitude or emotion. For example, 'cruelty is wrong' is really expressing disapprobation towards certain types of behaviour—those types, non-ethically described, that are labelled 'cruel'. The second strategy concedes that the surface structure of ethical judgment is descriptive: 'cruelty is wrong' is an attempt at describing a fact, like 'apples grow on trees'. But the metaphysical account ensures that the attempt will fail: ethical properties are intimately connected with the subject—usually they are again thought of as attitudinal or emotional states—and speakers engaging in ethical judgment actually 'project' them onto things, but mistake their 'projected' attitudes for real properties that they are actually discerning.

Both moves are typically united in their metaphysics—a projection, or at least an attachment, of attitude to world.[14] The first move finds no error with speakers, and places weight on the expressivist hypothesis: the semantic claim that ethical discourse can be explained as expressions of attitude rather than reports of fact. The second move shifts the emphasis onto the metaphysics: it must support the view that ethics *cannot* be descriptive and it must show what it is that ethical properties lack but is nonetheless erroneously attributed to them.[15] The second move is more important, since it is based on the plausible idea that, whatever the surface structure of a discourse, it may be misleading. So not much is at stake in debating the actual surface structure of ethical discourse, unless a position about that can be supported by a plausible metaphysics of the object of discourse. Nevertheless, since the surface structure may supply a *presumption* of the underlying metaphysics, the first move must be addressed first; whether ethical discourse is on its face cognitivist or not, may affect the overall plausibility of each position.

The first move represents *non-cognitivism* (NC) in the strict sense. NC *sensu stricto* is best captured by views on which apparent ethical judgments lack assertoric force, but rather perform some other 'speech act'. But this claim makes strict NC vulnerable to the well-known objections to setting apart any class of expressions ostensibly having special, non-assertoric force. That objection derives from Frege

[13] Throughout the discussion I shall be alternating between evaluative and ethical concepts, since nothing distinguishes them in non-cognitivism. One cannot consistently be non-cognitivist about ethics and cognitivist about values, since whatever metaphysical and epistemological defect ethical properties have according to non-cognitivism—emotive nature, non-fabric-of-the-world status etc.—evaluative properties have it as well.

[14] 'Projection' is more apt for the error move, in which the attitudes are not only 'spread' on the world, but are also mistook for the real thing.

[15] Mackie's *Ethics: Inventing Right and Wrong* makes the second move. Notice the parallel between Locke's and Mackie's error moves: in *PFL*, Mackie has Locke accuse speakers of error even about the capacity of natural kind predicates to pick out real properties. Mackie himself concedes that capacity, while accusing speakers of error in the restricted ethical domain.

and was later developed by Geach. Susan Hurley has developed the Frege/Geach point in the following way.[16] If a sentence like 'X is wrong' performs a non-assertoric speech act, then it is unclear how that performance embeds in conditionals like: 'if X is wrong, then Y is wrong'. If such a conditional is used in *modus ponens* inferences (supplemented, say, by 'X is wrong' and concluding with 'Y is wrong'), then it is difficult to make sense of the inference. This objection appeals to the following intuition: the inference being drawn in the example appears to be the same sort of inference as that in the general case, viz. 'if p then q'; 'p'; 'therefore q'. Now the standard inference requires that the content of 'p' in both major and minor premises be the same, as it is indeed by taking the cognitivist line: in the unasserted 'if p', 'p' has the same content as in the asserted 'p'. But if 'p' expresses an attitude or performs some other 'speech-act', then it does not seem to match the content of 'p' in 'if p', since, in the latter context, 'p'—the alleged attitude—is described, rather than expressed. So the inference does not appear valid.

Non-cognitivists are faced with a dilemma. Either they must find a way to characterize the conditional so that the content of 'p' in the major premise matches that in the minor, and so defend the inference's validity on the standard *modus ponens* form; or they must characterize the inference itself as a different type of inference—a type not applicable to ordinary assertions, on pain of failing to show what is allegedly special about ethical utterances—*and* offer reasons for falsifying the intuition that it belongs with the standard *modus ponens* form.

There does not seem to be any way of attempting the first horn's task successfully, insofar as one seems bound to construe the major premise as appealing to the existence or propriety of a response, rather than actually expressing it, and thus bound to allow that the response is a normal (if subjective) fact, while insisting that the minor premise expresses an attitude would render the inference invalid.[17] One may take the second horn, and insist that the inference *is* valid, despite the mismatch of content in the premises. Such a move must amount to the discovery of a special kind of inference, since the expressivist reading of the ordinary *modus ponens* would not be valid. We may concede the validity of any such special inference, and still ask for an argument to the effect that it *is* special—that it is not what it appears to be, namely an ordinary inference (with the result that the descriptiveness of the major premise is matched by descriptiveness in the minor). Even if there were a valid inference for expressive discourse, ethical inferences

[16] Frege's objection had been made in connection with negation ('Negation', in *Logical Investigations*) and has been extended by Geach to cast doubt against non-standard force characterizations in 'Assertion', *Logic Matters*. See Hurley, *Natural Reasons* (hereinafter *NR*), 176–85; Ruth Chang, 'The Frege–Geach Point and Non-Cognitivism', (unpublished manuscript), for extended discussion.

[17] The best known attempts are by M. Dummett, *Frege*, 295–363; S. Blackburn, *Spreading the Word*, 189–96. Note Blackburn's attempt, in particular, to render the major premise as expressing an attitude (approval or disapproval) towards the *linkage* of p and q, where p and q are both thought of as expressing attitudes; this is ingenious, but fails since p and q get described, once again, in the major premise, rather than expressed. See again Hurley, Chang, opp.citt.

need not be of that kind. The missing argument cannot be NC itself—it would not be a good argument against our intuition (that the inference is normal) to say that ethical judgment is expressive—although of course independent arguments for NC may do the job.[18]

It appears, then, that evaluative discourse has cognitive structure: ethical and non-ethical concepts are used in the same way, that is to describe, reason about connections and logical implications, and so forth. But the central non-cognitivist thesis may yet survive: the surface structure of evaluation is cognitive, one may concede, yet this involves a projective error. People project their essentially non-cognitive attitudes onto parts of the world proper, and proceed to treat those attitudes as genuine properties in the world. Speakers do have a cognitive aspiration, namely to report genuine properties, but that aspiration is frustrated. NC in this wide sense is really global scepticism about ethics.[19] It takes the disillusioned stance—it seeks to expose the 'myth' of genuine ethical properties—and is therefore called to supply an account of value 'as it really is'.[20]

I shall turn, then, to a discussion of the sceptical task. NC claims that evaluation is composite, the pairing of an attitude, or other such subjective state, with an event. We need to see how that feature of subjectivity figures in the act of valuing on the disillusioned (or, according to NC, the objective) account, and whether that account is able to show that evaluation fails the standard of objectivity. I shall suggest that unsatisfactory conceptions of subjectivity and objectivity implicit in NC are to blame for this; rejecting those conceptions, however, allows for evaluative objectivism, properly conceived.

4. THE 'SUBJECTIVE'

In this composite picture, evaluation consists of a factual component (worldly events and states) and a human response. An account of the world that is purged of the tendency to believe that there is such a thing as evaluative properties in objects should be able to give a non-evaluative account of evaluation: it should be able to capture and explain evaluation in value-neutral terms. In the case of a

[18] For instance, if ethical concepts *could not* pick out properties for metaphysical reasons—like the ones I shall be considering below—then the move will go through. On its own, the semantic move (the claim that ethical discourse is in fact expressive) would not succeed even if expressivism had its own logic. The point is in response to an objection by Adrian Moore.

[19] Mackie clearly conceives his position as scepticist, in *Ethics*, 15 ff. See Hurley, *NR*, 186, who disputes whether this position deserves to be called non-cognitivist. I believe I follow standard, if loose, usage, in calling such positions NC.

[20] In confining attention to an error theory as an alternative to pure expressivism, I may be ignoring various intermediate positions. For example, a position that concedes that ethical discourse is descriptive, and yet insists that what it describes is the *occurrence* of some affective response. Even if any such positions escape the arguments against expressivism, they must all ultimately face the challenge put to error theories: they must give a response-based account of values that shows them to be less respectable than ordinary properties.

theory that locates value in the subject, it should be possible to state what it is for someone to believe that a cruel act is wrong, in terms of the appropriate states in a person's mind, as these are 'in themselves'. This requirement stems from the notion of 'attaching' (a response to a state of affairs, or an attitude): attachment is a relational notion, and we need an account of the *relata*—crucially, the mental component.

There seem to be two ways of going about splitting evaluation into two components. The first accepts most concepts used in evaluation as genuine or worldly: it accepts that 'cruelty', among other things, is a genuine category, a proper head under which torturing animals and other such nasty behaviour is collected. The subjective, non-cognitive, additional component consists in attaching condemnation to this class of events, attaching the 'contra' attitude (or the 'pro' attitude, in the case of commendable behaviour or events).[21] The second rejects all classifications used in evaluation, and seeks to expose as fallacious even the idea that certain events are grouped together, as they are by evaluative concepts. The grouping is, objectively speaking, an unprincipled, gerrymandered collection, which only appears to be principled by adding the subjective component: it is only thanks to attitudes or emotions that cruel acts come to seem (or feel) similar.

Under the first strategy, all that NC appears to claim is that cruelty need not be bad: badness comes about by adding the negative attitude. *Why* this attitude is usually added is to be explained, for example, by a socio-biological story that will show how 'hard wired' repulsion or attraction reflexes, owing their existence to the selective advantage conferred in connection with survival and reproductive success, came to be exploited in society in connection with socially important functions. But the attitude is in itself inert, and its connection with the class it happens to be connected with is not objectively important.

This first strategy fails. It supposes that one can neatly detach the evaluative aspect of concepts like cruelty and still be left with the same, or at least a different but coextensive, concept. It requires that concepts like 'cruelty', despite being used as evaluative, despite being perceived by their users as carrying evaluative significance, be *reducible* to equivalent coextensive non-evaluative concepts plus the relevant attitude. The task of reduction is this: one should be able to acquire the concepts (equivalent, but for the attitudinal component) and apply them without sharing the evaluative attitudes of ordinary users. There should be, then, non-evaluative properties shared by all instances of the evaluative property, i.e. all

[21] Cf. Mackie, who says that 'the kinds of behaviour to which moral values are ascribed are indeed part of the furniture of the world. . . . It is a hard fact that cruel actions differ from kind ones, and hence that we can learn . . . to distinguish them fairly well in practice and to use the words 'cruel' and 'kind' with fairly clear descriptive meanings; is it an equally hard fact that actions which are cruel in such a descriptive sense are to be condemned?': *Ethics*, 16–17. Mackie's cautiousness—evident in his use of 'fairly well' and 'fairly clear'—cannot avoid his begging the question I proceed to raise in the text: are there non-evaluative properties that collect together the class of cruel acts?

events and kinds of behaviour to which 'cruelty' is ordinarily applied to: cruel behaviour should be a non-evaluative *kind*.

There is no reason to suppose that this reduction can go through.[22] Instances of cruel behaviour, described in non-evaluative terms, exhibit no pattern; pattern comes about only through appreciation of the *evaluative* principles that collect such instances. There is no principle explaining why 'cruel' is correctly applied to a child dissecting an animal, yet incorrectly applied to a vet doing the same, other than an *evaluative* explanation of the circumstances in which infliction of pain and injury is acceptable. Pattern emerges only within evaluation. Explaining what collects together cruel behaviour is indicating other evaluative concepts that are interdependent with cruelty. A similar point applies in the case of colours: there seems to be no colour-neutral property (surface reflective properties, etc.) that collects together all objects that appear red.[23] What red objects have in common is redness.

The second strategy fails in an analogous way. There, the appearance of pattern in all events grouped together under 'cruelty' has to be explained in terms of feelings or emotions. But again we would need to know how it is that certain feelings combine together into a 'cruelty' response, others into a 'chastity' response and so forth. We need an account of individuation of different such feelings, that would explain why cat-tormenting strikes us as similar to certain jokes. Of course, a readily available answer exists: these events produce similar feelings in us. But this property common among the events cannot be what grounds the similarity of the responses produced: we cannot coherently explain the similarity of the feelings produced in terms of a common property of the events to which they are attached, where that common property is similarity-of-attached-feeling. We need an independent similarity criterion; everything is similar to everything else, in some respects, and it seems that the only respect in which cruelty-feelings are similar is *cruelty* itself.[24]

So both versions of the composite picture are unlikely to carry out the task of explaining evaluation in non-evaluative terms. Is this requirement, apparently impossible to fulfil, fairly put on NC? It is: it stems from NC's own claim that values are not part of the 'fabric of the world' (a notion I shall discuss below), and this carries a commitment to show *what* is not such a part, and how it relates to the world proper. As Stroud says, we need not simply a value-free conception of the world, but a conception of a value-free world.[25] So evaluation must be *intelligible* in the objective picture.

[22] See McDowell, 'Are Moral Requirements Hypothetical Imperatives?', *Arist. Soc. Suppl. Vol. 52*, 13–29; 'Non-Cognitivism and Rule-Following' *in* Holtzman and Leich, (eds.), *Wittgenstein: to Follow a Rule*; Putnam, *Realism with a Human Face*, 167–9.

[23] See D. Dennett, *Consciousness Explained*, 375.

[24] Cf. McDowell, 'Non-Cognitivism and Rule-Following', 158; B. Stroud, 'The Study of Human Nature and the Subjectivity of Value', in Peterson, G. (ed.), *10 Tanner Lectures on Human Values*, 227–9; Wiggins, 'Truth as Predicated of Moral Judgments', in *Needs, Values, Truth*, 159. Jonathan Bennett identifies the same error in Locke's view that 'ideas' are grouped together in virtue of their similarities and dissimilarities, which are not in terms of the objects they are ideas of, but of the ideas' similarities themselves—something Locke thinks need not be a problem. See *Locke, Berkeley, Hume*, 11–21.

[25] Stroud, ibid., 222.

From the intelligibility requirement it follows that every evaluative classification must be explicable in non-evaluative terms. One should be able to learn how to apply the evaluative concept (or its equivalent) without applying the evaluative concept itself, without having access to evaluation at all. This is not meant to contrast with *endorsing* the evaluative classification, in the sense of accepting that there is a genuine kind picked out by it. A *detached* explanation must surely be available. In fact, it is *elimination* of the evaluative 'kind' that requires that the evaluative classification be intelligible. For instance, if we want to eliminate centaurs from our inventory of genuine kinds, we must be able to account for centaur-beliefs in a way that makes sense of them. We may try to reduce them to 'man' and 'horse' in the context of a story that says, for example, that centaur beliefs are derived from mental representations of mens' heads with horses' bodies (here the story gives an account of what it is for one to have a representation of a man's head, etc.); and further explains how these beliefs are formed, say, by placing too much confidence in mythology.[26] The problem is that no analogous example has been constructed for evaluative properties. No story that explains the appearance of a principle guiding applications of ethical concepts has been supplied. Without such a reduction, the apparent principle must be presumed genuine.

Can we reject the requirement that ethical concepts be reduced? Rejection would entail that, in NC's objective conception of the world, values would be unintelligible. This would be to give up the claim of being able to make sense of their nature as responses, emotions or whatever else: values would become what Putnam calls a 'know-not-what'. Evaluation would become, NC-objectively speaking, sounds and marks.

What is the source of the difficulty in any attempt to reduce value to its objective counterpart? NC wants to capture reality as it is, not as it strikes anyone. Now values are essentially connected with things striking someone in one or another way—they are essentially connected with subjects. NC explains that connection on the basis of the contrast between appearance and reality. Values (as well as other things), NC claims, belong with the phenomenal. Yet only reality as it is figures in the objective conception, and therefore nothing essentially phenomenal has a place there.[27]

That line of thought is fallacious. Something's being essentially connected with

[26] Cf. Stroud, ibid., 226. See G. Evans, *The Varieties of Reference*, 369–72, for the explanatory task of negative existentials. Distinguishing the requirement that sense be made of appearances, from taking appearances at face value, is analogous to distinguishing intelligibility from truth, discussed in Ch. 2 section 5. Cf. the discussion of negative existentials like 'phlogiston does not exist', in Ch. 2, section 6. In Ch. 6, section 3, the distinction is discussed in the context of the question of external and internal criticism.

[27] T. Nagel has expressed this thought as the thesis of the 'incompleteness of objective reality'. The idea is that an objective conception of reality must inevitably fail to include subjective qualities since it has no access to the 'subjective standpoint'. Although the contrast seems to be more general, Nagel proceeds to assimilate 'subjective' with 'phenomenal' so that subjective qualities are things' appearances. See *The View from Nowhere*, 25–7; and ibid. 138–42 in connection with ethics.

subjects need not amount to its being phenomenal. But I shall postpone discussion of the alternative. Concentrating on the non-cognitivist picture, McDowell has convincingly argued that its inability to cope with values follows from the ban on the phenomenal.[28] Values, together with the so-called secondary qualities like colour, taste, etc., are thought of as pure appearances, in contrast to primary qualities—shape, solidity, etc.—which are essentially real (although they too have a phenomenal aspect since they may be experienced). As far as primary qualities are concerned, the objective conception (recall that this is NC-objectivity) can accommodate them on the supposition that the content of primary quality experience can be individuated in terms of the property of which it is an experience: the subjective (experiential) state corresponding to 'square' can be fixed by reference to what it is an experience of—a square—since the experiential and the real property resemble each other. I shall cast doubt on whether that way of individuating the content even of primary quality experience works. But what would be its analogue in secondary quality experience, say, of red? There should be a non-experiential property which should 'resemble' an experience of red, that should be 'just like red as we see it'. In order to say, with NC, that colour does not really exist, we would need there to be some such property, but there is none. The way the distinction between primary and secondary qualities is set up in NC, secondary-quality experience is, as it were, free-standing. There is nothing apart from redness to fix the content of red experience; and redness is banned, since it is not out there.

I noted above that there could be, in principle, successful unmasking explanations of appearances, viz. explanations that condemn what is perceived as imaginary. But such explanations involve *mere* appearances or illusions. They pertain to the contrast between veridical or non-veridical experience, rather than the contrast between the phenomenal and the non-phenomenal.[29] As such, they are able to distinguish non-veridical experience without being barred from recourse to the classifications that are being made by the subject under illusion. They are thus perfectly able to help in understanding what the content of the illusion is, and reconstructing it in non-'illusory' terms, rather like the case of dispelling someone's illusion that he is seeing a blue wall, when he is seeing a white wall lit by a blue light.[30] (In this case we use 'blue' and all the rest). What is not possible is to render non-phenomenal what is essentially phenomenal.

5. CAN THERE BE PRINCIPLED PROJECTIONS?

Before concluding discussion of the tension identified above and the suggested solution, I must digress in order to ensure that I have not failed to consider some

[28] See 'Values and Secondary Qualities', *in* Honderich, T. (ed.), *Morality and Objectivity*, 112–14; 'Aesthetic Value, Objectivity and the Fabric of the World', *in* Schaper, E. (ed.), *Pleasure, Preference and Value*, 11–12. Cf. Nagel, op.cit.

[29] See McDowell, 'Values and Secondary Qualities', 115.

[30] Stroud's example from 'The Study of Human Nature', used in a different context.

strategy available to NC other than the ones considered above: I argued in the preceding section that non-cognitivism (in a wide sense) must take either of two options, both of which I argued to be untenable. First, provide a sceptical explanation of evaluation, either by reducing evaluative concepts to equivalent non-evaluative ones onto which attitudes are explicably attached, or by eliminating ethical properties and explaining the appearance of pattern in terms of the attitudes themselves. Or, second, give up hope of providing such an explanation and yet insist that evaluative properties are unacceptable, therefore rendering evaluation unintelligible. The first option does not appear possible; and the second makes it a mystery why one should accept NC.

Simon Blackburn has argued that there is a third option. He claims to offer a projective theory that respects the explanatory requirement and thus makes sense of evaluation, and is not even sceptical. He claims that he can rescue most of the 'realist' conception of evaluation, without the wrong metaphysics, so that his projectivism is non-revisionist.[31]

In what sense is Blackburn's theory projectivist? First, he says that a naturalistic explanation of evaluation that does not use evaluative concepts is available. The example he cites is a game-theoretical analysis that shows that altruistic behaviour would have been naturally selected.[32] It is unclear how a full explanation of evaluation would be built up from that analysis. But the important issue is how such explanations work. Blackburn suggests that such explanations would be analogous to explanations of colours and colour perception: there, we have a story that explains colour vision as facilitating spotting and keeping track of objects (and therefore attracting the usual selective advantage). That explanation, Blackburn claims, explains colour without using colour concepts. He does not see, nonetheless, that such a colour explanation is neutral on the respectability of colour properties. Such explanations are *genealogical*, i.e. they account for acquisition and transmission of colour concepts or colour vision. They *assume* the concepts' or properties' content, and are silent on the question of whether the properties are genuine or not. They do not tell us what is wrong, if anything, with grouping red objects together, nor do they give us a colour-neutral property in their place.

Blackburn has a further proposal that may flesh out his projectivist claim in the expected way. He suggests an analogy with modality and causality: these concepts are best thought of, he claims, as a 'decision to archive' certain issues. We will not consider, that is, the suggestion that 1 + 1 = 3, and this is the sense of the notion of necessity associated with 1 + 1 = 2.[33] Now the concept of 'deciding to archive'

[31] See 'Errors and the Phenomenology of Value' *in* Honderich (ed.), *Morality and Objectivity*; 'How to Be an Ethical Anti-Realist', *12 Midwest Studies in Philosophy*, edited by French, Wettstein, and Uehling, 361–76; 'Morals and Modals', *in* McDonald, G. and Wright, C. (eds.), *Fact, Science and Morality*.

[32] See 'How to be an Ethical Antirealist'. See Allan Gibbard's *Wise Choices, Apt Feelings*, for a full statement of ethical scepticism built on a Darwinian as well as game-theoretical model.

[33] See 'Morals and Modals'.

suggests a choice: perhaps we might change our minds and decide to reconsider the archived claims. That is not possible, Blackburn says, because not respecting necessity and causality, as we now understand them by virtue of the constraints captured by the archive metaphor, is blocked by an imaginative limitation: we cannot conceive of any alternative. We have no access to a 'sideways' position from which to conceive necessity and causality as matters of choice.

So what is the point of describing necessity etc. as decisions? We avoid, Blackburn suggests, conceiving them as constraints imposed by an independent reality, made true, or compulsory, by virtue of some independent fact. This alternative, which Blackburn seeks to block, is not at issue here. The point is that, were values like necessity and causality, they would not be threatened by serious scepticism. But Blackburn does not think that values can be insulated from scepticism in the same way. *There is*, he claims, a sideways perspective on values—we *can* conceive of alternatives. So values are not on a par with necessity and causality, with respect to our imaginative limitations.[34]

At this point, then, Blackburn's claim that his projectivism does no harm to evaluation seems dubious. If we have access to a sideways view on values, then how is it that we cannot be globally sceptical, eliminate them or choose to change some or all of our evaluative outlook? Blackburn admits that, were alternatives imaginable, modality and causality would be affected.[35] Why does not the same hold true in evaluation? There is an internal–external distinction, Blackburn explains, that does the job. The external account of value, available as it is, cannot carry any weight within evaluative argument. The latter involves moving within the space of our evaluative commitments and tracing their implications, interrelations and so forth. The external story cannot do any work there.[36] But why can't it? Notice that this is not the acceptable claim, made for instance by Dworkin in the context of legal interpretation, that external scepticism is inert.[37] Blackburn *would* have recourse to the inertness argument in connection with necessity or causality, where his insistence that alternatives are unimaginable may allow him to shrug off the question, say, 'are causal relations *really* real?' But the argument cannot be used for value, if Blackburn is right to think that here we have access to the sideways point: to have such access *is* to be able to think of alternatives, to be in the position to mount and give content to external scepticism—or else there is no content to

[34] ibid.

[35] ibid., 136. Strictly, Blackburn says that *explanations* of the modal and causal imaginative limitations are not forthcoming, and he illustrates the relevant kind of explanation by an example of an explanation of a child's failure to imagine, in the sense of visualize, a space relation. Part of the explanation of that failure is a method for overcoming the limitation; so the explanation suggests how to imagine what initially appeared unimaginable. Having an explanation of the analogous limitation in ethics is, therefore, having a way to supersede the limitation and acquire the ability to imagine alternatives.

[36] See 'How to Be an Ethical Antirealist'.

[37] See the discussion of internal and external scepticism in Ch. 6, section 3.

'sideways perspective'.[38] The mere existence of an 'internally coherent' practice of evaluation cannot block the external story. A unicorn society that goes about applying the concept of a unicorn on some occasions and not on others, debates unicorns' real nature, and speculates on unicorns' evolution cannot be immune to 'external' scepticism about unicorns.

Blackburn claims that 'we do not hear' the external story. The only argument he gives to that effect is that our commitments have an affective grip on us from which we cannot be released even if we realize how it comes to grip us. Can the lover, he says, overcome his passion by realizing that his love is metaphysically suspect?[39] But surely he overrates the affective grip of evaluative commitments. We could learn to be unmoved by values, as long as a sceptical view were given content.

It seems, then, that Blackburn's success at reconciling projectivism with respectability of evaluative judgment is simply explained by the emptiness of 'projectivism'. With two reservations which I shall consider in a moment, the only content given by Blackburn to the idea that values are projected is that they are intimately connected with human responses and depend on discriminations we actually make. These claims are not contentious, and do not distinguish values from modality, on Blackburn's account. So 'projectivism' is harmless, and the debate loses its edge; or else, if projectivism makes any claim at all, evaluation cannot really survive undamaged.[40]

Blackburn's two points that seem to flesh out projectivism in answer to my accusation of emptiness are the following. First, he claims that values do no explanatory work, and are therefore less than causally efficacious properties. Second, he claims that values involve conative or affective, rather than cognitive, capacities, and so they cannot figure in ordinary judgment.

I shall dispute both points in subsequent sections. The point that must be made here is that, even if we concede that values are not causally important, and that they involve the sentiments, the concession will not make Blackburn's picture any more compelling. In that picture, values are not explained away, even if they do no explaining themselves, and the projectivist label is not justified for that reason. Further, values' conative or affective nature would make a difference if Blackburn supplied an argument to the effect that the mere occurrence of conative or affective properties in evaluation rules out the cognitive character of evaluation. However, no such argument is given (after all, snakes are both perceived and

38 Notice that a sideways view would *give* a fact in virtue of which value's content would be fixed—the biological or whatever facts that supposedly explain it. Unlike modality and causality, where no such fact gives them content, the badness of cruelty would derive from a fact, although not an evaluative fact: *that* would render the external story sceptical. In short, on Blackburn's picture it does not make sense to say that modality is *really* real, but it does make sense to say that values are *really* unreal.

39 'How to Be an Ethical Antirealist', 371.

40 Cf. Hurley, *NR*, 301, for the suggestion that the projectivism–objectivism debate is losing its point as long as both sides agree that evaluative judgment is principled. My point is that projectivists should not be allowed that conclusion.

affectively significant), and so projectivism gets no mileage from the effect values have on the emotions.

I conclude then that the 'principled projections' thesis is not an intellectual option. We must either be genuine projectivists and debunk evaluation, or accept genuine evaluative properties and principled evaluative discourse.

6. THE OBJECTIVE WORLD

I have argued that proper projectivism cannot allow values in its objective conception. But someone trying to construct an 'objective' account of evaluation (as it would be termed by NC), i.e. purge evaluation of the aspects inappropriate to the objective picture of the world, would, on the strength of the above remarks, have to picture evaluation as unintelligible; he could not at the same time pretend to salvage a conception, however austere, of value.[41] But this should generate suspicion about the cogency of the conception of objectivity here envisaged: we should not allow that conception to define away value.

What is the supposed error implicit in taking values to be genuine properties? The claim is that cognitivists go wrong in being committed to the objectivity of value, which amounts to picturing values as properties of things that in no way depend on subjects experiencing them or even on subjects existing at all, and yet are such that subjects manage to perceive them by interacting with the objects. In effect, cognitivists are supposed to go wrong in taking values for primary qualities. And, since evaluation is typically cognitivist in aspiration, that is the picture that evaluative judgment allegedly presupposes.

But it is wrong to attribute such a tacit presupposition to evaluative judgments. Surely such judgments do *not* rest on a presupposition that what they involve is not conceptually linked with human psychological states, just as colour judgments do not involve denial that colours are conceptually linked to experience.[42] What *is* presupposed by a colour judgment is that the properties involved in the judgment are, in McDowell's words, 'there to be experienced, as opposed to being a mere figment of the subjective state that purports to be an experience of [them].'[43] But to claim that colours fall under the first part of the contrast is not to claim that colours are primary qualities, in the sense that they can be understood without reference to objects' 'disposition' to give rise to subjective states.[44]

In section 4, I sketched McDowell's diagnosis of non-cognitivists' refusal to allow for the distinction between subjective properties that 'are there to be experienced' and subjective properties that are 'mere appearances'. McDowell

[41] McDowell, similarly claims that projectivists cannot have it both ways. Cf. 'Value and Secondary Qualities', 122–3, esp. n. 46.

[42] Cf. McDowell, 'Secondary Qualities', 113–14; McGinn, *The Subjective View*, 118, defending the common-sense view of secondary qualities from the supposed projective error.

[43] ibid., 114.

[44] I am using McDowell's formulation, ibid. 113.

traces the resistance to bad philosophy of mind, and particularly to a certain conception of the content of experience.[45] On that conception, the content of experience consists in 'ideas', i.e. mental states independent of the environment. The primary–secondary quality distinction is then supposed to amount to the following contrast. Primary qualities are properties of things in themselves, which are 'resembled' by relevant 'ideas'; secondary qualities have nothing to resemble, so they have the status of mere appearances.

The problem with that conception is that, if 'ideas' have a merely phenomenal content, then not even perception of primary qualities seems possible: the resemblance relation cannot possibly secure the correspondence of a content which is essentially experiential ('ideas') to a content essentially non-experiential (properties of things in themselves). If experience has no access to anything outside itself, the possibility of veridical experience seems problematic even where primary properties are concerned.[46] By contrast, the contrast between primary and secondary qualities can be retained by thinking of it as the contrast between those properties which are essentially subjective, and those which are not, where both types of property are 'there to be experienced', in McDowell's words, i.e. capable of being the object of *veridical* experience; the result is that the different distinction between veridical and non-veridical experience will cut across the distinction between the two types of properties.

The question then is whether the claim that colours are there to be experienced can succeed, and whether an analogous claim may be made for values. In connection with colours, it seems that we can have a coherent view of them as essentially identifiable subjectively, only insofar as subjectivity is taken to mean that they are conceptually linked with psychological states. Yet the psychological states involved in colour perception cannot be individuated except by reference to the content of the perception, which is colour-based. We have, therefore, sufficient grounds to distinguish specific instances of veridical and illusory perception, the grounds being whether, in fact, something is or is not thus and so (e.g. whether it is red). For all its subjectivity, colour judgment can be true or false depending on how things are.

The essential subjectivity of such properties is captured by the claim that correct application of the associated concepts depends on the *actual discriminations* made by subjects with these concepts. Colour patterns depend on there being sentient beings that discriminate such patterns.[47] The concepts are therefore response-dependent, but there is an important distinction to be made among different such concepts. Are objects red because we judge them to be red, or do we judge them

[45] See ibid., 113–17.

[46] Cf. the discussion in Ch. 2, section 5: if the mind deals only in its own intrinsic contents, then even something's really being an appearance of something objective is threatened.

[47] Dennett's 'Real Patterns', *88 J. Phil.* 27–51 argues that any pattern is necessarily discernible in principle. Perhaps secondary-quality patterns must be thought of as necessarily discernible in fact (allowing for one's being in a good position epistemically; I shall discuss the qualification in section 7.3).

to be red because they are red? Philip Pettit recently proposed a test:[48] if the question is unambiguously answered in the first way (something is X because we judge it to be X), then the concept is strongly response-dependent, that is, its application is really unprincipled. 'Chic' or 'cool' may be like that (at least for the so-called trend-setting group), as well as all the concepts that have to do with etiquette, and the sort of reduction discussed in section 4 can go through there. But if the answer is ambiguous, i.e. there is a sense in which something is X because we judge it to be X, as well as a sense in which we judge it to be X because it is X, the concept picks out a genuine property. Something is red in some sense because we say so; but in some other sense it is not up to us—we say so because it *is* red. In my terms, red is irreducible, although it is perfectly true that redness depends on the contingency of colour vision, and hence the judgments colour vision supports.

Values pass the test. Evaluative judgment depends on states or events (in the world) being such as to *merit* the relevant response. Postponing discussion of the precise way value is discerned, why should evaluative judgment look inferior to the truly objective?

One possible ground of inferiority must be that, in Bernard Williams's words, the analysis of value cannot figure in the 'absolute conception of the world'. The absolute conception is such that it cannot include anything that depends on some point of view, and value fails that criterion. The natural candidate for the absolute conception must be science. Williams himself expresses scepticism about a claim to the effect that science occupies the 'Archimedean point' apparently necessary for the absolute conception, but seems to think that science may still be a reliable route towards that conception, not simply because it is about the world, but also because it tries to represent it in the least perspectival way—the way least dependent on any peculiar point of view.[49]

Again we must appeal to McDowell's distinction between essentially subjective properties and mere appearances, and distinguish between two ways of understanding 'non-perspectival'. The first applies to an analysis which excludes possible objects of inquiry that are conceptually linked to subjectivity, e.g. colours and music. The second applies to an analysis which excludes, for some object of inquiry, how it merely appears, as opposed to 'how it really is'. The first option is unmotivated: why exclude those lines of inquiry that attempt to illuminate such essentially subjective facts as colour perception and the like? The second option represents a legitimate cognitive aspiration, i.e. to know how things really are, but it would exclude ethics only on the supposition that there is no such knowledge to be had in that domain; and that is to beg the question which the non-perspectival argument seeks to answer. Unless further argument is added, the distinction between seeming and being will cover both science and ethics.

[48] 'Realism and Response-Dependence', *100 Mind*, 587–626 at 614–15.
[49] See *Ethics and the Limits of Philosophy*, 138–9.

A further such argument could follow from the very notion of the Archimedean point: given such a point, access to how things are would be obtained in a way that would exclude both senses of 'seeming', viz. being conceptually linked to experience, and being 'mere' experience, as opposed to representing how things really are, on which I relied in making my distinction between the two senses of 'non-perspectival'. From the Archimedean point, 'seeming' would fall out of the picture altogether. But there is no reason to suppose that science occupies such a point; rather, it can lay claim to being able to distinguish veridical from non-veridical appearances, i.e. being good at avoiding the second sense of 'seeming'. Only if science did not yield veridical representations, but rather gave us access to bits of reality as it is in itself (with which to compare representations in order to see whether they 'resemble' or 'match' each other) could the claim to its exclusivity be justified.

Of course the unavailability of the Archimedean point does not count against science's reliability, but only against misconceiving the source of its reliability. If we agree that the Archimedean point is an incoherent notion, then we can hardly conclude that all knowledge is inferior, contaminated or whatever, since this pessimism precisely requires that the notion be coherent. Science derives its reliability by presenting satisfactory accounts of its objects; it makes no general argument to the effect that its world is all there is.

7. NATURALISM

Assuming that the above leaves room for non-scientific knowledge, at least in the sense of allowing for essentially perspectival knowledge, we should say more about *how* evaluative reasoning is supposed to constitute such knowledge. This discussion will present further possible grounds for distinguishing evaluative from scientific knowledge, and perhaps for reiterating the charge that the former is inferior.

G. E. Moore sought to demonstrate that values could not be natural properties, by arguing that whatever natural condition X we substitute in an identity relation with 'good', it may always be possible that something is X and yet is not good. The conclusion he drew was that value is *sui generis*, and is perceptible, if at all, with a special sort of faculty (epistemically similar to visual, olfactory or other faculties).

Moore's argument is mistaken. First, Moore's reasoning rests on the supposition that, if goodness were natural, it should be analysable into a set of (natural) necessary and sufficient conditions. But if 'goodness' is after all a K–P-type predicate, its content may be given by substantive, non-reductive theory rather than definition, and the scope for discovery afforded by the substantive nature of the theory allows that novel applications may require any given theory to be adjusted.

Second, the perceptual point is misdirected. Why do we need an extra faculty to discern values? Why not say that we perceive a cruel act, in its physical aspects, through the normal perceptual faculties, and further exercise the usual intellectual ability of concept application? Do we need square-detectors to identify a square? Rather, we need normal vision, and the concept of squareness. Further, the emotions may play a role in *identifying* certain basic ethical patterns; they may be part, in other words, of the cognitive exercise of identification.[50] We cannot just *assume* that cognitive capacities cannot be mixed with the emotions—that would amount to assuming NC.

Failure to attend to both points above has allowed Mackie to claim that if values are part of the world, they can only be queer, and knowable in a queer way.[51] However, Moore's argument does not work. Ethical properties can be instantiated by the occurrence of normal (natural) states and events, but the relation may be such that it will always be a substantive task to judge whether particular combinations of such natural states and events should be collected under an ethical head. Ethical properties may not be exhaustively definable *per genus et differentia*, and may be irreducible to natural properties. So values need neither be queer nor discerned in a queer way.

Nevertheless, the charge of epistemological queerness may rest on a thought like this: if I say water is clear, part of the explanation of the possession of the belief is that water is clear, yet there seems to be no clear analogue in ethics. But why not? If I believe that slavery is unjust, part of the explanation of my holding that belief is that slavery is unjust. The queerness objection needs a further thought: in the case of water, there is a causal transaction between me and water that warrants (via perception) my belief; my belief is built out of direct knowledge, afforded by perception, and certain valid inferences. In the ethical case, the analogue of that would have me enter into causal transactions with values, and form perceptual beliefs etc. *That* is where the queerness would emerge.

In response to this charge, Susan Hurley has exploited a distinction made by Davidson.[52] We first have to distinguish between causal *relations* and causal *explanations*. As far as causal relations are concerned, no queerness seems to arise. Causal relations hold between events and so may hold between a cruel act and the appropriate belief. It does not matter how the events are described: the cruel act is a natural event, and perhaps the belief is a neurochemical one. They do not have an extra 'layer'—ethical or intentional—by virtue of their instantiating an ethical and a mental kind, respectively. To say events are ethical (to concentrate on the important class here) is to say that they are appropriately grouped together under an ethical concept. But their being described in those terms does not affect their standing in causal relations with other events—such relations do not hold by virtue of the description. So an ethical belief can be causally related to ethical facts, without any queerness.

[50] See Pettit, 'Realism and Response-Dependence', 620. [51] *Ethics*, 38 ff.

[52] See *NR*, 97. Davidson's distinction is in 'Causal Relations', *Actions and Events*, 149–62. See William Child's *Causality, Interpretation, and the Mind*, 100 ff, for an especially clear and thorough discussion.

Hurley's argument shows that there need not be any causal relation between metaphysically suspect entities, but the problem may arise in connection with causal *explanations*. In explanations, which concepts are used is important. Both *explanans* and *explanandum* may be described in an indefinite number of ways, and which description is used may affect the explanatory power of the explanation offered. 'The event a claim was filed for to the insurance company was caused by the event described in the evening news' is a worse explanation than 'the yacht's capsizing was caused by the gale'.

Causation works, ultimately at least, at the micro-physical level—it is an object's constitution, and hence its micro-physical properties, that ultimately determine its 'causal powers', viz. its particular involvement in causal mechanisms. The causal efficacy of less basic properties may be questioned, and hence their causal explanatory relevance, viz. the explanatory force of explanations in terms of such non-basic properties. There may be, in other words, pressure for preferring causal explanations that are in terms of such basic, micro-physical properties, and this poses a problem about the explanatory relevance of ethical properties, not only in explanations of possession of ethical belief—the queerness issue—but in any explanation where ethical properties figure at all in the *explanans*, e.g. in explanations of action in terms of the agents' ethical makeup.[53]

Regarding the issue of queer epistemology in ethics, the important factor is the *explanans* cited in an explanation of belief possession (leaving aside the question whether beliefs are proper *explananda*, or should be replaced with the appropriate neurochemical events). Now in a paradigmatic case, the fact that a proton's going through the cloud chamber causes my belief 'there goes a proton' is supposed to explain my holding the belief. Would that work for colour—does an object's redness explain my belief that it is red, in the same way? One may insist that the proper explanation should be in terms of the object's surface physical properties (and move from there through the appropriate 'sensation' or whatever to the belief). But redness *ensures* that the appropriate micro-physical properties will be there. Pettit suggests this analogy:[54] a one-inch peg's squareness explains why it won't go through a one-inch round hole, by ensuring that there will be *some* overlapping part. It does not matter that an actual blocking is explicable in terms of certain overlapping parts; given the right dimensions, squareness guarantees that some or other part *will* overlap.[55]

In order to determine whether the analogy goes through in the ethical domain, we must deal with the complication of the judgment involved. Since we want to explain possession of an ethical *belief*, the explanation of one's forming, or failing to form, a belief that an act is cruel must be in terms of the act's cruelty, as well as the proper functioning of one's intellectual, as well as one's perceptual, capacities. The

[53] See Child, ibid. 188–204, for a discussion of causal explanatory relevance in general; and ibid. 204–16 on mental properties in particular.

[54] Putnam originally used the analogy in defence of explanations in terms of mental properties, in *Mind, Language and Reality*, 295–8.

[55] See Pettit, 'Realism and Response-Dependence', 614.

kind of intellectual capacities relevant here is evident in cases of mathematical or semantic judgment. (Note, however, that the first case is 'purer' than ethical judgment. In the ethical case the intellectual judgment is used in discriminating ordinary empirical events.) We may say, then, with Wiggins, that an act's cruelty explains the relevant judgment through a schema like 'there was nothing else to think, so no wonder one thought so'.[56]

Now this kind of explanation may seem inferior to the one available in the proton case. We may accept that the explanations that involve the basic physical ground are superior, and yet insist that, since there is no coextensive non-ethical concept to replace the ethical concept, explanations in terms of ethical properties are more illuminating. They are more illuminating in the same way that, in the above example, explanations in terms of a peg's squareness, are more illuminating than explanations in terms of such and such overlapping parts. But this response may not do: a non-cognitivist will say that *there is*, in the case of ethics, a proper causal explanation, so that, even if there are good explanations in which ethical facts figure (as in the 'there is nothing else to think' schema), they will be superfluous: the proper causal explanations will not involve commitment to ethical properties, since they will be in terms conceptually independent of the properties superficially involved in the judgment. A belief that some act was cruel will be explained by reference to factors independent of the act's cruelty. We will call explanations where the *explanans* is conceptually independent of the content of the belief figuring in the *explanandum*, *conceptually independent explanations.*

7.1. *Conceptual Independence*

There is no reason to deny that there *can* be explanations that appeal to conceptually independent properties; but the crucial question is whether the explanation could make sense of what it explained without itself presupposing the content of the crucial concepts, i.e. without theoretical commitment to the relevant ethical property. To return to colour once again: we may have explanations of beliefs in redness in terms of wave-length surface reflective properties and visual apparatus properties, but not without supposing that what we are explaining is redness *qua* a property of objects.

Consider, further, the case of a scientist's believing that a proton went through the cloud chamber. Notice that, in that case, some explanation in terms of psychological facts about the scientist is available, i.e. in terms of the scientist's beliefs in cloud chambers, particle mechanics etc. Does this—conceptually independent—explanation involve commitment to protons? The answer we give to this question should be the same as the one we give to the analogous question

[56] Cf. Wiggins, 'Moral Cognitivism, Moral Relativism and Motivating Moral Beliefs', *91 Proc. Arist. Soc.*, 80–81. See also Hurley, *NR*, 277.

concerning the explanation of a belief that an act is cruel by reference to other beliefs, rather than the act's cruelty.

The objector might say that there *is* a simple explanation of ethical beliefs that only makes reference to the believer's cultural background, upbringing, influences, and the like. Yet here again the same kind of explanation is available in the scientist's case: surely the scientist's holding a belief is explicable by reference to his education, culture, etc. The problem with these explanations is that they constitute explanations of belief *acquisition* or *transmission*, while they are silent on what it is that is so acquired or transmitted.[57] Citing one's education surely explains how one came to have the views one has on various—not only ethical—issues, albeit by presupposing their content: content is given to these views in other ways. So the mere availability of such explanations does not imply anything concerning the content of the relevant belief. On their face, the explanations are neutral towards the truth of the beliefs involved.[58]

Suppose that explanations of ethical beliefs typically presuppose commitment to the relevant ethical properties. Then the objection to the effect that values are superfluous in explanation may take the following form: explanations of value *may* involve explaining someone's judgment that X is wrong by pointing to X's wrongness. But there is a more interesting kind of explanation, namely a causal explanation framed in terms independent of the ethical concepts figuring in the *explanandum*, and this is the only kind of explanation that is worth taking seriously in the objective inquiry.

That this objection rests on prejudice should be obvious. It seems natural to suppose that the only kind of knowledge worth having is reductive, but this excludes for no good reason (and without being justified by such a causal explanation) the illumination offered by the sort of explanation that addresses human action and explains what it is (about the world) that makes an action appropriate or not, as the case may be.[59] And if there is no independent motivation for excluding this kind of explanation, then the parsimony advocated is unfounded.

Preferring conceptually independent explanations could perhaps be motivated by a concern for circularity. However, although explaining ethical judgments in terms of ethical properties may seem circular, the point of ethical inquiry is to provide accounts illuminative of the concepts involved, and this can still be done

[57] Compare the causal theory of reference transmission (in fact Kripke's theory), which is silent on the reference relation itself: it does not *explain* reference causally, but *presupposes* reference in order to say how it is transmitted amongst users of an expression. Recall the discussion of Blackburn's explanation of evaluation in section 5.

[58] Compare 'he came to believe in unicorns by reading this book, which he considered epistemically authoritative' and 'he came to believe in particles by reading that book, which he considered epistemically authoritative'. Some further assumptions are necessary in order to distinguish the two explanations: on their face, neither is sceptical.

[59] Cf. McDowell, 'Value and Secondary Qualities', 120; Hurley *NR*, 283–7, for discussions of the non-exclusivity of reductive causal explanations and distinguishing non-exclusivity from disallowing such explanations: if a good reduction is available, then it is surely acceptable.

while at some level the inquiry is circular. The illumination may consist in giving examples of the relevant property, noting interrelations with other concepts and the like, short of giving a reduction.[60]

The circularity involved can come in varying degrees. Here is an example from Jackson and Pettit's discussion of a related issue.[61] Explaining a vase's breaking upon impact in terms of a structural property—in terms of its fragility—involves a rather small circle: fragility just *is* the tendency to break upon impact. Still, that the vase has this *tendency* or disposition is informative: we learn that there is something about the vase, some or other configuration of its molecules, that ensures that some or other chain of events at the micro-physical level will be set in motion in all sorts of different circumstances, so that it was not anything peculiar to *this* configuration of the vase's molecules or *this* impact that brought about the breaking. In other cases the circle may be larger, and the information carried by the structural explanation more important. Squareness of a one-inch peg is more than its tendency to stick in one-inch holes, and it may be interesting to know that, among other things, squareness carries this tendency. Further, we learn that, although some particular configuration at the micro-physical level caused the sticking, it did not matter that it was that particular, rather than some other, configuration, that did the job. The analogy holds with explanations framed in terms of ethical concepts. Explaining A's refusal to be bribed in terms of his virtuousness reveals an interesting connection between virtue and bribery and shows that it was not something peculiar to the particular circumstances or the particular brain and neural states of A on that occasion that brought about the behaviour. It shows that A's virtue would ensure the occurrence of different but relevantly similar reactions to a host of different attempts to corrupt him.

Structural and ground-level explanations are not competitive. One's truth does not rule out the other's truth—in fact, they are complementary, and choosing among them turns on particular interests. If we must drive the peg into the hole no matter what, we need to identify the offending overlapping parts in order to file them away. If we want to know what to avoid next time we shop for pegs, we need to identify the offending structural property. The mere existence of alternative explanations framed in terms conceptually independent of each other does not entail that either must be rejected.[62]

[60] Cf. Hart's defence of non-reductivist yet informative explications of legal concepts; see Ch. 3.

[61] 'Functionalism and Broad Content', *97 Mind* 381–400 at 396. Jackson and Pettit discuss explanation in terms of structural properties with a view to vindicating explanations of action in terms of 'broad content', i.e. mental states individuated by aspects of the environment. The scepticism they are concerned with is to do with the explanatory role of broad content, as opposed to narrow content, i.e. the specific environment-independent 'internal' mental states to which transactions with the environment give rise, since the latter are the ones that are thought to enter into the causal chains leading to behaviour.

[62] Cf. Brink, *Moral Realism and the Foundations of Ethics*, 172–97, for support of the relevance of explanations in terms of structural (or 'higher-order') properties, and the lack of competition between them and explanations in terms of ground-level properties.

7.2. *Counterfactual Independence*

Explanations are tested for success by imagining the alleged *explanans* away, and seeing what happens to the *explanandum*. We may test, for example, the explanation of an ice cream's melting in terms of the room's temperature, by imagining the temperature to be different and asking whether the melting would still occur. If the melting would occur regardless of the temperature, then temperature explanations would be shown to be misguided: *explanans* and *explanandum* would be shown to be counterfactually independent.

Notice that the counterfactuals that test for explanatory relevance must hold everything except the *explanans* constant. In that way, ethical properties do not fail the test: if A were not virtuous, he could have accepted the bribe; if B had not behaved cruelly, I would not have believed that he did. But where we are concerned with the availability of more than one explanation, the suggestion may be that we not only hold facts other than the suspect *explanans* constant in the counterfactual specification, *but that we hold the explanans' ground-level description constant as well.* For example, we may try to imagine in the ice-cream example, that temperature varies, not only with everything else not related to temperature held constant, but with facts about kinetic molecular energy held constant too.

In that example the counterfactual should be blocked—temperature *is* (mean) kinetic molecular energy, so we cannot separate them in thought-experiments. So the counterfactual has an impossible antecedent. But it is interesting to consider different ways in which such counterfactuals can be blocked.

We have assumed that the counterfactuals try to separate two conceptually independent properties both of which are claimed to figure as *explanantia* in different explanations of the same *explanandum*. One way such a counterfactual could be blocked is by conceptual necessity: contrary to hypothesis, the two properties are conceptually dependent—we find ourselves trying to vary bachelorhood while keeping unmarried-manhood constant—and that ensures counterfactual dependence. A second way is metaphysical necessity. Temperature and kinetic molecular energy are not conceptually, but metaphysically, connected: to consider temperature as not being (mean) kinetic molecular energy and yet explaining melting ice-creams is not contradictory, but, provided temperature-theories and kinetic energy theories, together with the 'bridging laws', are right, it would be to consider a metaphysical impossibility, and because of *that*, rather than because we have flouted some definition, we would be considering a concept different than temperature.[63] As in the case of G.E. Moore, discussed in the preceding section, the K–P framework opens up the possibility for ties between concepts other than definition, and in the present case allows for conceptual independence without counterfactual independence. Note, however, that in the temperature example, the ties are looser than conceptual, but tight enough:

[63] See Putnam, *Reason, Truth and History*, 208.

temperature is fully reducible to kinetic energy. Given the 'bridging laws', it should come as no surprise that conceptual independence does no damage—the two *explanantia* are different, but one can be derived from the other. There can be a theoretical, rather than a definitional, reduction of one to the other. What if the two *explanantia* are not reducible to each other? Why in that case cannot they vary freely?

There is no reason to allow the move from irreducibility to counterfactual independence. Irreducibility implies that propositions using one set of concepts do not entail propositions using another. This does not rule out cases in which, as a matter of necessity, the properties picked out by one set cannot vary independently of the properties picked out by the other (that is, in the usual terminology, cases in which there can be no variation at the supervening level, without variation in the level supervened upon). There is no logical relation between propositions in terms of pegs' squareness and propositions in terms of pegs' micro-physical properties; nor is there some particular physical relation that is metaphysically necessary. But it can be logically necessary that *some* such relation exists, that changes in one level will be accompanied by changes in the other. This should be not surprising, since squareness is not an extra property of pegs over and above their micro-physical ones. Rather, it is a *kind* of configuration of *those* properties, a pattern into which some arrangements of those basic properties fall. It should be expected, then, that variations in these basic properties may well affect the pattern (despite the fact that there is no way to tell *which* variations will do that without using the structural concept). Hurley has expressed this point formally in terms of the relative scope of the existential and modal quantifier: it is one thing to say that there exists a relation R and that it necessarily holds (the reducibility case); and another to say that necessarily there exists some relation.[64] Co-variance is necessarily guaranteed in the second case, *without making the particular relation itself necessary*.[65]

It is important to note, then, that the relation among ethical and non-ethical properties can be as weak as the third type discussed above, viz. supervenience, and still be strong enough to disallow them to vary freely. We need not take sentences relating ethical and non-ethical facts to express analytic truths; neither need we take them to express reductive identities. This implies that we may consider slavery not being wrong as a conceptual possibility. We may accept that there could be 'counterevaluative' worlds in which slavery is the same in its non-evaluative characteristics, and yet not wrong. But, for counterfactual worlds, we

[64] See *NR*, 299–300. Hurley gives the theory–data relation as a good example of supervenience *cum* irreducibility: no particular relation is entailed between data and theory, yet if a theory varies data must necessarily vary. Hurley does not use the notion of structural properties in her argument.

[65] In this case, it is metaphysically necessary, but discoverable *a posteriori*, that Fs are Gs, where F stands for a structural property like squareness, as applied to pegs, and G for micro-physical properties of parts of pegs, to use the example discussed above. The reason that the necessity does not carry over to the relation R between Fs and Gs is that pattern is discernible only at one level (F), and there seems to be no way to make it discernible at the other level through bridging laws.

may insist that, if slavery were not wrong, enough non-evaluative facts would also have to be different (say, ownership would not be what it really is).[66]

The slide, then, from conceptual to counterfactual independence is motivated by either analyticity-or reduction-prejudice. The latter especially is surprising: paradoxically, irreducibility, which seemed to work for cognitivism earlier in this Chapter, appears here to be held against cognitivism. Irreducibility claims were used to support ethical properties' distinctness, the impossibility of deriving them from non-ethical properties. Here, the reductivist prejudice is employed to embarrass cognitivism: if irreducible to natural properties, ethical properties must be supernatural or otherwise mysterious. They must be a different kind of property, belonging to a special realm. But cognitivism is not committed to any mystery. Ethical properties are natural properties—they are some arrangement of physical properties. They supervene upon, but are not reducible to, basic micro-physical properties, i.e. they necessarily stand in some relation to such properties, though that relation cannot be expressed in a formula that will hold true necessarily.

8. SELECTIVE AND GLOBAL SCEPTICISM

So far, then, it seems that ethical properties create no metaphysical problems in connection with either causal relations or explanations. But this long discussion of the relation between conceptual and counterfactual independence is necessary, since it further bears on epistemology. Nozick has suggested a 'truth-tracking' test of knowledge.[67] A belief cannot be said to constitute knowledge, unless it is shown to track the truth: for any belief B, it must be true both that we would have believed B if it were true, and that we would not have believed it if it were not. The negative condition cannot be considered in the slavery example, if it is interpreted as requiring a possible world in which everything stays the same except that slavery is not wrong.[68] Nozick himself does not think this is a problem: we do not need to worry about tracking the falsity of B's content, since B cannot be false. Nozick relies on conceptual necessity, and he takes ethical beliefs to be analogous to mathematical beliefs. Now non-cognitivists may think that blocking the negative condition is somehow disingenuous. But if the discussion above is right, we may insist that framing the negative condition in a way that separates the ethical property from its non-ethical base is absurd, not because of any conceptual necessity of their relation, but because of the necessity that there be some such relation, since ethical properties *are* some arrangement of natural properties.

We can still use Nozick's test provided that the negative condition does not separate the relevant bases. We may consider attempts to debunk ethical beliefs by

[66] See Hurley, *NR*, 296. [67] See R. Nozick, *Philosophical Explanations*, 172–8.
[68] See Dworkin, *Law's Empire*, 428. Cf. Hurley, *NR*, 296.

claiming that we would hold an ethical belief even if it weren't true. For example, if my belief that I was treated unfairly is motivated by self-interest, rather than fairness convictions, then I would tend to persist in my belief even in a situation in which, although I would not really be treated unfairly, my interests would still be damaged.

Hurley provides an elaborate account of the way conceptually independent explanations may support *selective* scepticism by providing testable hypotheses for truth-tracking failure. I shall only sketch the account in order to illustrate the indirect way in which conceptually independent explanations may support truth-tracking failure.[69] I shall then rely on a feature of such explanations to show why they cannot support *global* scepticism.

In order to test for truth-tracking, we do not need to know what the truth is concerning an ethical question; we just need to know what kind of considerations could possibly be relevant, and therefore to be in a position to know that, unless one's ethical claims are formed on the basis of such considerations, they cannot track the truth. Whatever the plausibility of an ethical belief, if it is not held for the right reasons, it cannot constitute knowledge. Genealogical explanations of ethical belief may then make us suspicious about the credentials of one's ethical beliefs. They tell us how one came to possess the relevant belief: for example, 'he believes in racial equality because he was born into a black family in South Africa'. Here, a tacit suggestion is that the believer's interests or 'biases' drive his conviction, rather than the reasons why racial equality is a good thing. But note that nothing is yet established by the explanation: how one comes to possess a belief is logically independent of the reasons for which one holds the belief. The believer in the example may have been favoured, in fact, by his circumstances in getting to see the horrors of racism, and may have been granted an opportunity to cultivate his ethical judgment and reach his anti-racist beliefs for the *right* reasons—just as going to University gives a good opportunity to form true beliefs, for the right reasons, about physics.

But the availability of possession explanations *may* make us suspicious, and suggest ways to test truth-tracking by driving apart the suspected interest or 'bias' and the belief's truth. We may imagine an alternative form of national service that equally affects a draftee's interests and yet does not offend his ethical convictions in order to see whether his actual belief that the draft is ethically unacceptable tracks truth or interest.[70]

We can use Hurley's account of the way conceptually independent explanations debunk, when they do, to see why general explanations of ethical belief—say, socio-biological—cannot undermine the possibility of ethical knowledge at large.[71] Such an explanation would seek to damage (each and every) ethical belief in the

[69] See *NR*, Ch. 14. [70] Hurley's example, *NR*, 311.

[71] Hurley does not use the argument that follows to discredit global 'debunking' explanations. My argument derives from a view of the structure of debunking explanations that I believe is consistent with Hurley's.

following way: we can explain holding any ethical belief in terms of the believer's education, upbringing, and, generally, cultural position. Briefly, we can explain ethical beliefs as the products of culture. Can this suggest that our beliefs suffer an epistemic defect analogous to the biased draftee?

It should be obvious that the global version does not work. In the draftee case, the sceptical power of the suggestion that the believer has a personal interest in, or stands to gain from, his ethical view, derives from the implicit supposition that there *are* standards for correctness of the relevant belief, and that personal interest does not figure in them. It supposes, that is, that personal interest ought not to come into fairness beliefs, *because* other considerations—e.g. equality—ought to. If we find someone's reasoning not respectable, we thereby suppose that it *could* be respectable, that there *is* a standard by which it fails. In another of Hurley's examples, we seek to debunk someone's belief that Ferraro would not make a good Vice-President, by claiming that the belief was caused by her TV appearance in a pink dress. We presumably suppose that the belief could be properly held if it were based on the right considerations—political ability, virtue or whatever.

What could be the tacit standard, if we were to regard culture-dependence as an epistemic defect? Presumably culture-transcendence would be the standard which ethical beliefs would fail to meet. Here the relations to culture are not a matter of *scope*—of whether ethical principles are valid for specific cultures, or for humanity as a whole—although one may of course, starting from 'culture-dependence' build an argument for restricted scope of ethical standards. Rather, the relation is to do with the source, as well as the content, of ethical concepts. 'Culture-dependence' stands for the claim that we can only acquire ethical concepts by participating in a practice of using such concepts (rather than, say, by divine revelation); and that these concepts' content is essentially connected with actual ethical practice (i.e. the way they have been applied in the past). Correctly applying 'cruel' is not a matter of correspondence with some heavenly manual, but a matter of there being good arguments in favour of classifying some behaviour together with paradigmatic cases of cruel behaviour. It is this sense of 'culture-dependence' that the sort of scepticism discussed here must turn into a defect in ethical reasoning.

But this would be an absurd accusation of defect, coming from the non-cognitivist position. The claim that *motivates* NC is that ethics is essentially connected with human understanding and culture. NC takes the 'disillusioned' stance against the view that ethical knowledge is a matter of seeing things 'in themselves', or of being in tune with natural or divine order. It builds a strawman, a position that holds that the content of ethical concepts is a matter of 'independent fact', and proceeds to destroy that strawman by showing the position incoherent. Correct application of ethical concepts is necessarily dependent on how the concepts are actually applied in human practices, NC claims. How can NC then proceed to turn this discovery into a defect? Why does the (demolished) strawman reappear as the standard by which ethics fails? If the strawman does not represent a distinct possibility, then what is it that ethics fails to be?

This syndrome of 'the strawman's charm'[72] is rather common. In Chapter 6 I shall be discussing the case of Rorty and Fish, both of whom expose foundationalism in epistemology and some form of semantic realism as incoherent, and then embrace the views they attack by supposing that they, after all, represent standards that could (and should) be met.

Culture-dependence cannot then be a defect precluding ethical knowledge on the model that justifies selective scepticism; it remains a truth that is idle with respect to ethical reasoning. This is not to say that some other defect cannot be found (after all, culture-dependence itself could be a defect, if, for example, a theistic ethics could be made out). The point is that there is a limit to how global ethical scepticism can be: in finding some alternative that ethical epistemology, as it stands, does not meet, the sceptic is committed to there *being* ethical knowledge—even if it has consistently eluded us so far.[73]

My argument against conceiving culture-dependence as a defect of ethical judgment would not damage a form of NC that does not conceive that dependence as a defect. It appears that there could be a form of NC that considers culture-dependence a *virtue* of ethical judgment. On that version, ethical judgment *just is* learning to apply one's own culture's concepts as that culture requires, learning to move within some particular folkway. Consequently, ethical knowledge is available, as long as it is restricted to cover knowledge of application of local concepts, without any claim that these concepts are the best one could have.[74] Yet my argument is not weakened by such a form of NC. That form relies on the assumption that *different cultures use different concepts.* That assumption is necessary in order to give content to the question 'whose concepts are better?' But that assumption locates the real disagreement between cognitivists and non-cognitivists.

Cognitivists insist that education and other forms of cultural training supply *conceptions* of concepts, and that different cultures supply, at worst, different conceptions of those same concepts. They claim that the local nature of the *source* of ethical knowledge does not entail the local nature of the *content* of ethical knowledge. There is no reason, they claim, why the concession that ethical concepts are not divine, that their extensions are not written in secret books, nor do they stem from physical laws of nature that are independent of human responses, should amount to the concession that we cannot disagree in substance with people whose education appears to be very different from our own. Whether such differences result in different concepts, cognitivists maintain, is a matter to be established substantively, and often the opposite is established. Moreover, where it is established that different concepts are involved, cognitivists are still not troubled: the question whose view is right has no sense, in such a case, and the

[72] I am indebted to Susan Hurley for suggesting a similar name for that syndrome.

[73] Notice that this *particular* form of scepticism cannot be global. Recall that there could, in principle, be a fully sceptical picture, albeit based on a proper reduction.

[74] Williams's non-cognitivism seems to be of that form. See *Ethics and the Limits of Philosophy.*

disagreement should not have arisen in the first place. Non-cognitivists need equivalence of the competing views, and hence competition among them, not mutual irrelevance. Finding that 'cruelty' picks out different concepts in our own and someone else's vocabularies is no more troubling than finding that 'cruelty' and 'chastity' pick out different concepts within the same vocabulary. Non-cognitivists really need cases of disagreement in which 'cruelty' picks out the *same* concept, yet somehow the competing views are equally good.

The present form of NC makes no such case. Its conception of culture-dependence as a virtue masks the fact that that 'virtue' has all the implications for the possibility of ethical knowledge that cognitivists reject. If there were independent arguments to support the move from the 'virtue' of culture-dependence to the claim that different cultures use different concepts (and yet competitive ones, in the sense characterized above), this form of NC would be different from the standard form, under which culture-dependence is a defect. Pending such an argument, the move appears to be tacitly supported by the usual argument: only secret books could render different views competing views of the same concept. In relation to what would be required for ethical concepts' respectability, the 'virtue' is after all a defect: what would be required, for this as well the standard form of NC, is the familiar strawman of the secret books.

9. CONVERGENCE

Finally, I shall consider another ground for suspecting defective epistemology in ethics, namely the absence of convergence. Unlike science, ethical claims do not seem to aspire to convergence of opinion, and even less do they seem to achieve any such convergence.

The last complaint is related to conceptually independent explanations, by conceiving absence of convergence of ethical belief as a natural result: *because* ethical beliefs can be explained as the result of independent causes, it should not be surprising that opinion does not converge. Ethical judgment is driven by factors irrelevant to the possible truth of its content, normally having to do with cultural circumstances, upbringing, interest, and so forth: we should thus expect it to vary with different social, cultural, and personal (non-ethically conceived) circumstances. I shall not consider the scepticism based on culture-dependence that is implicit here, as I have argued that it makes no sense. Instead, I shall discuss how an objectivist account handles the absence of convergence.

We should note that alternative explanations of disputes are available. First, the existence of the dispute itself does not entail the impossibility of convergence: we frequently stand to learn by arguing for our ethical beliefs, and are compelled to give up what cannot be properly supported. In many cases what Wiggins calls the 'counsel of perseverance' is appropriate, which consists in the injunction to try to examine and support our beliefs in the face of objections, rather than take the very existence of disagreement as a sign of an unbridgeable gap.[75] Where divergence shows no hope of evaporating, it may represent a case of ethical systems so different, that perseverance will not make sense. But more often than not, in such cases, opposing claims will not even manage to be competitive with one another: the disagreement will not be such as to threaten each side's views, because that requires that the two claims be inconsistent with each other. Finally, it may also be the case that the claims in dispute *are* competitive, yet no side is prepared to give up on its position.

The last sort of divergence is of interest here. Cognitivism is not frustrated by the existence of such disagreements. They may be explained (and typically are explained) by two factors influencing the capacity to obtain ethical knowledge. The first involves the recognition of differing degrees of sensibility to ethical reasoning, and hence differing capacities to achieve ethical knowledge. The second involves precisely the sort of debunking explanations that NC invokes. The two types combine into a theory of error (not of Mackie's type): assuming that an ethical claim is as supported as it can be, one who does not endorse it is committing an error.

Concerning defective sensibility, Hurley says that perhaps a 'division of epistemic labour' is in order: just as many scientific beliefs are only available to the few skilled scientists on whose opinion the rest of us rely, some ethical beliefs may be reliably available only to a group possessing the relevant skills.[76] Of course, there is no guarantee that the 'experts' are going to converge, since there is no guarantee that they will hit upon ethical truth: the division of labour tries to distinguish reliable and unreliable ethical thinkers, but reliability is no guarantee of success. There is no *reduction* of the form 'whatever the experts say goes', just as there is no such reduction in the case of scientific experts. The point of appealing to experts in the sciences is *not* to equate the nature of, say, water, with current expert opinion; that may be in error.[77] The appeal is made rather to the *possibility of there being experts*, viz. to water's having a discoverable nature. This analogy holds (pending further argument) in ethics as well. Now in specific cases of dispute among people who appear to hold credentials of ethical expertise, we cannot but charge one or the other with inability to see the defects of his position, and this is a possibility that still exists in the case of the *prima facie* most reliable expert we might come across.

Alternatively, we may find that our putative expert suffers the second epistemic defect: there is an explanation of his belief such that the belief is not at all grounded on considerations that could plausibly be said to support it, but on independent considerations. In such cases, we debunk the ethical belief held in the way illustrated above.

[75] Cf. Wiggins, 'Moral Cognitivism', 75–6.

[76] Subdivisions within ethics may correspond to different sorts of expertise.

[77] This point is for clarification; I do not mean that Hurley intends her division of epistemic labour in the reductive sense.

10. ETHICAL ERROR, REAL OPTIONS, AND CIRCULARITY

I argued that ethical scepticism can only be selective. The necessary 'internality' of ethical criticism suggests there is no debunking ethics by appeal to culture. Culture may be responsible for different conceptions of ethical concepts, which may or may not be wrong. This implies that there is clear scope for cross-cultural criticism, and this makes for a perhaps very strong version of cognitivism. The allegedly excessive objectivism is to do with the scope for the attribution of error involved. An objective account of evaluation must allow for error, and indeed this is essential to objectivity. As was already mentioned, this implies that failure of convergence attracts a charge of error: if values are objective, then someone dissenting from the right ethical view is in error. If, when we realize that one (actual or hypothetical) interlocutor disagrees with us on an ethical matter, we do not claim that he is in substantive error, then this amounts to our ethical claim not really having ethical content but being perhaps a rule of etiquette, or some such evaluative standard which is essentially optional. For example, we do not care much about a culture's refusal to adopt our table manners. I think that much of relativism's motivation lies in exactly the realization that many ostensibly abhorrent ways of life are after all different options, ethically and morally unimportant. But here the correct conclusion is the opposite of relativism. It is, rather, that two apparently competitive concepts fail in fact to be competitive.

Williams's 'real option' idea is pertinent here: he thinks that the truth in relativism lies in its insight that we cannot really engage in criticism ethical outlooks that do not constitute a real option for us, and he cites the life of a medieval Samurai as an example.[78] However, what seems to make that life an unreal option is its (unimportant) 'external' make up: it is surely 'unreal', in the sense of ridiculous, for one brought up in Western twentieth century culture, to dress and behave (in a superficial sense of behaviour) like a medieval Samurai, but it is far from clear that the *principles* of Samurai life, in the sense of conceptions of duty, community and self relations etc., are not real options. Another way of putting the point is that, if we accept Williams's argument, there does not seem to be any principled way of distinguishing the 'unrealness' of the Samurai option from the unrealness of many contemporary options. Samurai life seems no more unreal than 'Yakuza' life, as far as I can see, yet that latter life appears to be well within the ambit of ethical criticism.

It may seem that I am missing the point that some options may be *practically* unreal, in the sense that, although they make sense as options and therefore appear to be candidates for judgment of their moral worth, they cannot in fact be taken up. For example, even though one may think that Samurais' life is sensible and

[78] See 'The Truth in Relativism', *in Moral Luck*. Note that recently Williams has weakened his thesis: see *Ethics and the Limits of Philosophy*, 220, at n. 3. I here address only his earlier view, although my argument can be easily adapted to cover his more recent view as well.

desirable, one cannot take that life up on one's own: there must be many similarly minded neo-Samurais for the option to be pursuable (because, say, competition for the greatest feat is constitutive of Samurai life). Therefore the 'option' is utopian, and thus not really in the domain of ethical appreciation.

Again, it is crucial how options are individuated. Suppose I contemplate the life of a Sicilian don. There are obstacles to my becoming one—not being Sicilian by origin, I do not stand a good chance even if I emigrate there. But this is a trivial obstacle: it is an obstacle to being a *Sicilian*, it is not an obstacle to running organized crime etc. (if it is true that this is what the life of a Sicilian don involves). Such trivial obstacles rule out too much; I cannot be a French lawyer, for that matter. Williams needs an obstacle that is relevant, that is a constitutive part of the way of life contemplated, so that, despite the way of life's being intelligible as an option, the impossibility of engaging in the relevant part renders it not a real one. There must be, therefore, a feature in the contemplated alternative way of life that makes it both competitive with the reference way of life *and* impossible.

The crucial feature that makes an ethical alternative both competitive and impossible to pursue must be *individuative*, at least partly, of the ethical alternative. It would not suffice for it to be *typically* associated with the alternative. This is not to define Williams's argument away: the requirement is entailed by Williams's own claims. His supposed unreal alternatives must be *alternatives*, they must be individuated by conceptions of ethical principles that compete with the conceptions that individuate the way of life of the person contemplating the alternative. Those alternative conceptions, therefore, should require courses of action that are impossible, or extremely difficult, to pursue. The difficulty should be required as a matter of ethical significance.

There is a complex theoretical requirement, therefore, for Williams's view. He must present some examples in which, first, what makes an option difficult to pursue is required by an ethical principle that is an essential part of the option, but, second, the option cannot be evaluated on ethical grounds: the option is blocked from criticism irrespective of its merits (that is, the option will not be pursued on account of the sheer difficulty of pursuing it, regardless of whether it is good or bad).

Williams's examples do not respect this complex requirement. In some of his examples, like the Samurai one discussed above, the features that seem to make the option difficult to pursue are ethically insignificant. They do not individuate an ethical option that is impossible to pursue, but one impossible way of pursuing it. As I argued, the impossibility concerns superficial aspects, which are contingently associated with the ethical outlook that a Samurai life realizes. More precisely, whether the difficulty is a necessary part, or just one way among many, of pursuing the ethical principles in pursuit of which Samurais used to live the way they did, is left unargued for by Williams. As things stand, it seems that the crucial, impossible to pursue, aspects of Samurai life are indeed beyond the ambit of ethical criticism, because they are not candidates even for academic such criticism. The aspects that *are* ethically significant do seem to be theoretical as well as practical objects of criticism, unlike the difficulties, which derive from details.

On the other hand, where the difficulty does not derive from detail, it is not the *sheer* difficulty, but critical evaluation of the option, that supports its rejection. For example, we will not take up the way of life of an 'out of the way people' on a remote island, at least in part for general cognitive, as well as specifically ethical, reasons. Such a life requires, among other things, that certain moral choices turn on the weather or other irrelevant considerations. We know too much to subscribe to such superstition; further, our ethical outlook requires that we do not make important choices on the basis of superstition, but rather upon deliberation that carries personal responsibility. It is for these reasons that we decline to take up that 'out of the way people's' way of life. Of course, here as elsewhere, there are a number of further inconveniences involved in joining such a 'primitive' way of life, yet nothing in our ethical structure requires that we do not subject ourselves to such inconveniences, and so no issue is to be joined between our own and that ethical outlook. Hence, there are no philosophical insights to be derived from the supposition that some, though convinced of the ethical superiority of such a way of life, may decline to take it up for the sake of habit or comfort.

Williams may have no more than some strong sense of inconvenience in mind, since he writes about being able to take up options in a 'sane' way.[79] If that is correct, the point that ethical principles should not lead people to alienate themselves from their own cultures and traditions, and drive them into bizarre ways of life with the purpose of serving ethical causes, is sound. But it owes its soundness to the fact that ethical principles require no such thing. Most utopias are silly not because they overrate moral worth, but because they have none—they require that one attempt to emulate the ethically insignificant features of moral outlooks, lifestyles rather than ways of life.[80]

Williams concedes that his 'real option' argument supposes that there is no ethical truth: phlogiston theory is not an interesting option, he says, not because it is not real but because it is false. So where questions of truth are relevant, relativism is false and options do not come into it.[81] So no new issue has been joined in the debate about the status of ethics. But his 'real option' may seem to work independent of the debate, to be an extra difficulty for the ethical objectivist, rather than what it is in fact, namely an attempt by someone *already* convinced by NC to account for the fact that sometimes we *do* engage in ethical criticism. Williams' essay should be titled more accurately 'The Truth in Objectivism', since he starts from a position that would disallow *any* kind of criticism, and seeks to show how closer-to-home ethical outlooks (which are routinely the object of

[79] Paul Sourlas has pointed out to me the Freudian overtone of Williams' argument: in arguing for the 'unrealness' of certain options, Williams may be concerned for the 'neurotic' effects pursuing certain ethical alternatives may have.

[80] On the other hand, where utopias carve out an ethical alternative, their utopian character is due to ethical unsoundness, rather than practical difficulty.

[81] 'The Truth in Relativism', 143.

criticism) may be distinguished from the ones for which NC may be easier to accept. My argument is that there is no distinction to be drawn.

Williams has expressed a further complaint.[82] Note that selective scepticism is in effect an argument for objectivism: scepticism that can only address particular beliefs presupposes vindication of the broad field to which the belief belongs. Selective debunking explanations, along with explanations of error on the basis of lack of the required sensibility on the part of our opponent, were appealed to as part of insisting that disagreeing with someone implies a claim that he is in error. But we cannot, Williams claims, offer one's 'not being in the right position' as an explanation. Such an explanation may hold for ordinary belief: someone's belief that he is seeing a blue wall, while actually looking to a white wall lit by a blue light, may be explicable by reference to his bad position (he cannot see the light from where he is sitting). Now in the case of ethical belief, any such explanation seems to be circular, i.e. seems to presuppose that one's belief is the wrong one. Consider a general such explanation: someone's belief that amputation is the right punishment of theft is explicable by the fact that he was raised in the wrong culture; all too often unacceptable ethics are charitably explicable along such lines. But the culture's wrongness seems to consist, partly at least, in the fact that amputation is condoned. So nothing is added to the claim that the belief itself is wrong: we have given no reason, that does not depend on amputation's being wrong, to reject some relativist position according to which the holder of the belief belongs simply with a *different* ethical system.

We must distinguish two readings of the objection. The first concerns the kinds of reasons that support the claim that one is committing an error. The second concerns the distinction between one's being in error and one's using a different concept.

The first reading is not really a problem. Surely what makes it the case that one is not in a good position to make a good ethical judgment cannot but be ethical facts. What makes it the case that one is not in a good position to appreciate the fact that one is seeing a white wall lit by a blue light is the laws of optics and collateral hypotheses in physics (light reflects on surfaces at certain angles, white surfaces reflect all light wavelengths, etc.). Similarly, one is not in a good position to appreciate ethical truths, if one is, say, placed within a culture where the sovereign is thought to carry divine powers and where dissent is punishable with death. There need be no circularity of the form: 'one is not well placed to appreciate that amputation is wrong, because one is placed in a culture that teaches that amputation is not wrong', where the appeal to culture is used in the sense of 'disposition to produce beliefs that amputation is not wrong'. (This explanation *wouldn't* be circular if the appeal to culture were meant as the claim that dissent would not be tolerated.) Invoking cultural obstacles to forming ethical judgment may involve facts independent of the particular belief criticized, e.g. general

[82] *Ethics and the Limits of Philosophy*, 145–52.

intolerance of freedom of expression, non-recognition of any form of civil rights etc.; or specific debunking considerations, e.g. that the specific belief, or collateral beliefs supporting it, track the sovereign's interests, rather than the truth.

The demand that the specification of what is or is not a bad position should not be circular cannot be so strong as to amount to a demand for reduction. Why should it be the case that being in a bad position for ethical judgment is specifiable in ethically neutral terms? In effect, this would make the complaint a reiteration of the desire that ethics should be reducible, and no new argument for reduction is being offered.

The second form of the objection is *not*: what makes it the case that one's epistemic position is bad, where it results in a belief that amputation is right? The objector may accept that this question is answered by other ethical considerations such as the wrongness of cruelty etc. Rather, it is: what makes it the case that belief in the propriety of amputation *constitutes a wrong belief about punishment*, rather than a different belief—say, a belief about punishment*, where punishment* is, precisely, a different concept, immune to criticism?

There does not seem to be any clear criterion for making the distinction involved (and this should not be surprising in view of the substantive, theoretical nature of semantic analysis discussed in Chapter 2). As I have argued in Chapter 2 (and I shall argue in Chapter 6), the distinction turns on a theoretical appraisal of the situation involved, constrained by some charitable presumption that makes the subject as rational as possible. The judgment that one holds a punishment belief is supportable by substantive considerations taking into account the subject's own beliefs about interdependencies of the belief with other beliefs (his sense of what is relevant to the content of the crucial belief), the actions that appear to be connected with it, and so forth. There is no denying that the borderline between same concept/wrong belief, on the one hand, and different concept, on the other, may be blurred. But insistence that an *a priori* specification of the distinction be supplied amounts to a demand for an *a priori* specification of the relevant concept's content: claims that a belief is a wrong belief about 'punishment' belong with the effort to specify the content of 'punishment'; and the claim that the objector attacks is precisely the claim that specifications of conceptual content *are not a priori*. So further argument is needed to show that this claim is misguided; as the objection stands, it simply notices what we have been arguing for, namely that substantive argument is needed to make or dispute a claim about the content of ethical and other semantically deep concepts.

11. THE NATURE OF VALUES AND LAW

The discussion so far suggests that no suspect metaphysical commitments are required by ethical cognitivism, and that there is no reason not to see evaluative and specifically ethical judgments as knowledge-bound. Ethics is undoubtedly causally dependent on the mind, and more specifically on cultures or 'forms of life'. But this causal dependence is compatible with ethical properties' having discoverable natures. As Wiggins puts it,

> [y]ou can say, if you like, that we create a form of life that invests certain features of people, acts and situations with the status of values. (Surely that is not false.) But this is not to say that *values* are created thereby. Rather, values are discovered by those who live the form of life that is said to have been created.[83]

Values presuppose, therefore, the existence of social practices, but that claim does not entail that we do not discover them, that what it is for something to be good or cruel is not to be established substantively.

To assume that there is no scope for ethical discovery needs an extra gloss on the claim that values are subjective. It needs the supposition that value is something situated 'in the head', in the sense of individualistic mental entities; and further the supposition that this something is available by virtue of the mind being transparent to itself. But I have argued that value cannot be constructed out of materials 'in the head', and that, at best, our responses are responses to properties ('outside' it, although the precise claim is that of interdependence, undermining the sharp distinction between 'internal' and 'external'), among which is the property of certain actions or events to affect us in certain ways. And I have cast doubt on the availability of features 'in the head' that manage to resemble features outside it.

I have argued that the line of thought under attack is encouraged by a general picture of the mind–world relation. In that picture, the world impinges on the mind through the senses. The senses convey information that is directly graspable and on whose apparent content we are incorrigible, and thus provide the content of foundational beliefs about the external world against which more complex beliefs are to be tested. On the other hand, the mind itself invents truths that cannot coherently be doubted, providing foundational beliefs whose purpose is to organize experience. Since values cannot be plausibly thought to be known in the first way (on pain of accepting a picture of queer faculties perceiving queer properties), they must fall (if there is any content to ethical judgment, i.e. if it is not to be 'pure' emotion etc.) under the second head: they must constitute a degenerate sort of truth, a stipulation that may not coherently be doubted. I have cast doubt, in Chapter 2, on this conception of the relation between mind and world, and I have argued in this Chapter that rejecting that picture makes evaluative objectivism a natural position. The next two Chapters will examine more closely the possibility of objectivism combined with the concession that concepts essentially depend on social practices.

I have argued that, even if we accept that ethics is in an important sense the product of culture, this thought does not help in answering questions of applica-

[83] 'Moral Cognitivism', 80.

tion of ethical concepts. A quick way to make that argument is to say that there is no 'sideways' perspective on values allowing us to examine evaluative judgment without engaging in it.

This way of putting the point may lead to the following objection: law does not involve the perspective obstacle. Law is the product of specific communities, and thus not something which we cannot but presuppose in our thinking. After all, the law can at any time be changed, whereas our 'form of life' at large is not something with which anyone has the power to tamper. Hence to the content of law, at least, some suitable conception of the community *does have* a privileged access.

This objection conflates scope with content. Law's scope is community-bound, and this leads to a parallel relativization.[84] No one thinks that English laws apply in France. But this relativization does not carry over to the determination of law's *content*. To determine that we must use the same method we use everywhere else. The arguments that support the claim that evaluative concepts' content is substantively determined do not turn on scope. The claim is *not* that, because ethical concepts range over any culture, because they embody humanity-wide principles, they are objective and anyone or whole cultures may be in substantive error about their conditions of correct application. Rather, the claim is that, because reduction of value to individualistic (environment-independent) mental states fails, concepts' content is objective and amenable to discoveries. Content is *analytically prior* to scope: scope conclusions follow upon, rather than being an assumption for, determination of content.

We may illustrate this insight in Burge's style. Law's scope depends on a community, in the sense that a community's choosing to enforce a certain rule makes it valid for that community. Now we can see that no implication about our capacity to disagree, doubt, and make discoveries about the content of law follows from that. The assumption about the community's role is not violated by these epistemic activities. When we doubt whether, say, the community chose to enforce X (where X is the purported content of the rule), we are not doubting whether what the community chose to enforce is what the community chose to enforce (much less are we doubting whether the community may choose to enforce what it likes); we are doubting whether what the community chose to enforce *is X*. What this doubt may breach is not the community's authority; the object of our study is undoubtedly the law, and we have agreed that the law is what the community has done (loosely speaking); the most the doubt may cover is any individual understanding (one or many) of what the community has done.

My distinction between scope and content considerations *would* collapse if what the community has done—the practice, for short—were reduced to communal understanding. In that case, doubting whether communal understanding captures the content of the practice would be incoherent—it would amount to doubting whether the practice is what it is. But the necessary reduction is impossible. How

[84] Cf. Hurley, *NR*, 289 (n. 2 to Ch. 3).

are we to conceive communal understanding? Presumably as an aggregation of individual understanding.[85] But if we are to get a foothold on the reduction, we need an independent constraint individuating the content of individual understanding. We need a constraint that identifies individual understanding without supposing anything about practice (since practice is what we hope to construct out of individual understanding) or else the account will be viciously circular. If my arguments so far are right, there does not seem to be hope for such reduction. Assumptions about the content of practice are *necessary* in order to individuate individual understanding, so no reduction is possible. Doubting whether sofas are meant to be sat upon cannot be reduced to doubting whether what most people think of as sofas are meant to be sat upon: 'sofas' needs to get content in the reinterpretation as well, and further reinterpretation will launch us on a regress. Individual understanding is understanding *of* something (the practice), which individuates the content of individual understanding, just as red individuates the content of sensations of red.

I conclude that the claim that the study of law involves the study of particular communities does not undermine objectivism about the law's content. Communities can go wrong in understanding themselves. In the next Chapter I shall pursue the implications of practice-dependence of the law's content, and I shall consider further arguments from practice-dependence against the objectivity of legal content.

[85] This assumption is not material to my argument—the argument works in exactly the same way for communal understanding *simpliciter*. I am making the assumption in order to address the most natural interpretation of the notion of communal understanding.

5

Substantive Disagreement and Indeterminacy

1. INTRODUCTION

In Chapters 3 and 4, I defended K–P semantics against metaphysical objections that purport to make it inappropriate for areas like law. I argued that K–P semantics does apply to expressions that designate 'mind-dependent' entities or properties. In this Chapter I shall consider a different objection: namely that K–P semantics cannot work in law, since legal concepts are individuated by their conventional content. Theoretical disagreement cannot take place in the law, since it would require that shared criteria be coherently dubitable. But, the objection continues, if one may doubt that the application of legal concepts is governed by the criteria shared by lawyers, one will be vulnerable to radical scepticism: there will be nothing in virtue of which different interpretations may be better or worse.

The central question is: what are the constraints on the interpretation of a concept? The question is made natural by the following thought: if legal concepts are capable of being the object of *substantive* disagreement (SD), there must be a way to demarcate this sort of disagreement from *conceptual* disagreement (CD). SD consists in there being disagreement over whether something is X, which turns on different views of what it is for something to be X, so that different views are mutually incompatible. For instance, we may disagree over whether some state of affairs is a contract, despite agreeing on all relevant facts identifying the state of affairs (short of its being a contract or not), because we disagree over what is required for there to be a contract; for instance, we disagree on whether some unusual event that took place prior to the agreement is so related to the other, uncontroversial conditions, as to defeat the judgment that the overall situation is a contract. Or we may disagree over the concept of a person, although we agree that it includes potential persons and therefore fetuses, because we disagree about how the property of being a potential person is related to personhood proper: I think the relation is such that potentiality is constrained to cover only viable fetuses, whereas you think it ranges over fertilized ova at any stage in their development. In CD we simply appear to disagree, but in fact there is no real disagreement. For instance, we think we have a disagreement over whether something is a vessel, but it turns out that I am talking about ships and you are talking about arteries. Or it appears that we have a disagreement over cruelty, but I am talking about brutality whereas you are (for some reason) talking about cost.[1] In both those cases, we should be likely to find out quickly that we are having a CD. A more interesting case arises where our disagreement *cannot but* be conceptual, despite appearances that, in disagreeing about X, we are talking about the same thing, because the condition of X-hood is such that it may not coherently be doubted, say, because X-hood is a fiat created by stipulation. For example, we are disagreeing about whether water boils at 100^0 Centigrade. Consequently a view which appears to doubt that necessarily picks out something else, and hence is not competitive with the view under apparent doubt.

In this Chapter, I shall examine the question whether allowing for SD in law entails radical indeterminacy of legal interpretation, unless conventional constraints to the content of law are presupposed. In section 2, I shall consider the importance of the subject in connection with legal theory. In section 3, I shall discuss various misunderstandings of Dworkin's attack on the Criterial Model—his criticism of the 'semantic sting'. I shall be claiming that Dworkin's theory is compatible with the K–P model developed in Ch. 2, and, indeed, that the two models are mutually reinforcing. In section 4, I shall discuss Joseph Raz's argument to the effect that Dworkin's model *presupposes* the Criterial Model, since it would otherwise make for radical indeterminacy of legal interpretation. In section 5, I shall clarify Dworkin's notion of pre-interpretive agreement, which is alleged to constitute his covert conventionalism, and distinguish it from positivists' settled law. In section 6, I shall identify the major unargued assumption behind the dilemma posed by Raz, viz. that one must either rely on conventional meaning or else meaning will be indeterminate; namely, Raz assumes that only indubitable truths can play the role of constraints. In section 7, I shall discuss arguments attributed to Wittgenstein that are thought to support the necessity of conventions, and defend an alternative view, also attributed to Wittgenstein, which in fact reveals Raz's dilemma to be false. Section 8 will deal with the question whether the latter reading can be of help in controversial cases. In section 9, I shall return to Raz's objection and argue that the correct conception of the thesis that practices determine the application of concepts allows for theoretical disagreement in the law, and for the objectivity of legal interpretation. In section 10, I shall go back to my claim that Dworkin's theory is compatible with my K–P model, and discuss the possible importance of the fact that Dworkin avoids metaphysics. Finally, in section 11, I shall consider the argument that consensus in law is important not for semantic reasons, but rather for reasons having to do with the nature of law.

[1] Dworkin's example, 'Bork's Jurisprudence', *57 U. Chicago L. R.*, 657–77, at 662.

2. SUBSTANTIVE DISAGREEMENT IN LAW

The question whether there is scope for SD in law runs parallel to the question of the limits of law, once put in terms of fidelity (to the law) versus repair (of it), and more recently in terms of interpretation versus invention. The two questions are parallel in the following sense: unless SD is possible in law, any dissent from the standard opinion as to what the law requires in a particular case will necessarily violate the requirement of fidelity; it will be, at best, a call for repair. If the dissenting opinion is motivated by considerations of natural justice, then offering such an opinion must be tantamount to claiming that the law proper must be repaired to make it more just; if it is motivated by considerations of political expediency, then it will be a call for repair to help achieve the relevant ends; and so forth. Or, in terms of the interpretation–invention distinction, any such opinion will necessarily be an instance of inventing, rather than interpreting, the law (and it will be a different question if, and under what circumstances, inventing would be acceptable). Scope for SD, on the other hand, will just be scope for characterizing *some*, at least, dissenting views as attempts at establishing what the law requires. The relevant debates will therefore be placed within the boundaries of law proper.

In its more recent guise, the issue is familiar from Dworkin's attack on positivism. The positivist tradition has identified the content of law by means of a master criterion—like Hart's Rule of Recognition—which singles out the corpus of legal statements, the content of which is in turn exhausted in their 'conventional meaning';[2] outside these constraints the question of interpretation and application of the law loses its content, and any cases are to be resolved through the exercise of judicial discretion. Only CD therefore may obtain outside these constraints; and since the constraints themselves are constituted by agreement (in the form of consensus-based conventions), no disagreement at all can be SD. Dworkin's central claim is that the question of interpretation—what is the law—survives outside the

[2] Convention consists in a system of interlocking beliefs and expectations concerning a regularity, so that (a) everyone conforms to the regularity; (b) everyone expects everyone else to conform; (c) there is common knowledge of (a) and (b); (d) part of the reason why agents conform is that (a) to (c) obtain. There must also be higher order expectations (of infinite order of implication). A linguistic convention would consist in a word's being regularly used in order to communicate according to conditions (a) to (d). See D. Lewis, *Convention*; D.-H. Ruben, *The Metaphysics of the Social World*; G. Postema, 'Coordination and Convention at the Foundations of Law', *11 Journal of Legal Studies*, 165–203. I will not here enter into a thorough examination of conventions. For present purposes, we have a tolerably clear idea of conventionalist semantics as claiming that words are matched to meaning in the above fashion, so that (1) meaning is fixed; (2) speakers know it; (3) propositions expressing what a word means have the status of a degenerate truth, viz. a truth that cannot coherently be doubted. The first two claims are necessary for the system of expectations to be at all workable, and the third claim further reflects the arbitrary nature of convention. There could be a brand of linguistic conventionalism which would accommodate speakers' semantic ignorance, arguing that there are 'deferential' conventions by virtue of which fixing the meaning of some expressions has been delegated to the appropriate experts. Then (1) to (3) must hold for the delegating convention itself.

boundaries of conventional meaning;[3] the true 'limits of the law' are not charted by the master criterion-*cum*-conventions, but by the availability of a coherent interpretation of legal practices taken as a whole. The major novelty in Dworkin's critique of positivism lies in his claim that his theory is offered as an account of how *what the law requires* is established, an account that purports to cover both 'settled' and controversial questions, rather than taking for granted the methodology of establishing 'settled' law and insisting that further materials and different methods are necessary in order to resolve difficult or novel questions.[4] Dworkin's account purports to deal with easy and hard cases alike; earlier critics had taken Dworkin to suggest that, although easy cases are resolved on the basis of 'settled law', conventionally identified, 'more law' may be extrapolated from that to serve for the resolution of hard cases. Some critics still insist in attributing this picture to Dworkin. The objections by Raz and Fish, to be discussed at length below, attribute just that to Dworkin on the basis of semantic and epistemological considerations, and conclude that his theory is untenable. Others (discussed in section 5, below) simply think that Dworkin's theory is a 'hard-case theory' and therefore can happily live side by side with positivism, the latter being an 'easy-case theory'. I shall argue that all this is seriously mistaken.

Clearly, Dworkin's thesis depends crucially on its being able to distinguish between interpreting (the law, a text, a practice etc.) and inventing (i.e. altering it).

3. CONSTRAINTS: PRACTICE *VERSUS* CRITERIA

Joseph Raz and Stanley Fish are among a host of critics who have dealt with the distinction between interpretation and invention in the course of criticizing Dworkin. Their views coincide in attributing to Dworkin a way of drawing that distinction which depends on a conventionalist individuation of the object of interpretation. They diverge in that Raz thinks this is the consequence of an insurmountable difficulty, whereas Fish offers his own version, which allegedly avoids that pitfall.

[3] Dworkin's critique also implies that positivism fails by its own standards. It fails to provide an accurate description of its object: disagreement in endemic in legal practice, yet positivism is committed to falsifying disputing lawyers' perception of their disputes as having any sense.

[4] Note that Dworkin's claim is not simply that, since lawyers disagree, there *must* be something they disagree about; moreover, he claims that, since it is virtually always *part of the claims made* by disputing parties that they are about what the law requires, those who deny that there is a common object to their claims will have the difficult task of explaining the appearance of genuine disagreement either in terms of massive-scale deception or massive error, e.g. by claiming that disputing lawyers *cannot* be debating what the law is, since there cannot be controversial law (in the context of an error theory analogous to Mackie's error theory discussed in Ch. 4). See for example MacCormick, *Legal Reasoning and Legal Theory*, 247 ff., where he offers to explain disagreement through a version of the second alternative above: the disagreement is *practical*, and so unresolvable since it turns on different evaluative commitments.

3.1 Dworkin's Practices

What is the proper way to draw the distinction? Dworkin's answer comes in two steps. First, he suggests that interpretation is constrained by the history of the practice, in the sense of what counts as a concept's paradigmatic applications. Such applications are supposed to exemplify the property expressed by the concept, and a proposed interpretation must explain and justify them as paradigmatic instantiations of the property. In the case of a social practice, it is particular acts which serve as exemplars, e.g. giving up one's seat to women in the case of 'courtesy'.[5] Dworkin sometimes calls these constraints 'formal' and distinguishes them from the creative task of providing a substantive explication of a concept.[6] But this is qualified by the second part of his account. In spite of identifying such formal features, Dworkin maintains that no feature of the concept is immune to revision. He writes:

> There is no feature that any stage or instance of the practice [of courtesy] just must have, in virtue of the meaning of the word 'courtesy', and the search for such a feature would be just another example of the lingering infection of the semantic sting.[7]

And again:

> [N]o paradigm is secure from challenge by a new interpretation that accounts for other paradigms better and leaves that one isolated as a mistake.[8]

This picture is strikingly similar to the one painted in Ch. 2. A complication is introduced, however, by virtue of the fact that Dworkin takes his thesis to be anti-semantic, by identifying semantics with the particular semantic theory he is concerned to attack—the *Criterial Model*.[9]

3.2 The Semantic Sting and K–P Semantics

The Criterial Model identifies content with the shared descriptions of properties with which speakers associate an expression. These properties operate as criteria for the correct application of a concept, and their criterial status is a matter of conventional arrangement. Dworkin is often taken to concede that this sort of analysis may be appropriate in ordinary communication, where grasping subjective

[5] Dworkin's example, *Law's Empire*, (hereinafter, *LE*), 72.

[6] Dworkin seems to use 'formal' as opposed to creative, in order to capture the idea that the requirement that an interpretation account for paradigms and abstract characterizations of its object is a *constraint*. But this is not to say that any particular paradigm or abstract specification is necessarily part of the correct interpretation. In Dworkin's terms, therefore, we may say that any such 'formal' feature may be rejected as mistaken. This in fact is what Dworkin goes on to say. We might make the same point by saying that no paradigm, let alone abstract conception of the point of a practice, is *individuative* of the practice.

[7] *LE*, 70.

[8] *LE*, 72.

[9] See, however, 'Legal Theory and the Problem of Sense' *in* Gavison, R. (ed.), *Issues in Contemporary Legal Philosophy*, at 10: '[S]uccessful theories of law will always have or entail what will seem a merely linguistic aspect or component.' Cf. Dworkin's response to Gavison, *in* Gavison (ed.), ibid., 19.

sense is crucial, but to reject it in contexts where speakers have developed the 'interpretive attitude', i.e. where they have developed sensitivity to the 'point' of a practice or concept. The occurrence of this attitude seems to necessitate a methodological switch: for interpretive concepts, we must disengage content from subjective or communal sense.[10] In other words, Dworkin's apparent concession that semantics is based on criteria seems to entail that what his method tries to establish is not meanings but something more transparent, which would explain his talk of *commitment* or *conviction*, the content of which depends on substantive theories. K–P semantics, on the other hand, involves the claim that meaning by and large turns on such substantive theories. Consequently, unless there are independent motivations for distinguishing among cases in which the interpretive attitude obtains, K–P semantics should be perfectly consistent with Dworkin's model.

A possible difference would be that Dworkin's 'interpretive attitude' looks like a sociological criterion of scope for SD, whereas K–P semantics (and Dworkin's older notion of 'essential contestability') makes it a conceptual issue. Michael Moore has claimed that Dworkin's method is in fact based on such a sociological criterion.[11] But this cannot be Dworkin's view, because it would leave it open for someone to claim that SD is the product of a delegation-convention, embodied in the Rule of Recognition: SD would occur where only the broad contours of a concept are conventionally fixed, and discretion is granted to practitioners to fill it in as they see fit at any given time, perhaps on the basis of morality. In other words, law would still be individuated by the Rule of Recognition, which would itself happen to cover Dworkin's method. For this reason, the 'interpretive attitude' should be construed as a conceptual consequence of a challenge to conventional understanding: whether the attitude occurs or not depends on whether a meaningful challenge *can* be put forward.

There is another interesting question concerning the language of commitment: perhaps Dworkin, like Blackburn, would like to hold on to a picture that allows for SD, but avoid a full-blown 'realism' that would be entailed by treating legal concepts as expressing genuine properties, and interpretations as genuine substantive theories. But as I argued in Ch. 4, in connection with Blackburn's model of ethical commitment, the model of commitment may contrast with some kind of realism that is captured in the 'out there' or 'secret books' metaphor. It is doubtful, however, whether it contrasts with a sober conception of properties as genuine, i.e. whether there is is a viable account of 'commitment' as expressing something less

[10] Dworkin does suggest that this special methodology is in fact general, i.e. all understanding is interpretive. See *LE*, 53. Consequently, disengaging content from subjective (or communal) sense may not be enough; according to the picture developed below, the disengagement may be pictured not as a case of preferring 'objective sense' over subjective sense, with the latter independently specifiable, but as an exceptional type of case in which subjective sense, though generally interrelated, fails to match objective. See sections 6–9 below and Ch. 6.

[11] See 'The Interpretive Turn in Modern Theory: a Turn for the Worse?' *41 Stanford L.R.*, 871–957 at 945.

than a genuine property studied by some sort of substantive theory. Without the metaphorical, 'out there', realism to distinguish itself from, the commitment model may only contrast with sober objectivism by taking seriously its own claim that the properties involved are not genuine, that is by taking a properly sceptical view of the relevant domain. In that case, the commitment model cannot really help itself to the possibility of SD within that domain.[12] Given that Dworkin's principal claim is that there *is* SD in law, as well as his notorious rejection of the coherence of 'secret books' realism, I conclude that he does not subscribe to something like Blackburn's commitment model.

It appears, then, that Dworkin would agree with both central claims of the K–P model developed here, namely that challenges to conventional meaning of concepts make a *prima facie* case for concepts' depth, and that, without a demonstration that the perception of these concepts as indeed deep is wrong, the concepts should be taken to collect together genuine kinds. Is Dworkin's theory then K–P-compatible?

Kenneth Kress, noting that Dworkin's anti-semantic arguments are actually directed against *criterial* semantics, manages to derive the opposite conclusion: he notices that K–P semantics are not affected by Dworkin's anti-semantic arguments, since under K–P semantics controversy can be accounted for, and yet suggests that Dworkin's theory is incompatible with the K–P framework, while positivists may well help themselves to it.[13] The reasons behind this alleged incompatibility are difficult to pinpoint; it may be that Kress believes that K–P semantics makes sense only within the context of commitment to the existence of queer legal entities. He writes that

> if there are entities to which the term refers, or which stand behind the concept, those entities and their properties (essential and accidental) may ground communication. Realist or essentialist leanings may support communication in the face of disagreement. [note] This claim should be sharply distinguished from Dworkin's assertion [. . .] that interpretive communities achieve genuine communication despite disagreement in criteria because 'the competing interpretations are directed toward the same object or events of interpretation.' Dworkin's position undertakes no substantial metaphysical commitments and accordingly has less power to ground communication in the face of controversy.[14]

If that is the claim, then it fails: as I argued in Chapters 2-4, such commitments are unnecessary. The notion that objectivism can only be purchased at a high metaphysical price is just a conventionalist myth. Kress wants us to 'sharply distinguish' a position that countenances 'entities standing behind the concept' from interpretation's being 'directed towards the same object or events'. Presumably he thinks that one needs contracts to be *sui generis* concrete physical things in order to be the object of SD. But we saw that contracts can be normal events, and

[12] See Ch. 4, section 5, for a discussion of Blackburn's model of commitment.

[13] 'The Interpretive Turn', *97 Ethics*, 834–60, especially 855–60.

[14] Ibid., 855, main text and note 24.

dispute about them can focus on examples of contracts considered paradigmatic by all sides, as well as on parts of a specification of what it takes for an event to be a contract, which are common among all rival specifications.

Kress however has trouble about what kind of thing can locate SD. He says that Dworkin's 'preinterpretive data' are physicalistically describable behaviour and events, and as such are not part of the content of the concepts of which they are paradigmatic. Just after the passage cited, he writes:

> Indeed, to the extent that Dworkin takes preinterpretive data to be structurally simple, to be physicalistically describable behavior and events, and not principles or rules pregnant with social meaning, he makes less plausible the claim that pre-interpretive agreement grounds communication. [. . .] To claim that agreement about such entities could ground communication about legal concepts would be like claiming that agreement about the properties of molecules could ground communication about the properties of middle size objects in the absence of a reductive theory.[15]

This passage raises questions about the relations between Dworkin's pre-interpretive data and the theories that account for them. Kress seems to have difficulty with the general issue of the status of data that locate SD among competing theories. He seems to suggest that these data would either have to be describable in a 'physicalistic' way, and thus be neutral with respect to the theories involved but unable to locate disagreement, or else be 'pregnant with meaning', and so presumably not neutral enough. But this is a fake dilemma. The data involved here could be, *inter alia*, events that would be classified as contracts by one theory, but not by another. The required neutrality can be attained simply by agreeing on a description of the relevant events that is as full as possible, yet not committed on whether they are contracts or not. That need not be physicalistic; it may well mention, say, agreements made with the intention that they are binding, for a certain consideration, arrived at after free negotiation, and so forth. Such a description, nevertheless, may include an event, which under one theory renders the whole story *not* a contract, and yet is considered perfectly in order by another. As long as that particular event, offending under one theory, is described in a way that does not, on the terms of the description alone, prejudice the issue of contracthood either way, it may constrain competing theories without fully determining them. Competing theories must *account for* such data, but they may account for them in different ways.

The relations between data and theory will be further discussed in the next two sections. Now the further claim that Kress seems to make is that conceiving of the data as 'physicalistically describable behaviour' without a reductive theory connecting them to a legal description disallows explanations of SD on a K–P model. This claim is difficult to evaluate without a more detailed account of the relations between data and theory. But, even if Kress's claim were granted, it would not

[15] Ibid., 855.

render Dworkin's and K–P frameworks incompatible, since Dworkin does not have to conceive of his data as physicalistically describable behaviour, but can accept (as he does) that they are 'pregnant with meaning', in the way illustrated above.[16]

So far, then, no incompatibility between Dworkin's model and non-criterial semantics has been established.

It is even more obscure how Kress supports the claim that K–P analysis is available to positivists. He does insist that positivists can acknowledge the existence of theoretical disagreement by adopting 'non-interpretive semantic theories' available to them.[17] Assuming that he would not saddle positivists with metaphysical commitment to legal entities he seems to think necessary for everyone else, perhaps he thinks that the type of semantic theory available to them that would accommodate theoretical disagreement is a (supposedly) K–P semantics built around the socialized picture of meaning whereby experts' criteria determine extension and speakers defer to these criteria in their use of the relevant concepts. However, whether Kress actually intends that move or not, the move fails: this type of socialized theory is actually incompatible with K–P semantics, and indeed *vulnerable* to Dworkin's argument from disagreement. If the socialized picture is to have any bite, experts' criteria must have, of course, *criterial* status. A socialized picture would have concepts' extensions *be* whatever satisfies experts' criteria. If X,Y,Z are the experts' criteria of contract, then X,Y,Z* cannot count as a rival conception of what is a contract, whose holders are in substantive disagreement with the experts. Nor can the experts themselves split into two groups, each siding with one set of criteria, nor even can they all change their mind and adopt the new set. In both cases, nothing could make it the case that the new set consists of criteria of contract, so that the new set could support disagreement, or the experts' changing their mind. Both disagreeing and changing one's mind need locating—there must be something one disagrees or changes one's mind *about*. The semantics necessary to allow for experts to disagree or change their mind should specify that contract is *not* what experts think it is, i.e. X, Y, Z; but what experts *think* is X, Y, Z. If the semantics allows them, in other words, to disagree and change their minds, then the content of expert judgment on what is a contract loses its criterial status, and is therefore incompatible with positivism.[18]

A further misinterpretation of Dworkin's anti-semantic claims may be the

[16] Cf. Ch. 3, section 4, against the idea that K-P semantics only works for empirical objects because they can be identified by way of reduced, physicalistic, concepts. See Chs 2 and 4 more generally against the idea of K-P works where concepts correspond to 'bare facts', and hence not where concepts stand for human practices. See section 5 below, for further discussion of the nature of Dworkin's 'pre-interpretive agreement'.

[17] 'The Interpretive Turn', 858.

[18] See the discussion on Putnam in Ch. 2. Note that the semantics that makes room for theoretical disagreement is incompatible with positivism insofar as positivism is committed to the Criterial Model. Kress has an independent argument according to which positivism may give up the Criterial Model altogether, which is not relevant here: I am here addressing his argument that positivists who are committed to the Criterial Model can help themselves to a K-P based explanation of disagreement.

following. Although Dworkin's attack is directed at criteria, its scope sometimes seems to be rather more comprehensive, i.e. to include all that is claimed by the so-called communication model. That model, largely espoused by positivists, claims that: (a) communication is intention-based, i.e. the content of communication consists in the content a speaker intends to convey; (b) speakers' intentions govern their choice of words; (c) words' application turns on criteria, i.e. evidence supporting judgments about correct application, and the criterial status of such evidence is a matter of convention.[19] These principles are thought to cover ordinary communication, and their adherents may extend them to law, provided they somehow refine the notion of intention so that it can capture so-called legislative intention. Now the standard motivation of critics of this communication model is their conviction that the alleged criteria must be open to doubt: even though segregated schooling was not thought to be ruled out by the requirements of the Fourteenth Amendment to the US Constitution at the time of its enactment, to take the standard example, we must be able to see segregation as actually contradicting the principle enacted in the Amendment.

One way to allow for enforcement of (the true content of) equality is to accept the communication model, admit that segregation is not strictly speaking prohibited, and argue for repair of the law.[20] Another option would be to reject the applicability of the model by denying that law is communication at all. This is the line taken by a recent objectivist position put forward by Heidi Hurd.[21] (Hurd examines a model of communication based on speech-acts theory, but it is unclear why we should restrict our attention to that version of semantics.) She supports

[19] This seems to capture, *inter alia*, Raz's view. I am here relying on 'Authority, Law and Morality', *68 The Monist*, 295–324; 'Dworkin: A New Link in the Chain', *74 Cal.L.R.*, 1103–19 (hereinafter, 'Link'); and Raz's lectures. The model is not committed on the question whether subjective sense is directly identical with conventional sense (i.e. whether speakers know the content of the extant conventions) or indirectly identical (by virtue of a blanket deferring intention to mean whatever conventions mean).

[20] A variant of this route is to say that the communication model itself allows for applying the correct sense of the concept, since the legislature's enactment of a 'general' principle is tantamount to granting discretion to courts to apply the principle as they see fit. Cf. Raz, 'Link'. On that scenario, desegregating schools will not require repairing the law, but simply 'filling it in' on the strength of the assumed delegation. I am saying it is a variant of the 'repair' strategy since both strategies accept that the content of law turns on criteria. They thus agree that desegregation is not directly *required* by the law; the ingenuity of the 'delegation' strategy lies in that it would present desegregation as *indirectly* required, as it were.

However, the 'delegation' strategy fails. What is it to say that 'equality' is general? 'Animal', say, is in some sense general, but a law prohibiting animals from being carried on public transport cannot be said, except in a trivial sense, to include a delegation to determine what is an animal. Although not expressly so, that law surely prohibits dogs and horses—what is or isn't an 'animal' is a matter of fact, just like what is or isn't a 'vehicle', 'equal before the law', 'unconscionable contract' and so on. So prohibiting animals *is* prohibiting (*inter alia*) dogs. The 'delegation' strategy will therefore strangely be in danger of collapsing to its own opposition, that is the view that the content of law is individuated by what it is in fact for something to be X ('equal', 'contract', etc.). The only way to block that consequence, i.e. to distinguish between the sort of generality involved in the Constitutional provisions and the other, everyday, generality, is on the basis of the former's 'essentially controversial', and hence not 'matter-of-factly', nature. But this will blatantly beg the question whether controversy entails that there is no fact of the matter.

[21] See 'Sovereignty in Silence', *99 Yale L.J.*, 945–1028.

the thesis that law does not involve communication by arguing that the law's content is not intention-based, but is better thought of as a diary kept by the legislature in which its discoveries and refinements of the content of morally good law are noted.[22] Disengaging content from intention makes the 'real' content of equality available to Hurd, no matter what the 'intended' content was (which Hurd takes to be the content legislators had in mind).

Dworkin is sometimes read as taking a similar 'anti-intentionalist' line, and (for that reason) as appearing to concede that the communication model holds for ordinary communication: he is construed as accepting that, in order to serve his major motivation (reject the Criterial Model), he has to reject the idea that interpretation is normally directed at capturing the intentions of the speaker.[23] But what he in fact rejects is the very idea that intentions are somehow self-evident, and thus determine content. Instead, he clearly says that establishing intentions itself involves using the method of constructive interpretation, rather than the application of criteria.[24]

Dworkin's rejection of the (ordinary) communication model, therefore, does not involve a tacit concession to the effect that ordinary communication is captured by the Criterial Model. Rather, law is unlike ordinary communication because subjective sense (or speaker's meaning) may assume varying importance in those two contexts. But this difference is not fundamental: the method involved (non-criterial, theory-based) is the same in both contexts. If at all, it will be *as a result* of applying that method that we will see that we must assign different importance to subjective sense.[25] We must separate therefore Dworkin's two concerns: the first (and most important) is to deny that criteria are *anywhere* (i.e. either in ordinary or in special cases of communication) necessary for interpretation. The second concern is to cast doubt on the idea that the meaning of practices is to be established by aggregating subjective understandings, and it is here that Dworkin expresses some hostility towards intentions: not, as I argued, because intentions are established by a different method, but because the method recommended by Dworkin may assign a weaker role to them (or, in terms of Dworkin's concession, properly understood: interpretation directed at ordinary communication may assign a stronger role to the self-understanding of one's intentions). Different interests, although not

[22] See Hurd, ibid. The 'diary' analogue is at best an awkward way to say that legal concepts stand for genuine properties about which we may make discoveries. If I am right, this option is an overkill: it burdens objectivists with arguing more than they have to, namely that content is not determined by criteria. By the same token, it unnecessarily concedes that communication cannot turn on matters of fact. Note that despite Hurd's efforts, her model runs into the obvious difficulty of distinguishing between law and morality.

[23] Cf. S. Fish. 'Working on the Chain Gang: Interpretation in Law and Literature' *Doing What Comes Naturally*, 87–102.

[24] See *LE*, 54, for a clear statement of Dworkin's thesis that constructive interpretation is necessary for the individuation of intention and therefore fundamental; ibid., 55–76, for support of the thesis in general; and ibid., 313–54, for support of the thesis in the context of statutory interpretation.

[25] Cf. *LE*, 54.

different methods, may be operative in ordinary communication.[26] So Dworkin nowhere concedes the applicability of the Criterial Model, and no other evidence for his theory's incompatibility with the K–P model is found. But I must now address the objection that Dworkin *presupposes* the Criterial Model.

4. THE THREAT OF INDETERMINACY: RAZ'S VERSION

Raz refers to the methodological distinction between ordinary communication and contexts in which the interpretive attitude flourishes, calling them respectively the 'communication' and the 'coherence' model.[27] Simply put, his argument is that the coherence model does not dispense with the communication model. The latter is necessary in order to single out what coherence is to apply to. To single this out, he contends, a criterion must be used—something like the Rule of Recognition, in the case of law. Again, the legal material that has been identified in this way is meaningful, and more specific criteria are necessarily employed in order to individuate its content.

> [T]he coherence model applies to a given set of legal material, statutes and decisions, which constitute legal history. [. . . Dworkin's] method of coherence can only apply to the legal documents which are given their plain meaning. [. . .] To determine the content of law we need first something like a Rule of Recognition to identify what belongs to the doctrinal history, and that doctrinal history will be understood in accordance with the communication model to generate the material which sets the limits to what the coherence model can do.[28]

Once the job of individuating the object of interpretation is thus done, the coherence exercise is exposed as an unnecessary gloss: the coherence model presupposes the communication model, and represents an attempt to extend the content of legal sources—an attempt which Raz suggests is motivated by, or at least has the effect of, political conservatism.[29]

Raz sometimes seems to think that the crucial presupposition is simply something to which Dworkin's view happens to be committed. But in fact he gives an argument which purports to render the presupposition compulsory. Assuming that we have somehow identified the text of the Constitution as part of the law, we are

[26] For example, we may be more interested in identifying the precise way in which some member of the Congress that passed the Fourteenth Amendment misunderstood the content of equality, in the context of writing his biography; but less interested in doing the same in the context of applying the Amendment. It is not that equality means or requires something different in those two contexts. See Ch. 6, section 4, for examples of concept attribution to individual speakers and legal texts.

[27] Raz, 'Link', 1110–11. [28] Ibid., 1119.

[29] 'This combination [of the two models] has a political logic of its own: it represents a conservative political view of the role of the judiciary. The fact that almost all of Dworkin's political polemics are directed at the Right should not be allowed to disguise this fact. The two-stage procedure that his theory involves puts coherence at the moral service of the powers that be': Raz, ibid., 1103. While the last sentence quoted refers to an alleged defect of Dworkin's theory, the first seems to be about the motivation of its advocates. I shall take up the issue of the alleged conservatism of objectivism in Ch. 6.

bound to construe its content as something meaningful. Unless, now, we are prepared to accept the normal, i.e. conventional, meaning as constraining the content, then we must face the threat of serious indeterminacy: the text itself will reduce to 'a jumble of ink scratchings', and it may be interpreted to mean anything at all (we may read Hamlet into the Constitution). (And, presumably, at the prior level of identifying the legal material, in the absence of the conventional criterion like the Rule of Recognition, we might identify Shakespeare's plays as a legal source.) Raz writes that the legal material is

> not a set of meaningless inscriptions on paper etc. It is a body of interpreted legal history, of meaningful documents. Otherwise why fix on legal history? If you regard the Constitution as an uninterpreted jumble of ink scratchings and regard legal theory as designed to give it meaning in accordance with the best moral theory there is, then there is no gap between ideal law and interpretation of existing law. Under these conditions one can interpret the Constitution to mean anything at all. It can be read to mean the same as Shakespeare's Hamlet.[30]

The second component, then, of Raz's argument seems to be posing a dilemma, whose first horn is a threat and the second the only available solution. The threat is radical indeterminacy of semantic content; and the alleged only solution is conventional individuation of semantic content.[31] Only if this dilemma stands, in the sense of exhaustively representing the alternatives, will his charge that Dworkin's model embraces conventionalism be made plausible: Dworkin does in fact offer an account of constraints, and Raz must prove this an untenable *tertium* to his dilemma. But, before addressing the viability of Dworkin's account, we must examine the alleged similarities between it and Raz's own.

5. DWORKIN'S PRE-INTERPRETIVE AGREEMENT: SOME MISUNDERSTANDINGS

Dworkin makes use of the notion of 'pre-interpretive agreement' as necessary for interpretation proper—i.e. the domain of SD—to flourish. This comprises abstract characterizations of the practice to be interpreted and paradigmatic instances of the practice. That is, it comprises abstract judgments like 'contract is a promise enforceable in law . . . ', and judgments to the effect that certain agreements are paradigmatic contracts. But this account of the relation between the abstract characterizations and the paradigms or examples differs from Raz's picture in two important respects. First, it is not the case that an abstract characterization of, say, legal practices amounts to a concept of law, prior to and independent of the specific legal concepts like 'contract', 'tort' etc., so that the content of the latter would be determined by the former. This would be a version of what Hurley calls 'centralism', and is exemplified by legal positivists' insistence that the content of,

[30] Ibid., 1119. [31] The dilemma is in fact more complex; see below, section 7.

say, 'contract', consists in the satisfaction by some rule (specifying a particular sort of behaviour or events) of the conditions set by the prior general concept of law—the Rule of Recognition.[32] Dworkin's notion, by contrast, is built by extrapolating from the specific practices the features that can figure in judgments commanding widespread approval; these constitute the minimal content necessary to locate SD.[33] Such judgments may serve to locate disagreement by attempting to specify the (non-controversial) properties that collect the exemplary applications under the relevant concept, but they are responsible to the examples they strive to account for, rather than being themselves the benchmark of class membership: the pre-interpretive consensus is part of the process of explicating meaning, but the interdependence of examples and judgments figuring the consensus ensures that it may not assume the role of a criterion (as, e.g., Hart's Rule of Recognition does).[34]

The second point is also a consequence of the character of the meaning-giving process. The relation between the judgments figuring in the pre-interpretive consensus and examples is such that no judgment is secure from challenge. The judgment, for instance, that all laws are enforceable in court may be doubted, e.g. on the grounds that enforceability is founded on substantive correctness, so that some unjust laws are not so enforceable. It does not matter whether this is a plausible challenge; it only matters that it should be best characterized as a *challenge*—as a bold attack on our conception of law, rather than as an irrelevant misunderstanding. Similarly, no exemplary application is any more secure: in Dworkin's example, the speed limit provision is the archetypical example of law, yet it is conceivable that a cogent justification for not so regarding it may be offered.[35] In both cases, the vulnerability reflects the fact that the content of the pre-interpretive consensus does not involve or support a definition of, or a synonym for, the concept to which it relates: someone who claims that tigers are not striped does not contradict himself, unlike someone who claims that tigers are not tigers. Nor does the consensus constitute some sort of 'degenerate truth', i.e. truth simply by convention or fiat, so that challenges to it would be absurd. Rather, the content of the judgments that figure in the pre-interpretive consensus is vulnerable just because it is responsible to theory about the nature of the property

[32] *Natural Reasons*, Ch. 1.

[33] Thus Postema is wrong to write that, for Dworkin, 'critical interpretation is focused around a "purpose" or "point" defined entirely independently of the agreed-upon rules or recognized activities of the practice'; '"Protestant" Interpretation and Social Practices', *6 Law and Philosophy*, 283–319 at 300. See also ibid., 305. Perhaps this is a consequence of the fact that, for Postema, Dworkinian social critics are protestant: they violate communal practice. But to say that they do violate practice is to assume that the content of the practice (what it takes to respect it and what to violate it) is established otherwise than Dworkin claims it is. Postema shortcircuits this question by tacitly assuming that the content of the practice is constituted by what practitioners believe it is, which is exactly what Dworkin (and Postema himself, at times) wants to deny. I return to Postema in section 9 below.

[34] Recall the discussion of the importance of examples, especially in connection with Burge's arguments, Ch. 2. See Burge, 'Intellectual Norms and Foundations of Mind', *83 J.Phil.*, 697–720, at 705.

[35] See *LE*, 92.

to which the concept relates.[36] Calling those judgments 'pre-interpretive', therefore, is to some extent misleading, for it suggests that they are essentially unrevisable. But this is to mistake their role—their ***not being doubted***, in the context of some dispute—for their being ***indubitable***.

5.1 Extravagant Cases

Consider the proposal that the US provision of a minimum age for presidential candidacy be interpreted to read '50' instead of '35'—a somewhat extravagant example. The rationale for such a reading is that '35' in the Constitution's text was set as a mark of maturity, rather than age proper; and given the changes in life expectancy, length of education etc. since the introduction of the provision, the same level of maturity is now reached much later.[37] Now this proposal may seem either as a flatly contradictory one—as claiming that '35' does not mean '35'—or (more plausibly) as a coherent, if not convincing, proposal for genuine interpretation that takes into consideration the relevant changes in the social and biological context. Even if critical evaluation of the proposal yields the conclusion that '35' should be interpreted 'literally', this supplies no argument against the vulnerability of 'literal' meanings in general; rather, it may be best characterized as a case in which the standard interpretation still carries conviction.

It may be tempting here to weaken the case further, by conceding that certain expressions, including numbers, are not vulnerable to semantic challenge,[38] yet insist that it suffices that most types of expressions—and at any rate most of those practically important in legal issues—are thus vulnerable. But this concession is unclear. The challenge mentioned above concerns '35' in the particular context of specifying presidential candidacy restrictions. It is now a different question whether in an 'ordinary' context some expressions do not admit of semantic challenge, and hence SD. It is difficult to say what an ordinary context is, unless it is circularly specified as a context in which such challenges are not raised. It is true that, in some contexts, some expressions appear to be semantically stable. But this concession is innocuous: to say that stability in fact obtains is not to say that the standard meaning ascriptions represent analytic or degenerate truths, i.e. that the semantic limits are *constituted* by synonymy or consensus. It may still be the case that the limits simply *coincide* with consensus, and that they can be best characterized in the way the general case is: agreement, when it occurs, is *explained* by the

[36] See Ch. 2 for the conception of synonymy as based on substantive judgment, and the arguments to the effect that challenges to conventional understanding are coherent.

[37] See, *inter alia*, M. Tushnet, 'A Note on the Revival of Textualism in Constitutional Theory', *58 S. Cal. L. R.* 683–700 at 686–7.

[38] The temptation would probably be motivated by the appearance of certain areas of law like the law of taxation as virtually immune from any kind of difficulty in application, calling for creative interpretation. See Ch. 6, section 4, for discussion of such examples.

fact that the current characterization is substantively correct, rather than agreement itself *constituting* correctness.

5.2 Easy Cases

These remarks bear on the easy–hard case distinction. Notice that the distinction cuts across that between clear and obscure law, since we cannot tackle the problem of clarity independent of application. Clarity may only be the result of interpretation; it simply consists in the report that undoubtedly, and without the need for complicated justification, the law is thus and so on such and such case. But this is not to say that a hard case may not arise concerning some application of a provision found straightforward until that case. What we have been characterizing, so far, as clear law, may become the object of a hard case.

It is crucial to note how a proposed resolution of a hard case will affect the *entire spectrum* of actual and hypothetical cases. Suppose that the proposal of the above example, about age limits, is plausible enough to merit our attention, and is being put forth in order to disqualify candidate X in the next election. There is a sense in which this would not affect past easy cases—the candidacies of Reagan and Bush, for instance. The sense in which it does not affect them, however, will only be that these candidacies would also be justified under the new interpretation—yet *for a different reason*, namely that Reagan and Bush met the 50, rather than the 35, age condition. Some other 'easy' cases might have been affected; they might have been classified as mistakes on the new interpretation of the law. But this is not important: we might well have a new interpretation that preserved each and every instance of past applications as correct. Yet the novelty of the interpretation would *eo ipso* alter the justificatory basis of past applications (and therefore redraw the distinction between easy and hard cases: for example, new candidates whose 35th birthday would be a few hours after the crucial deadline would now be easily disqualified).

It is small comfort, therefore, for those who want to preserve the hard–easy case distinction to note that novel interpretations may not question the correctness of most 'easy' cases. That there are cases on whose resolution we are confident is beyond dispute; the point is to explain *the source and nature of our confidence.* The real issue is whether easy cases are special in being resolvable without recourse to a substantive theory concerning what is really required by the law. If such theories are allowed at all, then their scope can surely not be restricted to 'hard' cases. Hard cases only make plain the need for substantive argument concerning what the law requires anyway; they make explicit and questionable what has always gone unnoticed (or so those involved in a hard case dispute will claim). The hardness of a 'hard' case will therefore only consist in the complexity, apparent novelty, and controversial nature of the arguments put forward. By contrast, those who wish to preserve the distinction as important need to construe it as a sign of a methodological switch: the 'hardness' of hard cases must consist in the substantive nature of the argument that is required for their resolution, *as opposed to* the alleged non-substantive (analytic, stipulative, conventional) nature of the 'easy' applications.[39]

Once substantive theories *about what the law requires* are admitted, there is no way back to positivist simplicity. For this reason it is a serious error to believe that Dworkinian theories are innocuous complements to positivist accounts of settled law. Yet exactly that is being claimed by many critics. Steven Burton has claimed that positivism still stands as the theory of identifying the legal materials, and Dworkin's theory is in effect a method for stretching the materials when their import is unclear; hence the theories are compatible, and Dworkin's error consists precisely in his claim that the two theories are competitive. Kent Greenawalt has claimed that Dworkin's deferral to paradigms is straightforwardly conventionalist, yet the role of conventions gets underestimated by Dworkin's concentration on hard cases. And Ruth Gavison has claimed that Dworkin's 'pre-interpretive law' is the positivists' law, and his post-interpretive law is 'Dworkin's law', complaining that 'pre-interpretive law', which is supposedly captured by the sources thesis, is an important and legitimate concern of legal theory, despite Dworkin's insistence on relegating it backstage.[40] But it should be plain that Dworkin's 'imperialism' is far deeper than these critics think: Dworkin's theory stands or falls as a *general* account of the way the the content of legal materials is determined. It does not want to shift emphasis from the 'sources thesis'; rather, it insists on the sources thesis,[41] disputes whether the positivist account is successful in giving content to that thesis (it disputes precisely whether the pre-interpretive stage is really the law), and offers an alternative account of the identification of legal materials. To repeat once more what I have been urging so far, the issue on which battle is joined is: what is it to say that something is a legal source and requires such and such—is it a substantive account amenable to argument, or is it a degenerate truth not coherently dubitable?[42]

It will not do, therefore, to say that Dworkin admits conventionalism at some

[39] See K. Kress, 'Legal Indeterminacy', *77 Cal. L. R.*, 283–337, at 296–7, for the idea that the occurrence of easy cases in itself proves something about the source and nature of our confidence in the judgments involved in them. Kress's target is scepticism, yet he presents the easy-case argument as militating for conventionalism, omitting again the third option of *substantive* nature of those judgments.

[40] See Burton, S., 'Ronald Dworkin and Legal Positivism', *73 Iowa L.R.*, 109–29; Greenawalt, K., 'How Law Can Be Determinate', *38 U.C.L.A. L.R.*, 1–86; Gavison, R., 'Legal Theory and the Problem of Sense: Comment', *in* Gavison, R. (ed.), *Issues in Contemporary Legal Philosophy*, 30–31. Kress, in his 'Interpretive Turn' also claims that positivists may well argue that their theory is an easy case theory. Raz in 'Link', 1119, subscribes to the doctrine that Dworkin's theory is a hard case theory. Notice, however, that Raz's argument is that Dworkin *cannot but* presuppose a positivist picture of easy cases, drawing the correct conclusion (in contrast to the other critics cited here) that, if that presupposition is in fact compulsory, Dworkin's position becomes untenable, not complementary to positivism.

[41] This claim is somewhat gratuitous: 'sources thesis' is Raz's to define. I mean that Dworkin does not want to extend law beyond its sources, but to offer an alternative account of what are in fact the law's sources.

[42] By way of illustration, take Greenawalt's discussion, in 'How Law Can Be Determinate', of the perennial city ordinance which in this case requires that 'dogs be kept on leash'. Dworkin, he says, must recognize the ordinance as law, given his commitment to paradigms. Consequently, he says, if conditions obtain under which unleashing one's dog seems perfectly reasonable and harmless, one should still

interpretive stage, because he cannot coherently do so (insofar, that is, as his aim is to characterize how law is determined, rather than how to adjudicate cases outside the contents of law). If conventionalism is right, therefore, and Dworkin relies on it, then his theory will not only be superfluous, as Raz says, but irreparably confused.

As I have mentioned, Raz's main argument is that Dworkin *cannot but* assume conventionalism, since no other account preserving determinacy is available. But this is a substantial thesis, involving various contentious claims. Raz still helps himself to the idea that perhaps Dworkin assumes conventionalism, simply by virtue of his 'concession' that some prior agreement (the 'pre-interpretive' material) will help locate the issue to be debated in controversial cases. But the real question concerns the *status* of the material. The interdependence of abstract pre-interpretive agreement and paradigms, the vulnerability of both, and the status of meaning-giving characterizations as sensitive to genuine theoretical knowledge, all mark out differences between Dworkin's and Raz's picture.

I have thus glossed the *tertium* I am trying to defend, but have yet to show that it is available: can the picture work? Before attempting that, it is worth reiterating that Raz (and others) simply *assume* the inevitability of conventionalism. They simply assume it insofar as they move from the premise that Dworkin, just like anyone else, has to rely on some way to pick out the object of disagreement (and this way will more or less be based on what is uncontroversial relative to the dispute), to the conclusion that the common ground thus located is all there is to the object of dispute. More specifically, Raz assumes that the content of consensus judgments *determines* the content of the relevant concept, and the undisputed paradigms exhaust its extension. No argument, other than the sceptical threat mentioned above, is offered in support of the common ground's having that role. Unless the sceptical threat is substantiated, it is open to claim that the common ground constrains only by fixing the object of interpretation, by fixing what must be *explained* by competing interpretations.[43] Competing interpretations may explain

uphold the ordinance on pain of violating legislative supremacy. The force of this remark is unclear; legislative supremacy enters into a question 'what is the law of New York', which is asked with the specific purpose of identifying whose institutions' requirements are law—where we are asking who passes laws. In response to such questions we will most likely claim that a city ordinance is paradigmatic. The justifiable unleashing issue, nevertheless, enters into a discussion of what the law *requires*, i.e. it is to do with the question 'what is the law', where we need not only to answer who passes laws, but *which* are the laws thus passed. Once we have answered that question, we may of course dismiss alternative suggestions about the law's content as breaching the law's (i.e. the already identified requirements') authority. But without that answer, invoking authority will be beyond the point. For, if someone is motivated to doubt that unleashing the dog is never permissible, he will be doubting not whether the city has authority to pass ordinances, but whether that ordinance always prohibits occasional unleashing—his doubt involves the *content* of the ordinance. If he is motivated by Dworkin's theory, that is: he may be motivated to doubt the council's authority by other reasons (for instance by classical legal naturalism, or by anarchism). In the present case, perhaps, both sorts of doubt would seem to have the same result, viz. suggesting that the law be broken: but this would be so only insofar as it is assumed that the ordinance plainly requires that dogs be leashed no matter what (i.e. insofar as we *have* the answer to the question of content). This result, therefore, is arrived at after addressing the content-doubt in substance, rather than blocking it by appeal to authority.

[43] Postema also seems to think that what fixes the object (of interpretation) must fix its interpretation as well, despite the fact that he wants to allow for SD; cf. '"Protestant" Interpretation and Social Practices'.

it differently, just as competing theories may explain in different ways why gold is heavy and does not corrode, as well as why such and such samples are rightly considered as paradigms of gold. Further, competing theories may explain the controversial material differently, i.e. explain why other judgments are incorrect—e.g. that gold is not really yellow—and why some samples were wrongly grouped together with the real paradigms.[44] In view of the alternative picture of the common ground to a controversy as a set of *explananda* for competing theories of a concept's content, Raz takes too much for granted in assuming that the common ground exhausts the concept's content.

6. SCEPTICISM AND INDUBITABILITY

Turning to the sceptical threat: what sort of scepticism threatens the picture being defended? Raz's suggestion seems to be this: if everything is open to (re-) interpretation, then the apparent constraints—paradigms and abstract specifications of what is essential to the practice—are no constraints at all. I characterized these apparent constraints as dependent upon some substantive, if typically tacit, theory and therefore susceptible to doubt and revision. This must entail indeterminacy, the objection may go, in the sense that there is nothing—no hard fact, secure from challenge—on the basis of which we may resist the sceptic who challenges our most basic assumptions and re-interprets the practice in a way unrecognizable to us (say, by reading Hamlet into the Constitution).

The objector here concedes *arguendo* that the conventionalist picture overrates the role of consensus, and adopts the idea that the so-called conventional meaning is only a rough guide to be criticized and revised in the face of recalcitrant examples best explained by alternative theories. But he notes that revisability entails that this critical ability is radically unbounded; *any* interpretation, however wild, must be taken to raise a case of SD with the more familiar ones, and this is to say that the notion of SD has no content.[45] Conventions then are introduced as something like a necessary evil, something made compulsory by a dilemma: either one must adopt the idea that meaning turns on hard fact, or else one is lost. And, given that the first horn is unattractive—by the lights of Dworkin's theory at

[44] See Ch. 2 on Kripke's distinction between fixing reference and determining meaning, and Putnam's point that some of what count as paradigms may be wrongly—yet explicably—classified as such.

[45] This would further imply that the notion of CD has no content either. So *meaning* becomes impossible, insofar as meaning depends on there being a distinction between properly and improperly applying an expression to things, events, etc. If every application may lay claim to propriety, the distinction breaks down. See McDowell, 'Non-Cognitivism and Rule-Following', *in* Holtzman, S. H. and Leich, C. M. (eds), *Wittgenstein: To Follow a Rule*, who discusses a dilemma brought about by the possibility of scepticism similar to the one I discuss in the text. The erosion of meaning in sceptical (and also, I shall argue, conventionalist) views will be discussed below.

least—and the second horn seems unacceptable, one is bound to accept the sort of degenerate constraint constituted by conventions.

An obvious response is to point out that the objector conflates the idea that *anything* may be doubted with the idea that *everything* may be so doubted.[46] It may be the case that the possibility of SD is associated with the *complexity* of the concepts involved. A complex concept is such that its meaning depends upon other concepts, so that complexity provides internal structure; a characteristic form of disagreement then obtains where there is agreement as to what sort of other concepts application of the complex concept depends upon, but there is dispute concerning the exact formulation of and the relations among those other concepts. Consider Hurley's example: there may be agreement to the effect that distributive justice depends upon equality, and dispute concerning whether it turns on equality of resources or welfare.[47] Further, the parties to the dispute will typically agree on at least some of the applications of the concept as exemplary. Note that complexity provides *structure*, not *composition*—the latter could be due to some concept's being made up of simple ones, the content of which would be independently established. Rather, structure is provided by concepts' *interdependence*. For instance, civil liability, criminal liability, responsibility and agency in general may all depend on each other. The idea is that we may engage in SD with someone precisely where we agree on the interpretation of at least some of the concept's features, so that we can dispute over the meaning of the rest.[48] The vulnerability thesis, namely that any part may be the object of dispute, rests on the assumption that, in every such case, *some* part must be taken as given. We cannot make sense of disagreement as substantive, where no point of contact exists between our own and the challenger's conception. By contrast, where some common ground exists, it serves as a set of data, accounting for which will be a mark of comparative success among the competing views (i.e. in terms of explanatory power, coherence, simplicity etc.). Does this picture, usually captured in Neurath's metaphor of repairing a boat while under way, a plank at a time,[49] pose a threat of indeterminacy?

[46] That is to say that one may hold on to the dubitability of anything, without being committed to the dubitability of everything. This seems to preclude the possibility of *everything* being doubted, a possibility celebrated, it seems, by K-P semantics. But this trades on the ambiguity of 'doubting everything': what cannot be doubted is everything *simpliciter*. Surely, on the other hand, everything-about-water, for instance, may be doubted. This would be the case if one claimed, say, that what we took as water was actually hallucinations caused by Martians. But such a finding would engage water-theory 'further up'—with respect to explaining what water-theory sought to explain. See Chs 2–4 for defence of the possibility of scepticism as 'wholesale' as one wishes, consistent with the thesis that disagreement must be founded on agreement. As I argue in Ch. 2, to attribute to K-P semantics the notion of some non-conceptual facts on which concepts 'attach', and explain the dubitability of everything on that picture, is a result of the postulation of a content-reality distinction and the consequent oscillation between the two 'realms' that makes radical scepticism inevitable. The distinction is nonetheless undercut, if anything, by K-P semantics. I shall make a similar point, in connection with Wittgensteinian scepticism, below. See also Ch. 6, section 3, for discussion of 'wholesale' rejection of 'discourses'.

[47] *Natural Reasons*, 47. See ibid. for an account of contestability in terms of complexity.

[48] Features may include implications in other areas.

[49] Cf. Dworkin, *LE*, 111.

We must here make clear what sort of indeterminacy the objector must show to obtain: it does not suffice to show that indeterminacy *may* arise in some cases, e.g. when the common ground cannot suffice to distinguish between the two apparently competing views, because they both account for it equally well. The objector needs to show that the potential vulnerability of each and every feature of a concept presents a *general* problem, no matter which particular concept is under consideration. He must show, in other words, that the absence of *indubitable* features creates indeterminacy, and that it does so even with respect to highly complex concepts.[50]

The objector's commitment to indubitable, foundational features may be disputed. The objector simply claims, it may be argued, that there are easy cases—there are cases in which we are confident that a concept is applicable. But this is not disputable. As I argued in the previous section, the objector must supplement this truism with an account of *the source and nature of our confidence*. So the objector must further claim that the judgments involved in easy cases—the judgments concerning the application of a concept which command widespread approval—enjoy *special status*: they are true as a matter of conventional arrangement, and therefore indubitable. And the objector's argument from indeterminacy quite explicitly assumes that unless *some particular contents* are indubitable, then indeterminacy will ensue.

The objector is committed, therefore, to the thesis that some contents are privileged by being indubitable—a species of foundationalism in the domain of meaning. In Chapter 2, I sketched the foundationalist picture behind conventionalist semantics. To a large extent, the present Chapter has illustrated how the motivation can be traced within legal conventionalism.

In Chapter 2, I argued that the criterial view springs from a questionable metaphysics of the mind, and an epistemological prejudice. Both motivations figure here. The indeterminacy objection in effect assumes that only *indubitable* contents can provide the necessary constraint. And this assumption in turn implies that the object of interpretation itself is incapable of providing any constraints: unless an essentially arbitrary constraint is at hand, it will be impossible to judge any interpretation as better or worse—the object will afford as many interpretations as we care to think of. As was the case in connection with ordinary empirical objects, the criterial view *needs* the possibility of radical scepticism. It requires that Dworkin's sceptic, who asks to be shown, *per impossibile*, that the best interpretation is 'really' the best, represent a coherent view.[51]

[50] This global objection is distinguished by Dworkin from the weaker one, namely that legal concepts in particular just happen to lack the required complexity. The implausibility of this weaker form is, I believe, obvious. Cf. Dworkin, *A Matter of Principle*, 169–70.

[51] See Dworkin, *A Matter of Principle*, 169 and 171–7 and *LE*, 85–6, for the view that there is something wrong with the conception of the epistemological problem assumed by scepticism. Virtually the same point has been made by Fish, *Doing What Comes Naturally*, Introduction and *passim* (but he derives different conclusions from it, discussed below); and it has been echoed by Kress, 'Legal Indeterminacy', at 283. What is wrong is nevertheless unclear. I think that Kress thinks that the

I suggested in Chapter 2 that rejecting mental autonomy makes space for determinate content, whose determination is a substantive issue. Its being a substantive issue, i.e. having theoretical character, entails that interpretations are vulnerable, rather than indubitable. But this is not to say that they are unconstrained; that inference would only be justified on the assumption that no kind of contents other than indubitable contents may play the role of constraints. Theory does not add more grist to the sceptic's mill because there are external constraints, i.e. constraints of formal and substantive rationality: as Lewis puts it, in the simple cases of assigning referents to thought, egalitarianism does not hold. 'Rabbits' are better (more eligible) than 'undetached rabbit slices', in the case where we wonder which to assign to a speaker who sees rabbits passing by.[52] Theory, as it were, comes already constrained.

In the general case of determining the content of a concept, I argued that it is determined by the speakers' thoughts, intentions, desire etc. Yet these are not determined individualistically: they are not representations whose content is independent of the speaker's environment. Rather, they are determined in the context of a general account of the agent's linguistic as well as general actions and relations to his environment. Dworkin's analysis of legislative intention is an example of simultaneous determination of a propositional attitude (intention) and conceptual content (equality) structured by formal (consistency) and substantive (political and moral) assumptions, which, on pain of circularity, cannot be part of the object of interpretation (intention), but rather are what make its determination possible.[53]

The considerations discussed in Chapter 2 and sketched above show how contentious are the assumptions upon which the apparently simple indeterminacy objection rests. But it is widely thought that the conclusion, the thesis that it is criteria that constrain conceptual content, can nevertheless be upheld. The next section deals with much the same issues from an angle rather more familiar in legal theory: it deals with the so-called Wittgensteinian arguments widely assumed to support a conventionalist answer to the question raised above concerning the 'source and nature of our confidence'. In the course of that discussion, I shall attempt to make the objective-determination account more plausible, and support my claim that the 'solution' allegedly offered by criteria is not only uncalled for (since scepticism is not unavoidable), but actually shares the flaws of individualism.

sceptic's standard makes sense but is unattainable. I discuss Fish's oscillation between the same view and the view that the standard does not make sense. Dworkin should be read as claiming the latter. Perhaps his injunctions to 'stick to our knitting' may again be thought to move towards the view that the standard is coherent but unattainable. But note the alternative construal, namely that the right standard is to be found by attention to our practices—a construal that is supported by his claim that the issue of 'objectivity' (where objectivity is taken in the sceptic's terms as correspondence of 'interpretation with reality') is 'fake'.

[52] Note that the constraint is not the concept 'rabbit', but rather the sense of naturalness the compels us to assign *that* instead of something else.

[53] See *LE* Ch. 9; and a recent restatement in 'Bork's Jurisprudence'.

7. WITTGENSTEINIAN ARGUMENTS

What is it by virtue of which the rule of addition expressed by 'plus' (+) must result in 125 for '68 + 57' instead of 5? (Imagine that I have not computed any addition involving numbers larger than 56 before.) This is Kripke's example serving as the basis for the explication of Wittgenstein's reflections on the nature of meaning.[54] The obvious answer seems to be: by virtue of the meaning of the rule. But a sceptic may press the question: why isn't it the case that the rule means that the result is the usual one for arguments up to 56, and 5 for any arguments larger than that? To say that the apparently deviant result is a case of not going on as before (i.e. in calculations carried out so far) will not help, because if the sceptic's interpretation *did* capture the rule's content, then the apparently deviant result *would* be the one that respects previous applications. The sceptic is claiming that the weird content has *always* been what one meant by the rule of addition.[55]

The difficulty put forward by the sceptic is not: how we *know* that the addition of 67 and 58 must yield 125. Rather, it is: what *makes* some way or other count as going on in the same way as before? It is a question with quite general applicability. It may be asked in connection with the meaning of any expression whatsoever, insofar as meaning depends on correctly applying an expression in this or that situation. For it may always be asked: by virtue of what is it the case that this, and not that, constitutes a proper application?[56]

The usual picture purporting to answer this question has two components: a rule, in the sense of an algorithm—an instruction that extends into hitherto not considered cases—and a psychological mechanism that 'internalizes' the algorithm ('engages mental wheels with the rule's rails', in McDowell's metaphor[57]) and guides one in future applications. The scepticism put forward, nonetheless, poses a devastating challenge to this picture. There is no mental or psychological entity that can justify distinguishing between the standard and the deviant extension of the rule in novel applications. Note that the scepticism can be repeated at all levels, no matter how we gloss the content of the rule: if we try to reduce the rule of addition to (mental representations of), say, counting, then the content of 'counting' may be re-interpreted in a deviant way to yield the deviant result 5 when 56 enters the counting calculation.[58] This is the familiar insight, that

[54] See Kripke, *Wittgenstein on Rules and Private Language*, (hereinafter, *Wittgenstein*), Ch. 2.

[55] Note the parallel with the discussion of the character of hard-case related challenges in section 5: the sceptic *justifies* easy cases, rather than proposes to ignore them.

[56] The objection (by Blackburn) that the analysis is of no help concerning the semantics of controversial concepts is addressed in section 8.

[57] 'Non-Cognitivism and Rule-Following', 146; echoing Barry Stroud, 'Wittgenstein and Logical Necessity' *in* Moser, P. (ed.), *A Priori Knowledge*, 84.

[58] See Kripke, *Wittgenstein*, Ch. 2; also P. Seabright, 'Explaining Cultural Divergence: a Wittgensteinian Paradox', *84 J. Phil.*, 11 (hereinafter, 'Cultural Divergence'), for examples of the inability to secure the interpretation of the rule through reduction to more 'basic' rules. Notice the well-known analogy with Goodman's 'bent' predicates like *grue*, i.e. green if observed before time T or blue if observed after T, in the context of specifying the content of induction: T being some time in the future, what makes

adding more words to guide the application of a concept will not solve the problem, since the extra gloss will be as open to (re-)interpretation as the original word.

There exists a virtual consensus among commentators that Wittgenstein's critique succeeds in showing that the standard picture cannot guard against radical indeterminacy. But it is quite controversial what Wittgenstein regarded as going wrong in that picture, and what solution Wittgenstein recommends. I should make it clear that in the ensuing discussion I am not concerned with the exegetical task of characterizing the position most faithful to Wittgenstein's thought. The positions under consideration deserve attention in their own right, and may be appraised on their merits; it is a different question whether Wittgenstein himself actually embraced either of them.

There are three key notions to the investigation of the defects of the classical picture and the proposed alternative: the idea that rules embody patterns; the idea that the content of the rule is determined individualistically; and the (alternative) idea of a community-oriented conception of the content of a rule.

A very influential reading claims that the solution to the problem posed by the sceptic is that meaning is determined by the community, in the sense of consensus or widely approved judgments.[59] The correct application of the addition rule in novel cases is that which can command the consent of the community. This solution is directed, it is claimed, by attention to the classical picture's defects. It allegedly respects Wittgenstein's insight concerning individualism: as the sceptical challenge reveals, it is not possible to specify the content of a rule only with the help of materials derived from an individual's mental history, dispositions etc. These materials are insufficient because they collapse the notion of being right (about the way to go on) to seeming right. In the proposed picture, the indeterminacy is avoided since community-wide agreement will constrain the possible interpretations. But this way of overcoming the problems of individualism has some severe consequences concerning meaning.

To start with, the idea that semantic rules somehow embody patterns of application is rejected. The range of a rule's applicability is specified in a piecemeal

it the case that all grass that has been observed is green, rather than grue? See N. Goodman, *Fact, Fiction and Forecast.* The analogy is also pointed out by Kripke. Kripke addresses an exhaustive list of psychological entities that might be thought to serve in fixing the content of a rule, and shows that Wittgenstein's arguments militate against all of them—not surprisingly, since *any* content ostensibly determining the rule's content may itself be interpreted sceptically. See Moore, 'Precedent, Induction and Ethical Generalization' *in* Goldstein, L. (ed.), *Precedent in Law,* for discussion of Goodmanesque scepticism in the context of precedent individuation.

59 I have in mind Wright (cf. *Wittgenstein on the Foundations of Mathematics*, esp. 21–38), Kripke (*Wittgenstein*, Ch. 3), and Blackburn ('Rule-Following and Moral Realism', *in* Holtzman, S. M. and Leich, C. M. (eds), *Wittgenstein: to Follow a Fule*), running together, no doubt, several differences amongst them; note that I am referring to a reading of Wittgenstein, not an endorsement of it. That reading is often taken for granted: cf. Peter Strawson, *Skepticism and Naturalism.*

fashion by consensus judgments.[60] This is an extreme rejection of the 'rules as rails' picture, in the following sense. What adherents of the conventionalist solution are eager to deny is that rules' extensions in arithmetic, for instance, are fixed in a way independent of mathematics, i.e. by our familiar practice carried out in the usual way; independent, that is, so that our mathematics would only hope, but perhaps fail, to match the results. The target, then, of Wittgenstein, on the reading considered here, is the 'secret books' conception of mathematical truth, according to which we find the result 125 to the addition 68+57 compelling because we hope that it matches the true answer found in those books. In rejecting this, the proposed alternative reverses the picture: 125 is the right result *because* we find it compelling. Meaning seems like a matter of *etiquette*.[61]

If this is the way to conceive rejection of the pattern idea, then the picture is doubly unsatisfactory. First, it erodes the notion of meaning completely, insofar as it collapses meaning to free creative decision: for the community there is no standard to meet, and what seems right to it will be right. (There is some sort of standard for individuals, namely the community; I shall address this below.) Secondly, its break with individualism (which is, partly at least, responsible for the sceptic's victory) is insufficient to ward off indeterminacy (hence the standard alluded to immediately before is only illusory). Communal meaning is specified as the collection of individual interpretations, and the familiar problems start all over again. How are individuals going to be able to choose an interpretation that carries the community's approval, if the content of the latter depends upon that very choice? But such problems notwithstanding, the communal standard fails for another reason. If the alleged constraint is 'X has content Y if that interpretation agrees with most people's interpretation', then the sceptic may re-interpret 'agrees' in a deviant way, and insist that 5 is the result that agrees with the communal result; and 125 does not agree, but 'schmagree', where 'schmagree' means. . . Meaning collapses entirely.[62]

It may be said that the sceptic will not manage to get away with the whole community against him. But it is unclear what is the supposed effect of communal

[60] Note that it is not the case that some part of the content is antecedently specified, and only novel situations are 'decided'. On the consensus model, the range of applicability for the already encountered cases has itself been fixed by means of consensus judgments as well.

[61] Cf. Putnam, *Realism with a Human Face* Ch. 1, at n. 19.

[62] Cf. Kripke, *Wittgenstein*, 146, n. 87 (added by Kripke in proof). Virtually the same point may be put in Jonathan Bennett's terms: the proposed solution is competence-presupposing. In solving the problem of individual indeterminacy by appeal to the communal standards, by which we enjoin the individual to abide, we presuppose that the individual so instructed is competent in the language. But this is to beg the very question we have started to answer, in response to the sceptic's challenge, which is how meaning is possible at all. Any answer we give to this question must give us adequate materials to constrain the novice. If, by contrast, the individual has already a method for understanding and applying rules (necessary to grasp the content of the master 'follow-the-community' rule), then our instructions become superfluous. See Bennett, *Locke, Berkeley, Hume*, 11–20, for an application of the argument to Locke's theory of the relation of ideas to the world, with respect to what Bennett calls the problem of classification. I am indebted to Susan Hurley for pointing out the relevance of Bennett's discussion.

pressure. The sceptic's original challenge was for us to find something *by virtue of which* his interpretation is mistaken, and the point made in the previous paragraph is that nothing, including communal agreement, is there for us to appeal to: no matter what condition we cite as *justifying* one rather than another application of a rule, the sceptic *may* render it useless through deviant re-interpretation. Surely a sceptic may elect to concede his case, and admit that he may be wrong if everyone else says so. But this does not help us much: he might as well concede his case at an earlier stage, before we resorted to appeal to communal agreement, e.g. he might have conceded it already by the time we appealed to 'counting' in order to fix the meaning of 'adding'. The scepticism we are concerned with, however, is that expressed by the unswerving sceptic, the one that refuses to concede his case unless a knock-down proof of its error is offered. *That* sceptic is invincible.

Communal pressure may be construed, alternatively, not as a *condition*, but rather as a 'fact'. It may seem, in other words, that a way out of this picture is to claim that the community does not specify meaning in terms of legislating what is to be the correct application, thereby setting a condition that others' interpretations must meet. Communal agreement does not, in other words, enter into the content of an expression. In this way we are giving up the conception of meaning as truth-conditional at all, instead of holding on to that picture and simply substituting truth proper for community-defined truth. In its place, we have a picture in which someone seems justified in asserting something only where he may command communal assent. In order, nonetheless, to keep communal assent distinct from the content we are anxious to determine, (on pain of repeating the scepticism in determining what is to count as assent, dissent etc., as above), we are bound to construe communal agreement as something which *de facto* obtains sometimes. It is obscure what this fact of agreement would consist in. Communal agreement must be something pre-semantic, some 'brute fact'. The most obvious candidate for that role would seem to be *force*, coercion by the majority to ensure that (unconvinced) sceptics refrain from expressing their scepticism. In fact, the notion of the community would become less significant: the same sort of force could be exercised by an individual against the sceptic; and, given sufficient power, one or a few could enforce their own view on the community.[63]

But there are more fundamental problems with the notion of brute facts constraining meaning. Whatever such a brute fact consists in, how can it inform semantic behaviour? We are in a predicament akin to that envisaged in Davidson's argument in Chapter 2.[64] If the signs of agreement convey meaningful informa-

[63] It will be useful to recall Hart's desire to distinguish rule-constrained conduct from the pure exercise of force; see Fish, for the view that the distinction is untenable, offering a sceptical solution similar to that described in the text: 'Force', in *Doing What Comes Naturally*.

[64] Davidson's argument is that, if the world is supposed to constrain our beliefs about it by means of information-bearing items, then the information may always be false—the supposedly constraining items are just more beliefs. If, on the other hand, no information is carried, then the items can never justify our beliefs. See Ch. 2, section 5, for discussion and McDowell's conclusion that, once the problem is posed in terms of the relations between two independent *relata* (belief or representational

tion—perhaps some feeling of acceptance in the community—the threat of scepticism concerning them is present. If, on the other hand, they do not—if they operate at the level of brute experience—then they can provide no normative constraint, a demand that one go one way rather than another. The picture then is a degenerate one. Meaning is worse than radically unbounded interpretations: it rather consists in sounds, for we have given no substance to the idea of a constraint capable of turning sound to meaningful expressions. In fact, we are left with *no content at all.* If the ground level of communication is conceived as 'sameness' of either linguistic or general behaviour (to communal or whatever behaviour), then communication becomes impossible; samenesses and differences *require* a language, rather than being able to ground one.[65]

Blackburn, attributing the communal solution to Wittgenstein, writes:

> *If* [Wittgenstein] is right, then language becomes impossible. In other words, we can become gripped by what I call a *wooden* picture of the use of language, according to which the only fact of the matter is that in certain situations people use words, perhaps with various feeling[s] like 'that fits', and so on. This wooden picture makes no room for the further fact that in applying or withholding a word people may be conforming to a pre-existent rule. But just because of this, it seems to make no room for the idea that in using their words they are expressing judgments. Wittgenstein must have felt that publicity, the fact that others do just the same, was the magic ingredient turning the wooden picture into the full one. It is most obscure to me that it fills this role: a lot of wooden persons with propensities to make noises is just more of whatever one of them is.[66]

This position is worse than a 'sceptical solution', as Kripke calls it, insofar as it accepts the scepticism envisaged in the original dilemma (rules as rails or else indeterminacy). A more attractive reading is available, which starts from the thought that the sceptical dilemma is put forward as something to be ultimately rejected, once the misunderstandings motivating it have been exposed, revealing the third position available.[67]

content or sense data, on the one hand, and world, on the other), the mental side of the divide cannot really amount to contentful states.

[65] Cf. Davidson, 'Communication and Convention', in *Inquiries Into Truth and Interpretation*, 280: 'I suggest . . . that philosophers who make convention a necessary element in language have the matter backwards. The truth is rather that language is a condition for having conventions.'

[66] 'Rule-Following and Moral Realism', 183 (emphases in the original). This consequence *is* pointed out by Kripke: see Wittgenstein, 146, n. 87 (added by Kripke in proof); also Seabright, 'Cultural Divergence', 21; McDowell, 'Wittgenstein on Following a Rule', *58 Synthèse*, 325–63 at 350. Blackburn and Kripke appear half-hearted, at times, about the unworkability of the 'solution'—they appear to allow that there *could* be a language without the help of any notion of sameness. Again, Blackburn remarks in the passage quoted that the 'solution' renders language impossible.

[67] I have in mind here principally McDowell's reading: see 'Non-Cognitivism and Rule-Following'; 'Wittgenstein on Following a Rule'. Similar readings can be found in Putnam, *Realism and Reason*, Ch. 7, *Realism with a Human Face*, Chs 1, 21, and esp. in his recent Dewey Lectures, published as 'Sense, Nonsense and the Senses', *91 J. Phil.*, 445–517, where he explicitly adopts a McDowell-type naturalism; Stanley Cavell, *The Claim of Reason*; Stroud, 'Wittgenstein and Logical Necessity', who confusingly says (at 84), however, that Dummett steers the middle road between Platonism and constructivism which Wittgenstein would himself endorse; J. Lear, 'The Disappearing "We"', *58 Arist. Soc. Supp.* 219–42 and

On that reading, the misunderstanding centres on the individualism that informs the classical horn of the dilemma. The dilemma is fake, insofar as it trades on the idea that the question of meaning is the question how the mind succeeds in grasping a pattern, the relation between the two being captured in spatial metaphors: inside (the mind)—outside (the world) etc. The sceptical horn of the dilemma is what remains once the possibility that the two may always fail to match is revealed. It is this conception of the relation of mind to world that makes indeterminacy inescapable. The communal solution—the central thesis to any conventionalist account of meaning—seems workable only by supposing that the dualist picture is available. If it were, we would be able to identify independently the contents of individual minds, and aggregate them to a communal (majority?) standard of correctness. This standard would then be able to constrain individuals in their use of expressions, i.e. in applications of the expressions to bits of the world, themselves independently identified.[68]

This picture, however, is (if the above remarks are correct) unworkable. On the reading recommended, we must reject the premises on which the dilemma, and the sceptical 'solution', depend. This reading is based on a more radical rejection of individualism, by suggesting that the idiolectic meaning figuring in the interpretations available to individuals is constrained not by communal interpretations but by the communal practices themselves. The crucial difference consists in this: the boundaries of idiolectic interpretation are not the judgments that have wide currency in the community. The fundamental constraint to interpretation cannot be just some interpretation (what determines the content of *that*?). If communal practices are to act as boundaries, they must *limit*, not be, judgments. Communal practices, then, must be *built into* idiolectic interpretation. They must be shaping individuals' ways of thought by supplying a sense of naturalness, that marks out those interpretations that are eligible.

The notion of practices should be then conceived as follows: there are facts of our natural and social history (endowment with perceptual apparatus, initiation into customs, practices etc.) that determine our way of thinking and so limit what we may find intelligible. To recognize that our thought is shaped by those facts is to accept that our thought is in some sense contingent. Rules do not embody

'Leaving the World Alone', *79 J. Phil.*, 382–403. See also the introduction in McDowell and Pettit, (eds), *Subject, Thought, and Context*. Similar conclusions by a different route are reched by Burge, in a series of publications, most notably 'Intellectual Norms and Foundations of Mind', 697. This reading is most straightforwardly adopted by Hurley; see *Natural Reasons*, esp. Chs 2, 3, and 5. It goes without saying that several differences exist among these commentators. What groups them together is their apparent agreement that Wittgenstein's arguments are not meant as proving scepticism an insuperable problem, but rather as a *reductio* alerting us to the misconceptions that allowed scepticism to arise in the first place. That point apart, the authors cited here should not be held responsible for the alternative account developed in the text (with the obvious exception of any particular point specifically attributed).

[68] Thus the illusion of a workable answer to the problem of *classification* in terms of communal standard is brought about by a misconceived picture of *intentionality*, i.e. the relation between mind and world. I must again note my debt to Susan Hurley for posing the question concerning the relation between the two issues.

independent patterns, or rails that extend 'by themselves'; rather, they embody rails whose extension in an important sense 'depends on the route of the rails already travelled'.[69] But the dependence of the rails' extension on past practice does not support a relativistic conclusion; it does not support the conclusion that there could be alternative ways of thought, so that meaning would after all be unbounded.

There are a number of different reasons why conceiving of communal practices as constraints does not support a relativistic picture. First, as was mentioned, the conception of practices as constraints is meant precisely to reject the picture of interpretations trying to capture practice-independent patterns, (rails that extend 'by themselves'). The relativistic picture needs the latter, rejected picture: under that, practices could play the role of supplying an *aspect*, one among many possible, of that world of practice-independent rails. Rejecting that conception of the problem leaves no room for thinking of practices as metaphysical lenses.[70]

Second, practices do not magically turn one among many intelligible alternatives into the right one; rather they set the limits of intelligibility. The constraints they make available and necessary for determinate ascriptions of belief and meaning are what Lewis calls the constraints of 'eligibility'. They consist in a property of 'naturalness' that distinguishes the interpretations to be preferred. Addition, rather than quaddition, is preferred since, if we abandon the commitment to the natural construal, we will, eventually at least, find ourselves unable to solve the interpretive problem.[71] In the case of the quadder, discussed above, after a certain point in trying to connect his sayings with his other general behaviour we will start to lose sight of what he is saying—what it is that he doubts. Of course it is possible that we will manage to ascribe quaddition-beliefs, if we restrict our attention to the calculation problem upon which the deviant interpretation was offered. (Restricting our attention is an exercise of charity: we expect that the quadder is otherwise reasonable.) But if we really try to make sense of the quadder's beliefs, we are bound to discover major inconsistencies, which will require more and more relaxing of our sense of naturalness, eventually making the interpretation question intractable.[72] What is important in connection with the relativist claim, nevertheless, is that at no point will our 'form of life' come into question. For, although it is a platitude to say that our sense of naturalness derives from our living the form

[69] Cf. Stroud, 'Wittingstein and Logical Necessity', 84; echoed by McDowell, 'Non-Cognitivism and Rule-Following', 145 ff.

[70] Wittgenstein's argument cannot therefore be read as 'cutting the world down to the size of our minds', since the argument is supposed to establish the incoherence of thinking of the world as something over against which minds are set, and instead to undermine that distinction. At any rate, my argument here is only meant to provide a reading of Wittgenstein that is inconsistent with the Criterial Model; possible idealist tendencies of his argument are beside my immediate point, although if the Davidson—McDowell view I sketch in Ch. 2, section 5, is correct, no such problems should arise.

[71] Cf. Lewis, 'New Work for the Theory of Universals', *61 Austral. J. Phil.* 375–7. Recall, once again, Ch. 2, section 5.

[72] The next section illustrates this gradual disappearance of the sense of real disagreement with the sceptic, and thus the blunting of his sceptical power.

we do, this truth is perfectly idle in our interpretive efforts. Such platitudes point in a general way to the pedigree of our way of thinking, but arguments of pedigree cannot figure in the reasoning pertinent to meaning-giving characterizations, say by providing grounds for acceptance of one of them. Such a case would be to cite 'this is the way we do it' as a *justification* of the proposed answer (125) to the addition rule; and would allow one to conclude that this is what makes it correct. (What seems right to us would then be right; so we might at any moment do it otherwise, and then *that* answer would be the correct one). But that fact can only be cited where no justification is called for (the 'bedrock' level), marking a case of *conceptual* disagreement with an unconvinced interlocutor.[73]

The 'sub-bedrock' facts are not facts we can decide about, nor are they of any help in our reasoning about meaning—and this is the third reason why conceiving of practices as constraints does not support a relativistic picture. 'Sub-bedrock' facts being not optional, are also not part of our 'theory', i.e. the considerations we bring to bear, rather they constrain what sort of theories we may use.[74] 'Forms of life' are not something *upon* which, but *in* which we agree, in the sense of being in agreement throughout.[75] The relativist picture goes wrong because it transgresses the distinction of levels between the meaningful (which extends down to 'bedrock') and what lies below it.[76] In order for an 'alternative' to make sense, it must be above 'bedrock', and hence within our 'form of life'.[77]

In sum, then, the interpretation of Wittgenstein's arguments recommended takes Wittgenstein to be putting forth a largely *negative* thesis, to be arguing how *not* to attempt conceiving of what it is to apply a concept. According to that reading of him, what distinguishes correct from incorrect applications is not a pattern drawn in some secret books, but depends on practices or 'forms of life'. But 'practices' are *not* a particular interpretation of the relevant concept, which somehow has special status (interpretations cannot figure as the bottom-line

[73] This case should be sharply distinguished from the case of a fanatic, or otherwise impossible to convince, interlocutor, who *is* disagreeing with us about a concept: for him, the argument can always go on. By contrast, the sceptic discussed in the text is not, after all, disagreeing with us at all.

[74] Does the idea that we can never appeal to 'sub-bedrock' facts make causal explanations of social science impossible? Consider, for instance, a 'debunking' causal explanation: it seems that it is ruled out, because it purports to characterize our practices from an external standpoint, that is by citing facts belonging to 'forms of life' and thus transgressing the distinction between levels. I believe that this is a misunderstanding. For it to be 'external', and hence violating the distinction, it must purport to disqualify our way of thinking *simply* by appeal to the fact that it would be different, were we part of a different form of life; it could then be true, but not illuminating. Nonetheless, a debunking argument purports to disqualify some way of thinking by showing it to be inconistent with what we already believe, i.e. *by appealing to our practices*—hence, it is internal. Seabright seems to reach a similar conclusion; see 'Cultural Divergence'. See the discussion of debunking explanations in Ch. 4; and the discussion of the view that criticism is necessarily internal in connection with 'discourse autonomy' in the next Chapter.

[75] See Cavell, *The Claim of Reason*, 32.

[76] See McDowell, 'Wittgenstein on Following a Rule', for attributing this transgression to anti-realism.

[77] Note that this picture rejects the possibility of solving the problem without recourse to values, senses of naturalness etc., and hence the possibility of a solution that does not help itself to conceptual content at all. Constraints are therefore external for any particular case, but not 'external' *tout court*.

constraint on interpretation, on pain of circularity); *nor* are they one, among many, ways of looking at the world; *nor* something we agree upon (an option); *nor* can they figure as the ultimate justification, since that would erode, rather than support, the distinction between correct and incorrect application.

Wittgenstein's negative project can be described more abstractly as the denial that the normativity involved in applying concepts can be reduced to anything simpler. On the suggested reading, nothing non-normative—for example, the fact that many agree with an interpretation—can add up to one's *having* to do such and such, in order to follow a rule.[78] Wittgenstein's thesis should be taken to be that the normativity deriving from 'forms of life' is irreducible.

Finally, another negative Wittgensteinian point deserves special mention. As I mentioned (and this point is beyond dispute), Wittgenstein rejects interpretations *qua* ultimate constraints—justifiably so, since it is interpretations that the fundamental constraint is supposed to keep in check. This is how Wittgenstein's anti-interpretive stance, his insistence that there is no interpretation *at* the bottom level, should be understood. It must be read as insisting that interpretations cannot be the ultimate constraint, not that there is no interpretation *of* the bottom level, say because there are some concepts—perhaps the basic ones, on which Wittgenstein supposedly focuses—interpretation of which is ruled out. Rather, any concept can be the object of interpretation. However, where an interpretation makes clearer what a concept's correct application is, it is not the interpretation's special status that makes that application correct, but its having illuminated the way most consistent with past practice—its *substantive merit*. This is a point to which I shall return.

8. INTERPRETIVE CONSTRAINTS

Where does this leave us concerning constraints? Any attempt at interpretation that succeeds in presenting an intelligible alternative, is an eligible interpretation (although not necessarily correct—it marks a case of SD); and what fails is not (it marks a case of CD). It may seem that this makes for a trivial criterion: almost anything will pass the test. Is not the deviant addition rule intelligible?

The answer to that objection must be that such cases seem intelligible only when considered by themselves. But imagine what else must be true for the deviant addition practitioner: he must happy with the idea of selling his car for up to £56, or else for £5; he must hold that a year after his 56th birthday he will become 5 years old; that the speed limit on the motorway is 5 miles per hour; and so forth.[79] I do not mean that we will eventually manage to convince him of his error; for he

[78] Cf. Blackburn's remarks cited above.

[79] See Stroud, 'Wittingstein on Logical Necessity', for similar treatment of Wittgenstein's wood-sellers, soft-rulers etc.

may always re-interpret every new notion to make it accord with his original funny interpretation. (He may simply say that addition does not necessarily yield the same result in every occasion.) We have already established that glossing the rules is of no help. These are reflections *we* must make, to avoid the illusion that his proposal is intelligible; they are, in fact, the usual way we examine novel interpretations, the demand for consistency being part of our 'form of life', and the more we reflect on the possibility of a coherent life of a quadder, the more we must 'go out of our way', in Lewis' terms.[80] It is probably part of Wittgenstein's insight that meaning depends on the whole of our world-view, and part of the demonstration of the instability of meaning vis-à-vis the sceptic is meant to point out the fruitlessness of the attempt to determine content in a piecemeal fashion.

It should not again be thought that the intelligibility criterion is too strong, that it disqualifies any attempt at reconstructing our understanding. There are innumerable concepts over which intelligible debate is being conducted—ethical concepts being the most prominent, but not the only ones. In fact there seems to be a continuum of contestability, with what Hurley calls 'uncontestable' at one end (colour being the most obvious example) and essentially contested at the other.[81] In all cases, nevertheless, the availability of intelligible alternative construals marks their boundaries; and it simply so happens that the uncontestable ones seem, at the moment, the most secure—possessing them seems to turn on actual agreement over their application.

There are two more things to note concerning the analysis of disagreement. First, there is a general presumption in favour of a disagreement's being substantive, rather than conceptual. This is because it is *prima facie* more natural to take the disputants as having different beliefs about the same object, even if as we refine our understanding we may explain all the errors involved (involving the very error that they are engaging in substantive dispute) and end up characterizing the case as CD. We start by being charitable, an unavoidable requirement of making sense of others. This is illustrated in the case of the addition sceptic, in that we presume that he is a rational person, i.e. that he will care for consistency and find the implications of his position embarrassing, that he has the concept of car selling, reasonable price, age etc. (in order to make out the inconsistencies) and so on. Eventually our presumption is frustrated, but it is important to see that we have to start out with it. This is just an implication of the idea that 'forms of life' are not optional: we cannot help but think in the way we do, and we have to assume that the same way of thought obtains in others, in order to get started in understanding at all. The only way we may try to make sense is to place what is to be made sense

[80] Reasoning with hypothetical cases, as I have been doing, is standardly used in legal argument, *inter alia*. See Hurley, 'Coherence, Hypothetical Cases and Precedent', *10 OJLS*, 221–251.

[81] *Natural Reasons*, Ch. 3. Note that 'contestability degrees' are not on the concepts' face, as it were; rather, attention to the relevant practices, by actual challenges or counterfactual thought experiments, will reveal whether any concept admits of re-interpretation. Cf. the discussion of Dworkin's 'interpretive attitude' as scope for SD, in section 3.1, above.

of (utterances, sentences, beliefs etc.) in the system 'of familiar paths' and check for coherence—that is to say, to assume that our way of thinking also holds for the object of interpretation.

Second, I must address the 'irrelevance thesis', i.e. the objection that Wittgenstein's problems may not really be applied in controversial cases. Blackburn has pointed out (against McDowell) that Wittgenstein is concerned to examine the source of our confidence in cases where the extension of a rule is clear cut and unshakeable; but in controversial cases like ethics, we can perfectly well make sense of divergent ways of thinking.[82]

To start with, Blackburn assumes that Wittgenstein adopts the conventionalist solution, and thus begs the question raised by McDowell. He assumes that it is agreement in substance with the judgments current in the community that constitutes applying a concept correctly, and so naturally concludes that where there is no well-defined consensus to follow, there is no correct application of the relevant concept: where controversy is endemic, there is no rule to follow. But the alternative reading sketched above precisely rejects consensus as constraint. On that reading, consensus or its absence play no role in fixing a concept's application. Everyone agrees that 68+57=125 because it *is* 125; it is not 125 because everyone agrees that it is. So easy and difficult questions of concepts' application alike must be answered substantively, and there is nothing *in principle* disqualifying areas of controversy from being treated in the same way.

Further, Wittgenstein's motivation in focusing on non-controversial cases may more readily be explained as follows: given that Wittgenstein's target was the picture of meaning as made up of ideas in the mind magically determining their application, it seems natural that he chose to attack, through the device of a sceptical interlocutor, those very cases that seem more plausible candidates for the picture under attack, i.e. the cases in which application seems 'automatic'. In such easy cases the classical picture of minds grasping patterns in secret books would be more convincing, by contrast with more controversial cases where influence by non-mental matters (the relevance of engaging in the practice and trying to establish substantively how one ought to go on) would anyway be admitted by the classical picture. In focusing on areas which appear most secure, like arithmetic, Wittgenstein gets an opportunity to show that *even there* there is scope for challenge, and that it is arithmetic, rather than some mysterious mental entity aligned with a secret-books formula, that supplies the right answer.

Yet another reason why Wittgenstein's arguments have been argued to be irrelevant to controversial areas is his alleged anti-theoretical stance which I discussed in the preceding section. Where an argument about a concept's correct application needs support by complex theoretical considerations, the irrelevance thesis goes, it is beyond the ambit of Wittgenstein's picture of 'hearing the meaning in one's words'. But, once again, the picture of hearing the meaning contrasts with

[82] 'Rule-Following and Moral Realism', 170–71.

a picture of guessing at hidden patterns, *not* with engaging with substantive evaluation of theoretical arguments. Such arguments, as I have argued, cannot be ultimate constraints, which is not to say that they are irrelevant. Theory cannot guide future applications if we imagine that it is called to convince a sceptic, if we imagine, in other words, that it is supposed to provide the ultimate constraint to a language which is in principle unconstrained. Nothing could solve such a problem, Wittgenstein should be taken to say, no-one could build determinate meanings out of in principle indeterminate materials. Wittgenstein's point is not to contrast obscure meaning, that needs explanation and argument, with evident meaning, but to demonstrate the absurdity of adding more of that imaginary material—unconstrained language—in order to turn it into the real thing: constrained language, whose meaning can even be evident. *Given*, however, language as it really is—already constrained, as it were—theory is *not* more grist for the sceptic's mill, but an all important tool for discovering and illuminating what practices really require, how the pattern set in the past ought to be extended.[83]

There is no reason, therefore, to doubt that the analogy holds between cases of arithmetic and, for example, cases of ethics.[84] On the recommended reading, the extension of plus (or equality) is determined by arithmetical (or ethical) reasoning, rather than by mental entities grasping patterns. There is nothing to exclude ethics from such treatment in principle. Of course, Blackburn has a further point: that we don't see controversial concepts, (e.g. ethical concepts), as such that divergent conceptions of them are simply a matter of clarification and exposition, we don't think that if we had the time and energy required, all reasonable men would agree. It is in *this* way, Blackburn seems to say, that we can fully understand divergent practice.[85]

To be sure, Blackburn's view could be the right account of ethics. The Wittgensteinian arguments canvassed here cannot be decisive. Ethical concepts could be disqualified from treatment in a way that distinguishes between correct and incorrect application, if for example there were plausible substantive arguments that could show them to be no different than concepts of *etiquette*. Even if Wittgensteinian practices should not be taken as cultural options, some practices clearly *are* such, and ethics could well turn out to be one of them (although in Chapter 4 I argued that no substantive account supporting such a view of ethics has been proposed). On the other hand, the arguments that do support scepticism

[83] Cf. the discussion of Fish's position in the next Chapter. Notice a more abstract motive for Wittgenstein's anti-theoretical stance, viz. his thesis that philosophy leaves everything as it is. Philosophy should *account for*, but not attempt to reconstruct with outlandish theoretical apparatus, practices. That sort of respect for common sense may have plausibly motivated his injunctions against theory, i.e. bizarre theory that does not square with practitioners' intuitions concerning their engagement with practices, not theory *tout court*.

[84] This may seem a weak conclusion: if I am right, Wittgenstein's solution would not exclude ethics, although other considerations might do. Yet I think that the weak conclusion is important, since the imagined 'communal solution' rejected above has been a very popular ground for ethical relativism.

[85] 'Rule-Following and Moral Realism', 171.

about ethics can bc largely traced to a philosophy of mind that I argued to be defective. On the reading suggested in this Chapter, Wittgenstein's arguments attack that very philosophy of mind. If this is right, ethical sceptics should find allies elsewhere.

9. INDETERMINACY AGAIN

To return to the indeterminacy objection: Raz objected that there are two options—either evident and indubitable interpretation, or a thesis that everything is open to (re-)interpretation—and his objection was that, if the latter option were taken, indeterminacy would ensue. But I have argued that the dilemma is false, and that there exists a third option that Raz ignores. Raz rejects the possibility of theory providing the distinction between good and bad interpretations, on the assumption that theory *could not* act as a constraint. He tacitly accepts that scepticism is a coherent position, that nothing (save for the weak, second-best, constraint of conventions) can block crazy re-interpretation, once interpretation is allowed at all. But for all practical purposes, everything *is* open to interpretation, because the threat of scepticism is fake. The constraints we have identified do not take the form of interpretations not open to doubt (definitions, conventions etc.). Rather, practices act as constraints in a way that supports the objectivity of interpretation: to interpret is to engage in a practice and try to establish what it requires, how to go on consistent with what has been done in the past, and the best interpretation is the one that best accounts for past practice. Raz's dilemma is not an exhaustive set of alternatives, but an *absurdum* that can be ignored once the presuppositions that drive it are exposed, once, that is, it is plain that an interpretive claim to the effect that such and such is the correct way to go on can only be won by substantive argument.

The third option, what we may call for short the objective conception of practice, respects the difference between what the community is doing and what its members *think* they are doing,[86] by rejecting the individualism informing both realist and sceptical horns of the dilemma and exposing the individualism that still informs the conventionalist 'solution'. This insight has been echoed by Gerald Postema, a sometime adherent of the conventionalist model who recently distanced himself from it.[87] He writes:

'Common meaning' [. . .] does not entail consensus—agreement in belief among individuals—about that meaning. Of course, common meaning or a common world can be

[86] It does more than that: as mentioned above, even what members of the community *think* they are doing is individuated by reference to what the community is really doing. But the scope of error is there, and for present purposes error is important.

[87] On Postema's conventionalism, see 'Coordination and Convention at the Foundations of Law', on his more recent views, see '"Protestant" Interpretation and Social Practices'.

sustained only if there is some substantial degree of consensus. But to focus on agreement of individual beliefs is to miss the point; *it is to speak of the common in an individual way.*[88]

Preserving the distinction between what the community (the legislators etc.) have been doing and what they think they have, provides the basis for interpretations which may, if supported by good reasons, ignore, say, legislators' understanding of the Fourteenth Amendment, yet really respect legislators' intention. As Dworkin has shown, individualistic specifications of intention are hopeless; and the conventionalist solution is unnecessary and, since it relies on individualism itself, unworkable as well.[89] Seeing that intention is *constituted* by 'common meaning', in the composite sense of a practice, reveals the originalist–interpretivist debate as fake.

There may still be an alternative way to preserve the importance of consensus in law. But before turning to that alternative, I must deal with a particular reason some may feel uneasy with one of my claims in this Chapter.

10. IS DWORKIN A METAPHYSICIAN?

I have argued that Dworkin's model of legal practice is perfectly compatible with K–P semantics. To summarize, both models focus on the surface structure of a discourse; both note that key concept-words are intended to pick out the concepts they stand for, whatever their content may be, and that arguments on the content of these concepts are perceived as substantive, treating the concepts' extensions as having a discoverable nature. The models conclude that, unless speakers are guilty of large-scale deception or serious error about the relevant domain, the content of the relevant concepts is determined by substantive theory, which is constrained by paradigmatic applications and abstract characterizations of the relevant practice of application.

Indeed, the two models are mutually reinforcing. Dworkin's theory describes a domain where K–P semantics is *prima facie* applicable and musters arguments that work in favour of its applicability. K–P semantics supplies theoretical ammunition against challenges to Dworkin's model, drawing on similar challenges in other domains like that of natural kind words.

Yet there appears to be a great difference between the two approaches, and this

[88] '"Protestant" Interpretation and Social Practices', 315; emphasis added. Postema has some misgivings concerning how Dworkin understands these issues, which I believe spring from misunderstanding; if my interpretation of Dworkin in sections 1–5 is correct, Dworkin is not guilty of the 'protestantism' and quasi-formalism Postema attributes to him.

[89] *LE*, Ch. 9. Note that Dworkin's anti-individualism goes deeper than Postema's: Dworkin argues that we cannot identify intention at all except through enforcing charitable presumptions about what the intention *should* be. See *LE*, index entries on intention (general and legislative). But Postema's anti-individualism does not seem to doubt that individual propositional attitudes may be identified, but simply points out that they may be mistaken.

is to do with their respective position on broadly semantic issues, those usually described as metaphysical. Dworkin is perceived to be an adherent of quietism about questions metaphysical. This quietism hardly squares, it may be objected, with the solemn preoccupation of semanticists, especially those of an objectivist persuasion appropriate to the K–P model, with all things metaphysical.

Dworkin's perceived quietism has a stricter and a looser aspect. He is quietist in a stricter sense where he discusses typical metaphysical issues, namely the questions of objectivity, radical scepticism, and indeterminacy, and concludes that the sceptic posing these serious questions about the possibility of objectivity must be ignored—that we must 'stick to our knitting'.[90] He is quietist in a looser sense, insofar as he discusses the nature of legal concepts in terms more or less alien to the classical mode of metaphysical inquiry. Dworkin does not talk, or talks very little, about properties, entities, reducibility, supervenience, and so on, but rather couches his analysis in terms of interpretation, conceptual complexity and the like. In fact, even where he discusses those traditional problems like scepticism, he makes no attempt to connect his position to traditional or Wittgensteinian scepticism.

Given that looser quietism, one cannot say with confidence whether Dworkin would agree with some aspects of the particular way objectivity in law is argued for here—whether he would agree, for example, that legal properties supervene upon, but are irreducible to, more basic, physical properties, or whether the key to the rejection of conventionalism is individualism in the technical Burgean sense, or whether Wittgensteinian arguments are meant against, rather than for, conventionalism. Yet that difference in terms of analysis need not conceal any important underlying differences, since both models treat the legal domain in very similar ways, as was shown above.

Neither does Dworkin's quietism in the stricter sense mark an important difference from the K–P framework. Dworkin's treatment of the internal–external distinction and indeterminacy have important metaphysical implications that are in harmony with the K–P framework developed here.[91] Dworkin rejects the possibility of external scepticism, i.e. criticisms of substantive arguments made within legal practice that are not themselves substantive but express a demand for (and register the absence of) a fact, independent of that practice, by virtue of which substantive arguments lay claim to objectivity. And he dismisses the related allegation of radical indeterminacy, claiming that there is enough material to constrain substantive theory, even if that material does not have the status of indubitable truths.

[90] *A Matter of Principle*, 171. See ibid., 167–77, for a discussion of objectivity.

[91] Some aspects of the internal-external distinction are discussed in the next Chapter. In very recent work, which I had an opportunity to see after most of this book was written, Dworkin discusses in detail some issues in metaphysics. That work may help to evaluate my claim that Dworkin's model and my K-P framework are compatible; however, as that work is still unpublished, I cannot use it in support of that claim.

The K–P model developed here treats external scepticism and radical indeterminacy in a similar way, as was shown in the preceding discussion. Although the K–P framework starts by inquiring at length what 'the yarn we knit with is made of',[92] it concludes that the legal domain is metaphysically respectable and indeed is such that a claim to objectivity needs no support from facts independent of the original, first order substantive arguments. Once we have done our theoretical work justifying a concept's application in some case, there is no residual question, viz. what makes that interpretation the best.

So we are agreed in Dworkin's quietist conclusions. The K–P framework developed here explains and justifies how that residual question lapses; it does so in a way different perhaps from Dworkin's own, yet it joins Dworkin in the injunction that we need only 'stick to our knitting'. Once the inquiry about the yarn we knit with is concluded, we need not worry any more about it.

11. INTERPRETIVE POSITIVISM

Finally, let me consider a manoeuvre someone attracted to Raz's objection might make. Consensus in the application of a legal concept, it might be said, is important not for semantic but for legal reasons. Our legal practices themselves require that the absence of consensus over law's application count as the absence of law (with the relevant cases resolvable through discretion). The feature of legal practice that embodies such a requirement could be, for instance, law's authority, which would be endangered if controversies were allowed. From the standpoint of the law's authority, we simply register when consensus breaks down (why and how that happens being beside our legal interests), and take it as a signal for the exercise of discretion.

This formulation is an altogether different argument, and I am here considering it as a matter of clarification: it does not invoke indeterminacy to ground the indispensability of consensus, but rather poses as *an interpretation*, in Dworkin's sense, of legal practice.[93] This formulation would therefore make a significant concession, namely that attendance to our practices, rather than shared criteria, are fundamental to answering questions of application.

But the manoeuvre fails anyway, because it cannot avoid having a semantic basis. If the simple occurrence of controversy were to mark the limits of the law, then the limits would collapse: one could start doubting that cars were vehicles (and insist

[92] In the words of an anonymous referee. Chs. 3 and 4 discuss the metaphysics of that 'yarn', i.e. the nature of legal properties and their metaphysical standing.

[93] This formulation *cannot* be construed as Hart's position: for Hart, the boundaries of consensus are the consequence of 'our relative indeterminacy of aim and relative ignorance of fact', i.e. a result of the guaranteed failure of any attempt to specify fully our intentions as against a partially inaccessible reality—omniscient legislatures would presumably be able to make perfect laws. Hart's argument is therefore clearly semantic. Cf. Ch. 3, above.

that *that* is what everyone agrees upon etc.) and then the law would *ipso facto* be declared unable to guide the dispute. A variant of filibuster would suffice to obliterate any law.

What is needed is, of course, a way to demarcate reasonable from absurd challenges. Even the semantically liberal positivist must somehow disallow silly challenges, and to do that he must have some principle of identifying what the law really is. Given that the law is *ex hypothesi* identified by consensus, there must be a way to identify what is the content of consensus. So a semantic basis is indispensable for the authority-based view. Of course, we *do* have a way to do that: we have semantic theories that supply the necessary contents.

Now, if the proposed semantic basis is the Criterial Model, then the arguments of the preceding sections apply: the criterial view *presupposes* the content of 'consensus'. So it must be the case that: *either* the ultimate constraint, that determining 'consensus', is non-consensual, and therefore the view collapses into a non-consensus-based view of constraints; *or* we are launched on an infinite regress ('consensus' identified by consensus and so on).

If we take the first horn (which is to take the view actually recommended in this Chapter), then consensus *is* identified, but the argument from authority fails: for, on this view, there is something in particular that the law requires, controversy notwithstanding. Controversy may be the result of failure to appreciate what the law requires (or: what the law is need not coincide with consensus). So cases may arise in which the law requires something, although it is controversial what it requires. And it will be a very weird conception of legal authority that asks us to ignore what the law requires and exercise discretion instead, simply because some refuse to see what it is that it requires. (No doubt such a conception *may* be proposed with the argument that it is better to ignore the law when people do not understand it. Note that here the constraint of consensus comes about at too late a stage: it rules out contents that were already *identified as law.* I am not sure whether this is consistent with law's authority.)

Perhaps there is a more complicated way to do what is needed here, namely to obtain a principled combination of *political* consensus constraint and non-consensus-based semantic constraint, so that only non-controversial law is identified as such. For example, one may say that according to the best theory of law, what the statute book says is not necessarily law, despite there being consensus-independent constraints that determine what the statute book says; it is law only when there is no controversy about what it does say. This theory might have a sincerity criterion, a way to distinguish sincere controversy from the type of filibuster mentioned above. But the theory would be committed to ignore error: controversy should turn a decision required by a statute into a decision that is not required by law, despite the fact that those who resist the decision are just *failing to see* that it is required by the statute, that the best interpretation justifies it. Substantive error cannot, on that theory, disqualify a controversy from acquiring the role of blocking a statutory requirement from being the law, or else this model of interpretive positivism would become empty: it would ask us to respect controversy where controversy is neither insincere nor due to failure to see the right answer. What kind of controversy would that be? Presumably, it would only occur where no right answer exists, in which case the theory has no rival.

Provided, then, that the theory I am considering must respect controversy where it is explained by lawyers' sheer error, it is a bizarre theory.[94] It will be the business of substantive argument to see whether this conception of law is a satisfactory picture of any legal system.

[94] I think that there are deeper problems with it: each judge would have to wait for everyone else in order to determine which interpretation expresses the law, even if the preliminary issue of what is expressed by the statute had already been determined. Cf. Kripke, *Wittgenstein*, 146, n. 87 (added by Kripke in proof).

6

Conceptions of Practice

1. INTRODUCTION

This Chapter discusses several problems connected with the claim that legal practices determine the content of legal concepts. A common theme runs throughout these problems, namely a persistent tendency to conceive practices in conventionalist terms, identified by practitioners' agreement. The second section discusses the well known arguments of Stanley Fish, and shows how he oscillates between a conventionalist conception of practice, under which the mark distinguishing good from bad interpretations is their potential for approval by the relevant 'interpretive community', and an objective conception of practice, under which practices objectively determine which interpretations are the right ones: identifying *which* interpretations are in fact required by the practice may take substantive theoretical argument. Fish's views supply a good opportunity for sharpening the objective conception of practices, since he defends a sophisticated pragmatism that purports to retain some sceptical character, while avoiding the pitfalls of straightforward conventionalist conceptions. Section 3 addresses the objection that, if content depends on practice, then practices are self-validating: no external criticism is allowed. Section 4 deals with the objection that failure to respect conventional or legislators' subjective understanding of the concepts used in the law will result in substituting law for morality, and that only good law will be identified, so that the distinction between law and ideal law will collapse. Several different examples of legal interpretation are discussed in an attempt to show that no bias towards good law is implied by applying concepts in an objective way. Finally, section 5 addresses a variant of misunderstanding objectivism, under which it is thought to make for conservatism.

2. FISH'S PRAGMATISM

Fish is an anti-formalist; everything else he believes is directly or indirectly entailed by his rejection of formal constraints, as he has recently pointed out.[1] His anti-formalism then breaks down into a series of theses, most of which are put forward as boldly challenging, and indeed exposing as incoherent, almost every other position in the field. Dworkin's views are one of Fish's more persistent objects of attack.[2] On its face, Fish's critique establishes irreconcilable differences between their respective views, Dworkin being accused of falling into the 'positivist trap', a trap allegedly avoided by Fish on the strength of his pragmatism. But I shall argue that, despite appearances, the differences are really small.

'Formalism', in Fish's vocabulary, acquires many senses. First and foremost is the thesis that some interpretive claims are indisputable, they are just 'imposed' by the text, and therefore act as 'foundations'. Fish's denial of that thesis splits into two claims: first, any interpretation is in principle revisable; second, any interpretation depends on deeper-seated assumptions which are themselves vulnerable.

This sense of Fish's anti-formalism is evident in his earlier attacks directed at Dworkin. What Dworkin calls the 'formal' constraints on interpretation are, Fish insisted, as controvertial in fact as the substantive claims the interpreter is making. The superficial difference, namely that a particular interpretation does not challenge these 'formal' features, detracts nothing from their potential contestability. In the words of one of Fish's students: '[I]t is naive to think that the elements of the formal dimensions are being applied *except* through the deep structures that give shape to what we think'.[3] This is a reminder that, although any interpretation must take some elements for granted, what is being taken for granted is not really incontrovertible, inasmuch as it rests on some tacit substantive assumptions. The reminder should be necessary to anyone prone to think that Dworkin believes that 'the interpreter first determines the shape (or meaning) an object apparently has, and then wrestles it into another shape according to some prior sense of what it would be best for it to mean'.[4] Sure enough, the distinction between formal and

[1] *Doing What Comes Naturally* (hereinafter, *DCN*), 1–33.

[2] Fish and Dworkin have been engaged in a debate, consisting of the following papers: Fish, 'Working on the Chain Gang: Interpretation in Law and Literature', *60 Texas L.R.* (1982), 551–67 (responding to Dworkin's 'Law as Interpretation', *ibid.*, 527–50, reprinted as 'How Law is Like Literature', *A Matter of Principle*); Dworkin, 'My Reply to Stanley Fish (and Walter Benn Michaels): Please don't Talk About Objectivity any More', *in* W. J. T. Mirchell (ed.) *The Politics of Interpretation*, a version of which appears in *A Matter of Principle* as 'Interpretation and Objectivity'; Fish, 'Wrong Again', *62 Texas L.R.* (1983), 299–316; Dworkin, 'Not Really', (unpublished); Fish, 'Still Wrong After All These Years, *6 Law and Philosophy* (1987), 401–18, (hereinafter 'Still Wrong'; review of Dworkin's *Law Empire*, hereinafter *LE*). The Fish essays are reprinted in *DCN* (to which page references will be given hereinafter). The most recent exchange between Fish and Dworkin appears in Brint, M. and Weaver, W., (eds.), *Pragmatism in Law and Society*; their respective essays are 'Almost Pragmatism: the Jurisprudence of Richard Posner, Richard Rorty and Ronald Dworkin' and 'Pragmatism, Right Answers and True Banality'.

[3] J. Lane, 'The Poetics of Legal Interpretation', *87 Columbia Law Review*, 197–216 at 207. Lane seems to think that this erodes the notion of textual identity. Different interpreters, she maintains, are 'essentially disputing the identity of the text': ibid., 213. She thinks that this dispute of the text's identity represents a dispute about what was the author's intention. Intention, then, individuates texts, and disputes turn on different characterizations of it. Lane assumes that, since what individuates a text is in dispute, then there is no identity to the text. That seems to be very much a 'formalist' assumption.

[4] Fish, 'Still Wrong', in *DCN*, 362.

substantive elements is not to be taken as a two-stage recipe for the *production*, but rather as a *characterization* of, a proposed interpretation. (Recall the discussion of Raz's two-tier objection discussed in Chapter 5.) In this context, 'formal' should be understood as standing for those features that are not being challenged by a particular interpretive proposal, and hence do not call for argument, while 'substantive' for those that need to be defended against the orthodoxy or other non-standard suggestions. Some of the formal elements may (and do) appear as truly unassailable, but, once the lessons of traditional scepticism are understood, they are revealed as in principle vulnerable. Further, even the time metaphor is often apt: one often takes a certain interpretation for granted, only to be led, upon reflection or upon hearing a new argument, say, in court, to reject part of what one once took for granted. One does not need to just 'see' the answer—at least not to complex legal questions (although Fish seems to disagree with this, as will emerge below). But once the vulnerability thesis is conceded, there does not seem to be any reason for reiterating it every time suspect expressions like 'formal' or 'identity' are used.

At one point Fish *did* seem to reject the idea that some elements ever enjoy 'formal' status. But as he has now pointed out, in connection with anti-foundationalism, that thesis does not deny that there are foundations, but points out that the source and nature of the (necessarily existing) foundations are not what formalists take them to be (the culture-independent variety), but are intimately connected with history, culture and circumstance (thus avoiding, incidentally, the *tu quoque* argument usually levelled against the thesis: Fish freely accepts that there are foundations, he just rejects the 'formalist' picture of their source and nature).[5]

In view of the above, Fish's negative point clearly is that, whatever constraints there are to interpretation, it cannot be that they consist in the indubitability of some particular interpretive claim: some features are always foundational, yet what is foundational within an interpretive problem is intimately connected with certain background assumptions. But while it seems correct to deny that any particular *interpretations* operate as constraints, the question is whether there are any constraints at all, whether, that is, any old interpretive proposal may be put forward, as long as the relevant background assumptions have been suitably modified. The real issue then must be joined in connection with the positive implications of the anti-formalist thesis—the positive account of the source and nature of the 'foundations' actually available. But what exactly Fish's positive account *is*, is difficult to pin down.

Fish initially appealed to the notion of 'interpretive communities'. What provides the structure of constraints on which the eligibility of interpretations is judged is what is at any time accepted by the relevant—professional, in the case of literary and legal interpretation—community. But this lent itself to misunderstanding: Fish was widely understood as advocating something akin to the 'sceptical

[5] Cf. *DCN*, 30.

solution' sketched above in connection with Wittgenstein. Fish appeared to be claiming that there is no good argument against the persistent sceptic, so that the only constraint available is the insubstantial one of communal approval. Hence, there is no real content to the notion of the right interpretation but only the weak alternative of what happens to be accepted.[6]

This theory of interpretation attracts the objections levelled against its 'Wittgensteinian' counterpart in Chapter 5. First, communal approval cannot serve as a *definition* of truth or correctness of interpretation, because the sceptic may always insist that his *is* the accepted interpretation. Consequently, Fish was open to the challenge to explain what it is for the interpretive community to agree, given the general lack of real constraints to the content of anything, agreement included.

Fish seemed to be able to escape this objection by rejecting the idea that consensus is a definition or criterion of truth or correctness, opting instead for a conception of consensus as a 'brute fact', brought about by the exercise of any political power that happened to be carried by a particular interpreter. The picture then seemed to be that, in principle, anything goes, but in the end 'it's all politics', i.e. political factors determine which out of an indefinite number of equally 'good' interpretations will count as the correct one. But this picture attracts a second objection, namely that politics, force etc. must be pictured, on this view, as something literally meaningless—'brute' force, noises, senseless motions. As I argued in Chapter 5, once the sceptical possibility is admitted, the consensus solution is no solution at all: *either* the solution presupposes some meaningful materials available for expressing the communal standard, which is supposed to be the ground-level constraint (in which case the ground-level itself is otherwise constrained) *or* the materials are not meaningful and cannot actually constrain anything. So (on the second horn) the 'politics' slogan does not work, for lack of any meaningful materials out of which to construct a dominating view or purpose.[7] If, on the other hand, the materials used to express the dominant view acquire their sense otherwise, (the first horn), then the slogan does not capture what is basic to interpretation, since it relies on a prior standard of correctness, viz. that which fixes the content of the materials used. Then the dominant view may have achieved its persuasive power on merit. Its power may derive from the fact that it correctly interprets its object.

As I argued in Chapter 5, the picture of communal constraint, on both the

[6] Cf., *inter alia*, Dworkin, *LE*, 425 at n. 23; F. Kermode, *History and Value*, 103–4, 126, for a reading of Fish as advocating such a sceptical solution.

[7] Of course, the 'politics' slogan may work at a non-basic, and therefore non-threatening, level. Some, not all that brute, facts, may sometimes explain the prevalence of a view. High salaries, frequent citation, and other such facts *may* underlie an academic view's domination. But they cannot give content to that view—they cannot individuate *which* view aspirant disciples must subscribe to, if they want to get promotions; neither can they help the dominant-view holders to identify *who* their disciples are. In quasi-sceptical scenaria built around such facts the scepticism does not go deep: the dominating, as well as the heretical, views are individuated by other, non-political, constraints, and the question whether they are good or bad views remains open.

communal-definition and the 'brute fact' versions, fails by virtue of falling foul of the individualism that gives rise to the original sceptical problem. The problem of understanding is set as the problem of capturing autonomous mental entities (principally, intention for Fish's purposes); and, once it is shown that this results in radical indeterminacy (since *any* intention may be ascribed by adjusting the background story[8]), bringing more individuals into play cannot really help (how are we to ascribe content to their doings and sayings?).

But this cannot be Fish's view, and this has been made all too obvious in his recent essays. Fish's dismissal of 'real' constraints like literal meanings, indubitable truths etc. is not meant to allow for the unconstrained interpreter those constraints were supposed to hold in check. On the contrary, Fish rejects the idea of an in principle unconstrained mind needing such rails in order to be kept in line. What he now calls the 'enriched notion of practice' (presumably to avoid the positivist overtones of 'interpretive community') ensures that what an interpreter is allowed to claim cannot amount to the possibility of radical scepticism, a possibility made compelling by the individualistic picture. Our practices determine how we may interpret (i.e. what intentions, meanings, behaviours etc. we may ascribe) rather than serving as checks on independently determined contents. Fish has apparently embraced the satisfactory reading of Wittgenstein set out in Chapter 5, which dismisses as illusory the notion of mysterious entities whose content is autonomously specified and bears a contingent relation to the social environment.[9] Such autonomy would make the relevant entities empty (inner space dark, in the terminology used in Chapter 2). Rather, the social environment (social practices) bears a *constitutive* relation to the target of interpretation (intention, belief, meaning etc.): practices make content possible, by making available the conceptual content and sets of values that make ascriptions possible. Here is Fish:

> The demand for self-consciousness is a demand for a state of consciousness in which nothing has yet been settled and choices can therefore be truly rational. But if all concepts or constructs remained to be chosen, there would be nothing—no criteria, no norms of measurement, no calibration of value—with which or within which the choosing could be done; indeed there would be no chooser, for if the question of direction were totally open the mind (such as it is) would be incapable of going in any direction at all if only because it would be unable to recognize one.
>
> To put the matter baldly, already-in-place interpretive constructs are a condition of consciousness. It may be . . . that the thinking that goes on within them is biased (which means no more than that it has direction), but without them . . . there would be no thinking at all.[10]

We might say that the relation between practices and contents that Fish invokes here enables us to make judgments of intelligibility, i.e. judgments of what contents

[8] See one (among countless) of Fish's exercises in deviant interpretation in *DCN*, 8–9.

[9] I here ignore the natural environment.

[10] 'Dennis Martinez and the Uses of Theory' (hereinafter 'Martinez') in *DCN* 372–398, at 394.

would make sense of our subject, and to reject the sceptical threat that comes about by otherwise imagining (mysteriously) determined contents which our interpretations try, but may always fail, to match. Now the rejection of scepticism should lead to some sort of objectivism: disallowing the myth of the mysterious contents entails that there is no presumption against the ability of our practice-dependent interpretations to reveal what the case is, no presumption that practice-dependence must inescapably make for distortion. Fish goes some way towards such an objectivist account. First, in the passage quoted above, he argues that the constitutive engagement of practices with beliefs, intentions, meanings etc. implies that 'pedigree' or 'status' objections—those invoking the contingency, historicity and so forth of anyone's convictions—are idle. The alternative, i.e. some version of uninterpreted reality, over against which interpretations are set, does not make sense. Consequently, 'antifoundationalist thought deprives us of nothing; all it offers is an alternative account of how the certainties *that will still grip us when we are persuaded to it* came to be in place.'[11] This echoes Dworkin's dismissal of what he calls the external sceptic, the 'critic' who points out to the lesser pedigree of one's arguments, to their being 'tainted' by one's theories and convictions and therefore not 'really objective'; both Fish and Dworkin respond to this sceptic by exposing the idleness of the objection.[12]

A further consequence is that nothing relevant to a practice may be external to it, but is always put forth as a better understanding of it. This may sound paradoxical, but the paradox arises only by assuming that the boundaries of the practice are conventionally individuated, and this is the assumption rejected by Fish's anti-foundationalism: only if the identity of a practice turned on an indubitable criterion should any criticism put forth count as a request that the practice change its identity. Rejection of this assumption has the consequence that either an argument in fact engages the practice's concerns and is therefore competitive with claims made within it (it is a piece of criticism, raising a case of SD) or it fails to be competitive and is therefore irrelevant (not criticism at all, a case of CD). Here is the way Fish explains how it is that even the most radical criticism of literary interpretation is internal criticism, so that the practice retains its identity through countless changes in the orthodox understanding of itself:

> The answer lies in the nature of an interpretive community which is at once homogeneous with respect to some general sense of purpose and purview, and heterogeneous with respect to the variety of practices it can accommodate. Any one of those practices exists in some relationship of assumed justification to that general sense; both those who do and those who don't practice stylistics believe that they are engaged in the business of determining the meaning and value of literary texts, and if one wants to persuade the other to his point of view, he will do so by invoking the goal they both acknowledge and arguing that it cannot be reached except by the route he follows. . . . Each will have recourse to examples that would

[11] *DCN*, 26 (emphasis added); the theme is developed in every essay in the book.
[12] Cf. Dworkin's discussion of scepticism, *LE*, 75–85.

seem to challenge the other's assumptions, and so it would go until one persuaded the other.[13]

Stylistics, in other words, only appears as a self-contained practice challenging some other practice, but in fact all this happens under the umbrella of literary interpretation as an overarching practice. Continuity is thus ensured in Neurath-boat fashion:

> [N]ot everything changes at once. Interpretive communities are no more than sets of institutional practices; and while those practices are continually being transformed by the very work they do, the transformed practice identifies itself and tells the story in relation to general purposes and goals that have survived and form the basis of continuity.[14]

Further, although all justification comes in the form of beliefs, criticism and reconstruction of any belief structure is possible by virtue of a (no doubt provisional and itself vulnerable) ordering of beliefs:

> [B]eliefs are not all held at the same level or operative at the same time. Beliefs, if I may use a metaphor, are nested, and on occasion they may affect and even alter one another and so alter the entire system or network they comprise. Even though the mind is informed by assumptions that limit what it can even notice, among those is the assumption that one's assumptions are subject to challenge and possible revision under certain circumstances and according to certain procedures when they are set in motion by certain persons.[15]

For example, some of our beliefs are *epistemic* beliefs, which govern what is to count as a reliable source of information, and if we come to discover that an argument is supported by a more (less) reliable source, we are bound to revise our opinions accordingly.[16]

The resemblances with Dworkin's picture are remarkable. In fact, in the light of Fish's recent essays, all his earlier pragmatism seems to have disappeared, especially the reduction of meaning to politics: this seemed powerful precisely by virtue of posing as a reduction, by placing constraints *outside* the practices. That reduction claimed a *revelatory* effect for itself: it sought to expose fundamental fallacies in the practices, and in particular tried to establish that the practices were only apparently responsible to rules amenable to argument, whereas in fact all arguments and apparent standards were empty or degenerate. But this requires the coherence of external criticism (scepticism), which Fish has rightly rejected.[17]

[13] 'Change' in *DCN*, 149. [14] Ibid., 153. [15] Ibid., 146.

[16] Cf. Dworkin, *LE*, 426, at n. 27.

[17] This is not to say, of course, that we cannot dismiss the claims of a 'Pegasus society', whose members claim that winged horses actually exist. See section 3 below for discussion. Recall the discussion of phlogiston theories in Ch. 2; and of ethical scepticism in Ch. 4. Note that rejecting the possibility of 'external' criticism, and arguing for the necessarily 'internal' character of criticism has the unhappy result that the internal–external distinction appears to have sense. The correct position is that the distinction is senseless, and that is what the necessity of internality of criticism should be taken to mean.

Fish has shown a change of heart about his pragmatism by noting that he is now arguing 'for politics instead of Politics (the new transcendence)'.[18] But what is the modest politics he now invokes?

A clue is present in the first passage quoted:[19] rather than talking about interpretive proposals standing or falling depending on their ability to account better for the practices they are referring to, Fish talks about *practitioners* trying to *persuade* each other. Again, in the last passage,[20] he refers to *persons* (in position of authority) as setting in motion the belief-revision mechanism. The idea seems to be that, contrary to there being room for unforced, rational reflection leading to better understanding of our practices, the real engine of understanding is persuasion—the result of rhetoric. Hence the 'politics' slogan turns out to have content: the politics that govern practices should be conceived as the structure of power within the institutions of the practice, a structure that guarantees that the opinion which will carry the day will be the one coming from those sitting high up in the hierarchy.

But neither does this formulation escape the familiar problems. It is still the case *either* that the powerful practitioners' arguments manage to persuade by being good arguments, and so by speaking to the concerns of their audiences and claiming that, say, a particular reading is more consistent with the audience's own convictions (in which case 'rhetoric' is another name for 'argument'); *or else* the winning arguments work by freely re-interpreting standards whose content is not really constrained by anything, i.e. by being addressed to a community which is literally standard-less, and therefore impossible, as Fish himself has shown.[21]

Rather, Fish seems to want to say that *precisely* by virtue of realizing that the sceptical picture is incoherent, the distinction between practice-based and rhetoric-based arguments is undercut:

> *Any* reason that finds its way into a judge's calculations will per force be a *legal* one, and therefore one whose very existence is a function of that history (that is, of some view of it)—a history he could not possibly discount even if he declared himself to be doing so.[22]

That is, it is not that case that any old interpretation will do, since the background practice constrains what may be *intelligible as* an instance of the practice. Something violating those constraints will be unintelligible as an effort at interpretation—as a legal decision, literary criticism, and so forth. A judge finding

[18] Postscript to 'No Bias No Merit', in *DCN*, 179.

[19] Cited in note 13.

[20] Cited in note 15.

[21] I am here focusing on audience, and asking what sort of arguments may persuade it. Of course, the issue turns on the prior question—what sort of arguments are *available*. i.e. whether there exists conceptual room for good and bad arguments, notwithstanding whether actual audiences appreciate the distinction. Recall that the sceptical picture under discussion must capture the bottom-line of disagreement; rejection of the sceptical picture is not rejection of the possibility that the wrong argument *may* win for the wrong reasons, but quite the opposite: it is *because* the bottom-line allows for objective standards that the distinction between good and bad arguments—and good and bad reasons for accepting them—is made possible.

[22] 'Still Wrong', 366; emphases in the original.

against Mrs McLoughlin on the basis of race is producing something unrecognizable as a judicial decision, as Fish observes.[23] The considerations informing such wild proposals will have come not from one's pure 'preference': there is no such a thing as pure preference, but only other sets of institutional practices, say, a political theory endorsing racism, and thus such preferences really consist of principles, yet principles that are inappropriate as a basis of deciding a case in court, since they are inconsistent with the requirements of legal practice.

But, despite his commitment to the distinction between good and bad arguments and his recognition of the constraints of eligibility on interpretation militating for natural contents, Fish slides back into a version of *laissez faire* in the following thought. Since practices determine which interpretations are eligible, normally a trained practitioner will refrain from bringing what he sees as inappropriate reasons into his judgments, and thus will tend to opt for the most eligible interpretation he may find. But of course this tendency is no guarantee against considerations figuring in a judgment that are, in fact, inappropriate and Fish does not see how we may fault a practitioner who chooses to employ such considerations. He considers a judge who manages to make a case for his *prima facie* unconnected 'preferences' as actually representing a better way of understanding what the law requires.[24] This suffices, presumably, to make the opinion pass the test of intelligibility, and is a case of engaging in 'self-presentation', i.e. a 'pragmatic strategy by means of which decisions are successfully inserted into a field of practice'.[25] Despite, therefore, the fact that the imaginary judge's considerations are *ex hypothesi* inappropriate, since they are actually at odds with the best account of the practice (and despite having established that there *is* a standard of propriety which these considerations flout), Fish manages to find no fault with them.

How does Fish's pragmatism achieve that? In the case of a judge engaging in rhetoric, the trick of making the bad yet 'dressed up' argument indistinguishable from a good one is performed by insincerity: the judge in the example merely presents his argument as legal interpretation, whereas he is, in fact, up to deceiving his audience. But this is not important: the possibility of deceit proves that a legal argument's worth lies not in its resembling a good account of law, but in its *being* one. An insincere judge may manage to have his opinion considered as an attempt at good interpretation, rather than have it dismissed out of hand. But this is not to say that the opinion is made into a good one simply by being submitted for

[23] Cf. Fish, ibid., alluding to the case Dworkin uses to illustrate his point in *LE*, 177. 'Think of what he would have to do in order to "work" such "reasons" into his decisions', Fish goes on to say about the imagined judge who would like to decide the case on racial grounds. Compare David Lewis's notion of 'going out of our way', the less natural the contents we consider ascribing; see 'New Work for a Theory of Universals', *61 Australasian J. Phil.*, 343–77, at 376.

[24] 'Still Wrong', 367. In the course of that example Fish engages in the two-tier exercise he has accused of Dworkin as mistakenly espousing: the judge, on Fish's scenario, decides to 'wrestle' institutional history into a shape capable of accommodating his sense of justice, despite having already identified the institutional history (and therefore having discovered that his preferred shape is in fact inconsistent with it).

[25] 'Martinez', 389.

consideration. That conclusion could only be reached by an argument that collapsed correctness to admissibility; a way to make that argument would be to defend the idea that what makes a view a *legal* view is a matter of style. It is a requirement of legal practice that judges believe in their opinions, but it must also be the case that they correctly state what the law is. The interesting deceit would involve the second requirement, and it is hard to see how one could collapse what it is for an argument to be a good one into what it is for an argument to *seem* a good one.[26] Fish argues that a judge, as long as he tries to comport himself like a judge, will 'see' what the law requires—no doubt in the light of all his convictions that he thinks relevant. In that case, rhetoric is what he must engage in so as to make his decision presentable to a legal audience. The question is: what does it take to do that? First, he must presumably express himself by using the stylistic formalities—the conventions—of his office, but whatever these are, they are *ex hypothesi* not important (they are just formalities) and we can assume them away, say, by imagining the judge as presenting his opinion to an informal group of lawyers. To be convincing, he must probably employ legal concepts in characterizing the facts of the case and try to show that his opinion is grounded in the law. Now the insincerity may derive from the fact that some sort of reduction is available: the judge's opinion is expressible in non-legal terms, and its being grounded in the law is not really relevant to its content. So the specifically legal presentation is disingenuous. Again, this must be a picture capturing the *general* case—it does not suffice to say that such things sometime happen.

Fish gives a non-legal example of what seems just such a reduction: he considers a group of scientists discovering that paint brushes are 'sort of like pumps', and then proceeds to express this in terms of fluid mechanics in order to secure research funds. But this is surely no reduction: talking in terms of fluid mechanics is precisely what one has to do in order to talk about whatever is even remotely like a pump, because those devices *inter alia* are what fluid mechanics deals with. The trick supposedly performed still eludes us, and not surprisingly so: Fish has clearly rejected the possibility of such ground-level 'revelatory' findings about practices.[27]

We should further distinguish the sort of deceit we are looking for from a sort of second order deceit: a judge may be convinced that his arguments establish the true reading of the law, but may reflect that since his knowledge derives from contingent, historical belief structures, it cannot lay claim to truth; and he may choose to omit all reference to those qualms when writing his opinion. That judge thinks he is a sceptic, but if we know that he is not—if we know, as Fish does, that the pedigree of his beliefs does not debunk them—his deceit is uninteresting.

[26] Is Fish here rehearsing an 'argument from illusion', i.e. claiming that correctness is always a 'further fact'? He can hardly do so, once he has rejected the notion of the 'uninterpreted content' on whose inaccessibility the argument from illusion trades.

[27] See 'Critical Self Consciousness', in *DCN*; cf. Fish's denial that styles of presentation are conceptually connected to knowledge, *DCN*, 21; and his denial that changing one's mind may come about in any way other than by attendance to, and a better understanding of, the standards of the relevant practice, in 'Change', *DCN*.

There is some evidence that the latter sort of case is the one Fish wants to alert us to. In an essay on rhetoric, he distinguishes between the *homo seriosus* and the *homo rhetoricus*.[28] The former believes that there *is* point in talking about truth; he further hopes that our inquiries may lead us to discover truths that are untainted by human perpectives and interests. The latter rejects that hope, since he believes that the notion of such untainted truths is incoherent; but, while he has no reason to think that the essential dependence of our inquiries on human perspective and interest makes these inquiries less respectable and therefore also thinks that there is point in talking about truth, he likes to play with the idea that talk of truth is useless. The best way to confirm this interpretation of the distinction is to consider Rorty, who makes a similar distinction between what he calls the metaphysician and the ironist. The metaphysician is someone who believes in there being genuine distinctions among literary genres, fields of inquiry, correct and incorrect applications of concepts, and hopes that the distinctions we routinely use may correspond to some Platonic order. The ironist,

> would like to avoid cooking the books she reads by using *any* such [viz. genre, field of inquiry etc.] grid (although, with ironic resignation, she realizes that she can hardly help doing so).[29]

Given, however, that the grid is not Platonic but culture-dependent, the hope to avoid cooking with it is precisely the hope that Rorty attributes to the metaphysician (and Fish to the *homo seriosus*), namely the hope for pure and independent standards—the hope both theorists have devoted their careers arguing against. It is, therefore, (or so they are committed) a senseless hope.[30]

Consequently, we must construe Fish's pragmatism along the following lines: we may say that operating within a practice is nothing but rhetoric, but this is not to be taken as a threat. Rhetorical success turns on what is likely to carry conviction, but that can be nothing else but the practice's actual measures of success. (This seems to be the structure of Fish's latest criticism of Dworkin.)[31] We can even call those standards 'communal approval': the arbiters of communal acceptance, Fish might say, being themselves 'situated' within the practice, (cannot help but) appraise performance according to the rules and standards of that practice. They will judge their fellow baseball players by their ability to score runs (for if they judged them otherwise they would be unintelligible as baseball critics); or they will judge their fellow lawyers by their ability to present the most coherent account of legal practice; and so forth. We do not need to worry about the community going

[28] *DCN*, 471–502. [29] Rorty, *Contingency, Irony and Solidarity*, 76.

[30] Fish suggests as much in 'Rhetoric', in *DCN*, by reiterating his standard insight that all anti-essentialist, anti-rationality etc. arguments are really arguing for a better understanding of the old truth-seeking practices. Nevertheless, the 'metaphysician's' hopes appear to be irresistible: arguments for their incoherence tend to become arguments for frustration of a respectable epistemic standard.

[31] See 'Still Wrong'.

astray in their appraisal of their colleagues, for this is something they simply cannot do (on pain of being unintelligible as practitioners evaluating colleagues). If that is the proper way to understand Fish, then it seems almost satisfactory, and Fish's strictures must be seen as attempts to prevent careless slippage into believing that there are such things as standards of appraisals independent, outside, etc., of the practices they focus upon. The reservation is this: isn't it also the case that practitioners engaged in appraising others might go wrong? (this being necessary to ensure that it is not, after all, the support of the majority that grounds the approval, rather than the practice's own standards). But this is already taken care of, Fish might reply, for it is part of baseball, legal, and other practices that practitioners are judged on merit, rather than by vote. These last remarks indicate the cause of Fish's oscillation between an objectivist account, which we should expect to issue from his 'enriched notion of practice', and the pragmatism which ultimately rests on the spurious dichotomies Fish rejects in his more guarded moments. We can see the cause by focusing on this slide: from the idea that practices supply a background of constraints which make standards of objectivity possible, to the idea that whatever manages to get expressed within a practice must be objectively true. Or: from the idea that radical indeterminacy (which would make error impossible, since there would be nothing to distinguish correct from incorrect interpretations) is impossible, to the idea that error itself is impossible. Practitioners can do no wrong, Fish insists, since they are constrained. But the existence of constraints surely establishes the opposite, namely that there *is* a distinction between true and false beliefs, or between correct and incorrect interpretations.

This slide is reflected in Fish's persistent confusion of levels: while his 'enriched notion of practice' dictates that there is no 'critical self-consciousness' at the bottom-line (i.e. there is no space for scrutiny of what structures our practices, that would enable us to see their shape free of the 'distortion' brought about by our engagement with them, since that would require the incoherent notion of the 'given', the uninterpreted reality that constrains interpretations), he infers that there is no 'critical self-consciousness' at all; there is no way we may, armed as we are with the conceptual capacities our practices make possible, discover that some of our beliefs are wrong, or rest on unacceptable grounds, or consist of illusions. Or, from the (correct) claim that there is no sense in saying that our beliefs are 'biased' or based on 'preference' at the bottom-line (for the same reasons as above), he moves to the claim that there is no bias at all, that there is no space for us to discover that our beliefs track some particular interests, rather than the truth.[32]

An analogous confusion of levels is evident in Fish's insistence on 'doing what comes naturally', i.e. on the idea that trained practitioners grasp their interpreta-

[32] Recall the discussion on Nozick's truth-tracking in Ch. 4. Recall Fish's picture of belief revision, above.

tions 'in a flash', just 'see' the answers, and therefore do not need reflection and evaluation of different considerations in order to make up their minds (*ergo*, Fish thinks, only where their minds are *changed*, is a different, more reflective, way of making up their minds required, and that role is performed by rhetoric). Here he slides from the fact that no interpretation exists at the bottom-line to the claim that no interpretation is necessary at all.[33]

A form the last confusion takes is rejection of the relevance of theory to practice.[34] Read straight, the distinction endows practices with immunity from theoretical criticism, on account of the theory's being placed 'outside' practices. But how are practices' boundaries individuated? Since no conventionalist criterion is available to Fish, it is difficult for him to deny that challenges may come from anywhere, that no source of challenge may be *a priori* excluded, as long as it manages to make best sense of the practice.[35]

Fish invokes a different basis for his distinction. He calls 'theory' a body of abstract principles that are independent from any practice and purport to impose 'extraneous' standards on practice.[36] Of course we may allow Fish to use such a restricted notion of theory, under which theory does not concern itself with accounting for the practice but purports to bring extraneous standards to bear, and then the thesis is true: *that* sort of theory is superfluous, because it cannot speak to any of the practice's concerns; and the 'other' sort, that which manages to engage the relevant issues—well isn't that 'already' part of the practice? But then Fish's point about theory being superfluous is in danger of being *itself* superfluous, since it is unclear what theory that is 'independent of any practice' would look like, and whether there is any point in debating its relevance. Again, Fish's restricted notion of theory may have been held by some, and so he may be entitled to use it *ad hominem*. That is not to say that some may have invented practice-independent theory, but that some may have thought of theory as practice-independent. Fish's point then would not be new,[37] and anyway would not cover real theory, practice-dependent as it is. *That* theory would be relevant to practice, and Fish admits as much when he says that the demonstration that some such theory better accounts for the practice will certainly affect the claims plausibly made within it.[38]

But Fish has the further complaint against theory mentioned above: he claims that practitioners 'see' their answers and do not need any theory to figure them out. He thus wants as well to disqualify theory properly conceived, e.g. theory that is routinely employed in the process of legal interpretation, say, when we are offering accounts of what it is for something to be a contract in support of a particular judgment. Fish apparently takes exception even to the right sort of

[33] See 'Martinez'. Cf. the discussion of non-interpretive constraints in Ch. 5.

[34] 'Martinez', and *DCN passim*.

[35] In other words, to belong to a practice *is* to make claims engaging the practice's concerns; hence whatever is a challenge is by the same token not external.

[36] See 'Martinez', 378.

[37] Fish acknowledges the fact that Dworkin has been pressing the same point ever since 'The Model of Rules I' (in *Taking Rights Seriously*); see 'Martinez', 386–8.

[38] *DCN*, 15.

theory that takes the practice as its object and tries for the best account of it—and consequently Fish refuses to distinguish between judgments that are (even if tacitly) supported by better or worse accounts of the relevant practice.

Fish's anti-theoretical argument resembles the old American Legal Realist thesis about judges 'hunching' their decision. It is a commonplace, nevertheless, that responsibility to theory is not waived merely by the fact that one's application of a concept does not involve any active engagement in reasoning that is distinctive of theory: the question of theoretical responsibility turns on whether judgments on concepts' applicability need to be supported, potentially at least, especially in the face of challenge. However one arrives at the judgments, the real question is whether the judgments thus reached carry substantive commitments and are hence amenable to argument.[39] Fish's own account of change admits as much,[40] i.e. that our judgments *are* open to theoretical argument. His complaint must therefore be the deeper one that was mentioned above: he doubts not whether theoretical accounts are involved in practice, but whether this involvement may result in a distinction between good and bad interpretations. He doubts, in other words, that the correctness of a particular 'move' within a practice—say a judgment of application of a legal concept—may turn on theoretical support that can be mustered in its favour.

It seems that Fish's doubt stems from his confidence in sceptical power: adding theoretical argument is unlikely to make any headway with the sceptic that insists on re-interpreting whatever theoretical support we may find for our judgments. This motivates the following line of thought. Adding interpretations to a rule, as Wittgenstein made clear, is adding grist to the sceptic's mill.[41] So we cannot make any headway with real-life opponents either, for they may selectively re-interpret as they see fit and render their own judgments just as coherent. Hence theoretical considerations are useless in determining who has got it right. Fish concludes that correctness is ultimately determined by the practice, in the sense that practice moulds our ways of thinking and gives us the capacity for judgment; but, on that score, all 'embedded agents' are on a par—they can all lay claim to being shaped, and therefore constrained, by the practice. Hence, paradoxically, we get indeterminacy, after all.

The key to the paradox lies precisely in the realization that correctness is ultimately determined non-theoretically. The sceptic is rebutted by disallowing his premises—the demand to connect practice-independent with practice-dependent entities—and showing how practices provide the necessary constraints. Now *given* those constraints, interpretations are neither vulnerable nor useless. They are not vulnerable, since they get their content the usual way—on the strength of the

[39] Michael Moore makes a similar complaint against Fish in 'The Interpretive Turn in Modern Theory: a Turn for the Worse?', *41 Stanford L. R.* (hereinafter 'Interpretive Turn'), at 909–17. Note also that theorizing and arguing about our concepts is also part of our practice: we 'stand corrected', in Burge's phrase, in our hunches. See Ch. 2, section 4.

[40] Recall the discussion of Fish's account of belief revision, above.

[41] See Ch. 5, section 7.

constraints we have identified.[42] They are not useless, since they are not meant to rebut the sceptic, but to rebut erroneous conceptions of what the relevant practice requires. The sceptic helps us see where to look for the grounds of the distinction between right and wrong, and our conclusion is that there *are* some grounds, not that the distinction is impossible. The distinction is impossible if we *grant* the sceptic's question (we look for practice-independent grounds) and are therefore denied access to our conceptual capacities, senses of value and purpose etc. But armed as we are with those capacities, we can make the distinction.[43]

Fish gets into an ironic position when he shows the constraints available against the sceptic, and then proceeds, in effect, to ask for them again when he has moved up away from the bottom-line: he asks that interpretation, argument, critical self-consciousness, bias-based debunking explanations, theory, recourse to examples, and all the rest (the exercise of our conceptual capacities) determine content by themselves, unaided, as it were, by the constraints he has so convincingly identified.[44] As if he found himself looking for the mysterious entities the sceptic was asking for (a pursuit he has exposed as incoherent). It should not be surprising that radical indeterminacy becomes once again inescapable.

As before, there is a way to reconstruct Fish's writings to reconcile them with the above remarks: we should relax 'doing what comes naturally' to include theory and all the rest (or conversely: to restrict 'theory', 'reflection' etc. to exercises of reason unconstrained by practices). In that case, we should treat his 'pragmatist' remarks as available *ad hominem*, to show what the bottom-line cannot be. Even if we do not so reconstruct them, we cannot, in view of the bulk of his antisceptical insights, take them seriously, and should rather treat them as *lapsi calami*.

3. MOORE ON DISCOURSE AUTONOMY

It appears, then, that a properly 'enriched' notion of practice allows us to say coherently that the success of legal arguments turns on the best interpretation of

[42] This point is related to Lewis's remarks in 'Putnam's Paradox', *62 Australaisian J. Phil.*, 221–236, at 226.

[43] The structure of Fish's error here, as well as his various slides noted above, is analogous to the misunderstanding of charity discussed in Ch. 2, section 5. It is analogous to the slide from the presumption of truth of beliefs to the declaration of the truth of all beliefs, i.e. to the exclusion of error. As I argued there, charity enables us to identify belief, rather than enjoins us to declare true a belief otherwise identified. The belief thus attributed may well be *false*, and its falsity will be part of what charity enables us to identify. Similarly, given Fish's constraints, we can identify the content of what practitioners claim, and part of that content will often be in error.

[44] I am here indebted to Mark Greenberg's unpublished 'The Nature of Law: The Role of Values in Legal Interpretation and Implications for Dworkin's Legal Theory', Oxford B.Phil. thesis 1990, who notes the slide from 'interpretations are unable to determine content by themselves' to 'are unable at all'. Note however that the contrast between 'interpretation alone—interpretation at all' should not suggest a picture of *adding* constraint to content; rather, 'interpretation alone' stands for a conception of interpretation as an unconstrained mental operation trying to establish content, a conception precisely rejected.

legal practice, without any trace of pragmatism. Yet it is widely held that there is a fundamental flaw in the thesis that it is the practice that serves as the domain of meaningful disagreement. Michael Moore has argued that this results in deep relativism—it yields the 'discourse autonomy thesis'.[45] This is the thesis that practices are self-justified, allowing no external criticism. Attributing the thesis to Dworkin, he complains:

> According to Dworkin, we cannot criticize the practices of law, morality and literary criticism, except by employing the standards of validity prevailing in that discipline, nor can we raise wholesale questions within such discrete practices.[46]

This thesis, Moore alleges, entails that cross-disciplinary, cross-practice criticism is ruled out, and that apparently entails an *absurdum*.

> Presumably a Pegasus society could develop which became large enough to be called a linguistic community. If the society's members developed a complex set of standards towards which they also developed Dworkin's 'interpretive attitude', presumably the rest of us would have to admit that, in any meaningful (*i.e.* internal) sense of the words, that ancient winged horse really does soar through the skies.[47]

Now if this *were* Dworkin's position, then Moore would be right to stigmatize him as a 'deep conventionalist'.[48] Dworkin would be a deep conventionalist inasmuch as the position characterized above assumes that practices can be individuated according to some criteria shared among the participants. If that were true, then there could be a Pegasus-practice distinct from the well-known one. That well-known practice treats 'Pegasus' as standing for a mythical animal; the society's activities, on Moore's picture, would not just involve a different view on the old practice—namely that the animal really exists—but would constitute a new, independent practice. All that, nevertheless, holds only by assuming the thesis that practices are individuated by shared criteria. Yet that assumption is not compulsory, and anyway should not be attributed to Dworkin.

Moore is right in holding that cross-disciplinary arguments are admissible in disputes over the meaning of a concept. In fact, standard theory is vulnerable to attacks from 'any quarter', insofar as no kind of argument can be prohibited *ex ante*. To prohibit, say, scientific arguments in connection with disputes surrounding legal concepts, would be to prohibit arguments on the basis of their pedigree; and this could only be possible if the content of the legal concept were identified in a similar way, i.e. by appeal to a formal, unassailable criterion. But the semantics I have been proposing denies precisely that a concept's boundaries are individuated in that way. Rather, no critical attempt may be excluded *a priori*, but has to be tried out for substantive success.

Now this point must be reconciled with the commonsensical observation that there do exist many discourses; and, further, that some of the cross-disciplinary

45 Moore, 'Interpretive Turn'. 46 Ibid., 953. 47 Ibid., 954.

48 Cf. Moore, 'A Natural Law Theory of Interpretation', *58 S. Cal. L. R.*, 277–398, at 299.

arguments Moore envisages are inappropriate. The first component is easier to account for. We do have distinctions among disciplines (discourses, practices etc.), but these turn on *substantive* and hence vulnerable accounts of the kind of activity in which each engages. Consequently, the criteria we routinely employ to pick out the different practices are not necessarily individuative, but may consist in minimal abstractions to be evaluated, sharpened or revised in the face of challenges.

Something similar goes on concerning the propriety of arguments that may conceivably be brought into a dispute. Suppose an art critic looking at a painting says 'there is a unicorn there'. It is intuitively inappropriate for a biologist to object that unicorns do not exist.[49] It seems that we know *a priori* that this is inappropriate, it seems that we do not simply count this as wrong remark about the painting but as a remark about something else altogether. The quick conclusion is that 'artistic' and 'scientific' discourse are separate, autonomous, in the sense that 'unicorn' designates different things depending on the discourse in which it is used.

This conclusion is too quick, however. The expression 'unicorn' in the above example (*prima facie*, at least) designates the same thing, namely a particular mythical species, irrespective of the 'discourse' within which it is employed. 'There is a unicorn' should be construed as elliptical for 'this painting depicts the (mythical species) unicorn'.[50] The reason the biologist's objection is inappropriate is that there seems to be nothing wrong with art representing mythical species as if they actually occurred (which is not the case with biology). This is a substantive claim, drawing on our theories about what is good art and good biology. Like the identity of practices, standards of appreciation for each one turn on the substantive theory we hold (which is itself as vulnerable to criticism and revision as the more specific claims we make about more concrete examples of each practice).

The point is *not* simply that practices are individuated by some standard of evaluation—so that immunity could be conferred by different standards of evaluation across discourses, rather than by first-order claims made within them. This would simply move the issue one step up, to the standards of evaluation. Rather, the point is that what these standards are is a *substantive* issue. Consequently, it is a substantive issue whether a claim, apparently coming from outside a discourse, is properly made. Its propriety depends on whether the claim is *competitive with* some claim characteristic of the relevant discourse. In the above example, the scientist's and the artist's claims appear to be perfectly compatible, and it is for this reason that the former's criticism is rejected.

The point can be further illustrated by Moore's own example of the Pegasus society. The opposite conclusion, namely that scientific criticism *should* be allowed

[49] I owe this example to Dworkin.

[50] Are we allowed such a simplistic aesthetics? If that seems troubling, then let us simply say that the unicorn-remark does not, on the face of it, make any existential claim similar to 'there is a cat in the room'; this would be the situation the scientist is anxious to correct. As the unicorn claim stands, nonetheless, it seems *compatible* with the usual cat-claims.

there, rests on the assumption that the society is making a claim to the effect that what we thought of as a mythical species actually occurs, in the same way that cats and dogs do. Here, the society's claim competes with what we already believe, and it makes sense to ask that we are shown where we have gone wrong in thinking that no winged horses have ever existed. Issue is joined between the society and modern science by virtue of the competition between their respective claims, irrespective of whether the society's members are inclined to engage in the debate.

The distinction between the two cases turns on their respective relation to the ostensible criticism. In both cases, a claim faces a challenge from a scientific account of what it is for something to exist. The first claim, however, is not competitive with that account: it is not an existential claim about unicorns, which science may or may not interfere with. The second claim, by contrast, *is* such. So the relevance of the scientific account turns on whether it really constitutes criticism, a condition it fails in the first case, but fulfils in the second.

The question whether practices are immune to 'external' criticism is misleading. It is misleading in cases where, say, it is interpreted as the question whether the 'legal', rather than the 'scientific', understanding of 'death' applies to a statute. What this question really means is whether some particular conception of 'death', usually the one prevalent when the statute was drafted, rather than the modern one, should apply. Answering this question turns on whether the statute picks out death, or something else. If it does, then the modern understanding is applicable not *in lieu* of the legal understanding, but rather because *it is* the legal understanding. No 'external' understanding is brought to bear, i.e. an understanding that is not law's own. Conversely, if the statute picks out something else, the modern understanding of 'death' is inapplicable, not because the old one should be protected, but because the modern understanding is irrelevant. So whether 'external' criticism is admissible turns on whether, *first*, 'external' means 'external to some conception, which it attacks as a misconception of the law'; this is the case where 'death', conceived in eighteenth century terms, is attacked as a misconception of the law, the reason being that the law picks out *death*, not the criteria employed by eighteenth century science. Here the criticism is acceptable but 'external' in an uninteresting sense. Or, *second*, 'external' means 'different from the law's content'; here the law is independently identified, and differs from the 'external' view—for example, contract law requires that an agreement involve something in return for one's promise, not that one think carefully about the promise. Here, 'consideration' in the 'external' sense is unacceptable because it is *in fact* external; but the unacceptability involved is uninteresting: since the 'external' reading is irrelevant, it is unclear what the sense of 'allowing' or 'disallowing' it is.

Dworkin's internal–external distinction should be construed in the light of the above remarks. The distinction does not classify arguments on the basis of pedigree (stemming from, or prepared to embrace, some 'basic' features of the practice that is the object of criticism). Rather, it classifies arguments on the basis of their capability to be rationally appraised—to be *arguments*. If something is an argument, then it will not be external in the sense dismissed. Suppose a critic wants to argue that the standard analyses of the notion of constitutional equality are useless and misleading, since the notion is 'pure ideology'. As it stands, the criticism looks 'external'. But some emendation seems appropriate: the critic must be making the claim that the concept of equality is empty, that what we normally take as instances of its application are not so, and he must have an argument showing that. Perhaps he can show that no sense can be made out of these alleged instances, since they were actually based on other, less honourable considerations or were totally arbitrary. If he tries to do that, he will in effect be offering a theory which *would claim for itself*, as it were, the status of a more coherent explication of the (common) object—the alleged instances of application of 'equality'.[51]

The internal–external distinction has negative and positive import. Its negative import consists in denying illicit immunity to a party to a dispute, allegedly afforded by his refusal to engage in substantive argument. Its positive import lies in what may be thought of as a methodological maxim: if some apparently external criticism is being put forward, a construal which manages to engage the parties in substantive dispute should be sought and, if available, preferred. It is unimportant *where* the point of engagement lies. The distinction does not serve to prohibit any particular criticism from being offered, and so it is immaterial whether the critic challenges what we consider central or basic, or is just making a subtle point of detail. Notice that we are not here concerned with what is *obviously* a case of SD—this would probably turn on the status of the challenged material within the orthodoxy, i.e. whether that material is considered a controversial feature or a central tenet of the relevant practice. Rather, we are concerned with what is *in fact* SD, and the status of the material as controversial or not does not come into it.

The requirement that arguments be substantively considered, and indeed amended in the above fashion so as to facilitate substantive consideration, is not really an injunction: it is not a recommendation, but a cognitive point. Apparently external arguments, if they are really arguments, *necessarily* make internal claims, and the emendation is in order only to make sure that the immunity claimed on false grounds is not granted. In a recent essay, David Nelken considers various theses concerning the propriety of scientific arguments in the legal domain.[52] Typically, the form of the question assumes that the two discourses are demarcated according to some criterion, and consequently those arguing for the inadmissibility of cross-claims (which they are bound to characterize 'external') are in the awkward position of having to argue for each discourse's absolute epistemic authority over its 'own construction of reality'; this is a problem, however, only when it is taken to imply that the different 'constructions of reality' are really in

[51] Fish presents an array of pseudo-external arguments, and shows how they turn out to be internal upon examination; cf. *DCN*, especially 'Anti-Professionalism'.

[52] 'The Truth About Law's Truth', U.C.L. Working Papers 7, 1989 (mimeo), University College, London.

competition, making it necessary to fall back on either's authority to avoid engagement. Of course, the epistemic authority point is unable to do much work, because it can hardly be violated if the participants to a discourse elect to adopt some other's methods or findings.[53]

Conversely, those who stick with criterial individuation but support the admissibility of ('external') cross-claims are in the equally awkward position of needing a reason why unwilling discourses should surrender their epistemic authority. Thus Fish, for example, is able to construe Moore's claim for the admissibility of scientific criticism as an injunction to substitute one conventional truth for another.[54]

In fact, all this debate is misguided. It attempts to answer a senseless question, namely whether external criticism is justified—senseless because 'external criticism' is an oxymoron. For something to be criticism, it must put forward claims *incompatible with* claims made by the object of criticism, and so be internal; such an argument necessarily engages some of what is being assumed by the position criticized, and argues that the best understanding of those assumptions reveals them as inconsistent with the position under criticism.

Of course, one of the motivations behind this long-standing debate lies in a special type of 'external' critique, that of offering a causal (thus presumably scientific) explanation of beliefs (usually ethical and political, but possibly concerning 'ways of thinking about law' as well): for instance, the kind of explanation, considered in Chapter 4, of one's ethical beliefs in terms of one's training and upbringing. Given the above remarks, it may appear that such explanations are appropriate, and one will need to defend one's beliefs accordingly, say, by showing that one's beliefs stem from the structure of the universe instead. But the crucial question is precisely whether such explanations are really incompatible with the relevant beliefs, and as I argued in Chapter 4 and, in connection with Fish's pragmatism, above, there are good reasons to suppose that in general such explanations are entirely compatible with ethical, political, and legal beliefs.[55] At any rate, it is worth stressing that if a causal explanation is in fact competitive with

[53] Nelken makes similar points, but is in general more sympathetic towards immunity theorists, and does not, as far as I can see, challenge the initial assumption that discourses are individuated by some shared criterion; consequently, problems of authority arise when a competitive claim appears.

[54] See 'Martinez'. Moore escapes this point by arguing that people's intentions are transparent, i.e. they intend that their words refer to the real thing, whatever that may be, so that they have authoritatively surrendered their epistemic authority to the appropriate field of inquiry. This is almost right, except that it sounds like an empirical claim that speakers entertain such deferential intentions. But what if Moore's Pegasus society, on top of their claims about winged horses, added an explicit denial that they have delegated any questions to scientists? In fact, the issue is conceptual: it turns on whether what speakers say is responsible to theory about how things are, irrespective of whether they realize that or not. Consequently, rather than saying that Pegasus theorists defer to something external, one should say that in making existential claims they are making claims characteristic of science.

[55] As I argued in Ch. 4, such a 'critical' causal explanation of ethical belief acquisition does not in fact make any claim competitive with ethics, since no-one denies that one acquires ethical beliefs through cultural mechanisms.

what some belief or even field of inquiry presupposes, there is no denying that it is internal, and hence calling for defence.

It may be objected that if criticism is always internal, with the consequence of engaging some of the assumptions of the position criticized, then wholesale criticism is not possible: we will not be able to dismiss, say, psychoanalysis, and reject all of its assumptions. But this is the same mistake all over again. The objector assumes that discourses are individuated by what their participants are willing to accept, and thus he infers that there can be a discourse that manages at once to be self-sufficient and contradict what we believe. But a really self-sufficient discourse would fail to make any sense to us; if, on the other hand, we managed to disagree with it, then this would involve locating the disagreement in some joint commitment (though not necessarily one our opponent would *recognize* as such). In this way we are able to dismiss anything 'wholesale'—we are able to say that psychoanalysis is nonsense, for instance—without damaging the Davidsonian point that we cannot dismiss everything without losing sense of what it is we are dismissing.[56] Scepticism about psychoanalysis as a whole makes reference to the commitments common between the sceptic and psychoanalysis—the facts about desire, action etc. which psychoanalysis seeks to explain. Moreover, so-called wholesale dismissals of discourses typically involve an invocation of shared epistemic beliefs and the demonstration that the discourse under criticism flouts them.[57]

We may summarize this section's discussion by illustrating the difference between the present view and Moore's view. The way Moore attacks the problem of content lends itself to an essentially positivistic reading: he labels questions arising within legal interpretation as 'scientific', 'medical', 'ethical', etc., and proceeds to allot them to the relevant discipline for resolution, in a way analogous to the misinterpretation of Putnam's 'division of linguistic labour' considered in Chapter 2.[58] Like Putnam's picture, Moore's treatment may be misleading: it may suggest that people choose to substitute their own conceptions for someone else's, making the latter criterial of the relevant concept's content. In using 'death', legislators are pictured as making doctors' views determine the law, to the relevant extent. The idea seems to imply that for specifically *legal* concepts, legislators keep the privilege to themselves: for 'contract', legislators' views are the relevant criterion. In fact, no-one's conception—of deep concepts, at least—is criterial; people do not defer to anyone's conception but simply use concepts whose

[56] Recall the discussion of eliminative reductions in Ch. 3, section 3; and Ch. 4, section 4. The general form of the problem—negative existential sentences—is discussed in Ch. 2, section 6.

[57] Cf. Michael Williams, 'Coherence, Justification and Truth', *34 Review of Metaphysics*, 243–72, on the importance of epistemic beliefs against the possibility of self-validation of theories.

[58] Recall that Putman's point (that it is for the relevant experts to work out the true extension of a concept) is not the claim that concepts' extensions are to be decided by professional boards, rather than amateurs, but the claim that, in using deep concepts, speakers defer to 'the possibility of there being experts', i.e. to the possibility of the paradigms' having a discoverable nature. See Ch. 2, section 3, for discussion.

extensions they may be unable to discriminate. There is no reason why their own conceptions should be privileged, and consequently why these conceptions should be taken to individuate 'discourses'. Hence cross-disciplinary arguments should not be surprising. If the law says something about dead people, then the right conception of death is *part* of the law, and hence of legal 'discourse', not an external influence on it.

I conclude that Moore's argument from social dependence (viz. the thesis that concepts' content depends on social practices) to discourse autonomy (the silly form of conventionalism according to which, if a group of people agree on the extension of a concept, they may refuse to consider criticism coming from outside that group) does not work. The argument involves a *non sequitur* that can only be eliminated by tacitly assuming that discourses are individuated conventionally, and hence that different claims acquire their character as, say, legal or medical, by virtue of their pedigree rather than their content, by virtue, that is, of their being proposed by members of the relevant conventionally individuated discourse. Moore, no doubt, is no conventionalist. However, in deploying that argument against social dependence, he admits conventionalism by the back door, in quite the same way that those who read Putnam as proposing a 'professional', rather than conceptual division of linguistic labour, virtually embrace the conventionalism Putnam's point is meant to deny.

4. CONCEPT ATTRIBUTION AND LAW'S AUTONOMY

In the preceding section, I argued that 'discourse autonomy' is not a real issue. I argued that to say that a question arising within some discourse is the question whether some concept C applies is to say that that concept C is part of the discourse. In terms of disagreement, the picture is this: if different arguments bearing on a question are, or depend upon, different conceptions of C, then the disagreement is substantive (SD) and one of the arguments must be better than the other. A scientific discovery, for example, may lead to a challenge of accepted wisdom among lawyers, by being or supporting a conception competitive with the conception prevalent among lawyers, as the 'death' example illustrates. Once we locate the differing conceptions as conceptions of the same concept, then we can only think of the dispute as endangering the law's autonomy by assuming conventionalism, that is, by assuming that substantive disagreement with a shared conception is impossible—that groups' shared criteria individuate *concepts*, rather than conceptions.

It may be objected that my picture makes for too weak boundaries of the law. First, given that the law deals with many different issues of ethical and political importance, too many ethical and political concepts will be attributed to law's content, with the consequence that the law will lose its authority.[59] Legislatures'

[59] I shall use the locution 'attributing a concept to the law' in the sense of claiming that the law uses some particular concept.

power to *legislate* will be undercut by the very fact that they must inevitably use language. So that, simply by using the word 'equality', legislatures will have thereby implemented equality, on the best ethical understanding, often despite themselves; they cannot, say, have the power to exclude women—unethically, no doubt—from equal treatment, if ethical theory requires that they be equal to everyone else. But authority requires that one be able to do the *wrong* thing, and this ability will be blocked in principle by the concept attribution move. Law will be run over by ethics on the strength of a linguistic point.[60]

Second, it will be recalled that, on the picture defended here, concept attribution itself depends on evaluative assumptions. Faced with someone saying weird things about banks, I must judge whether to attribute *bank*, in the sense of financial institution, or in the sense of rivers' boundaries, or even in a special, indiosyncratic sense altogether, depending on which sense (strictly: which of the different concepts expressed by the word) makes best sense of the speaker, which makes him more reasonable, wise, and virtuous. And these judgments are inevitably made in the light of the interpreter's evaluations. Similarly, faced with the question whether the law is about *cruelty*, or whether it uses the word 'cruel' to mean expensive,[61] an interpreter must base his judgment on what would make the best sense of the law, and hence on what would make the law better.

Combining both points, the objection will be that, on my picture, ethical theories about what the law should be will be used to identify the law's content, and will attribute various concepts to the law, whose extensions will be determined by ethical theory. How can the law fail to be the same as ethics? The challenge, then, is to show that the picture defended here allows for bad law.

The objection fails; in order to see why, I shall start with the second point. Despite the fact that ethical assumptions are necessary, in the way the objector describes, to identify the law's content—to settle the question which concept to attribute to the law—one obvious way in which the law will differ from ethics is that a theory of law is under several constraints different from those affecting a theory of ethics. The former must take into account precedent, past interpretations, the systematic place of the particular legal rule within the law, and other institutional constraints.[62] Ethical theory has different constraints: communal practices are a constraint, as are interrelations of concepts that are the object of that theory with other concepts, but ethical theory can safely ignore precedent, judicial opinions, and the rest of the constraints appropriate to legal interpretation.

Further, there is no reason why assumptions about what the best law would be should make the law identical to ethics. There is no second-order assumption that the best law should not be different from ethics, and the assumption of what the best law would be is really weak: the *content* of such assumptions is not free-

[60] Compare Greenawalt's complaint, discussed in Ch. 5, section 5.1.

[61] Dworkin's example, in 'Bork's Jurisprudence', *57 Chicago L. R.*, 657–77, at 662.

[62] There may also be independent constraints, e.g. protecting citizens' expectations.

standing but is constrained by the parts of the law that are beyond dispute. Some parts must operate as data to be accounted for by a theory whose immediate object is a particular legal issue.[63] *Given* some parts of the law, the most reasonable way to fill in the rest may well be very unethical. To take an extreme example, given some of Nazi law, the most reasonable way to settle the question whether a statute that permits 'any religious activity that does not put the nation's interests in jeopardy', permits the exercise of Jewish religion, the answer must be that it does not—or else the rest of the law will be incongruous.

Still, the objection may be that the 'bias' of the picture defended here lies deeper: although, on its face, the basic constraint to attribute the content that makes best sense need not favour ethically best content, it is evident that somehow it does. It may be seen in what was noted by the first part of the objection, in the practice of attributing concepts whose mistaken conceptions are credited to practitioners.

4.1 The Intention Connection

The issue may be focused by considering the debates surrounding the US Constitution. The Fourteenth Amendment was apparently introduced to extend the right to equal protection of the law to everyone. Yet it was only in the 1950s that this came to be thought to require that racially segregated schooling be prohibited—or at least it was only then that a test case arguing that segregated schooling violates the Amendment (*Brown* v. *Board of Education*) was won. Dworkin has argued that the case was rightly won since the Amendment enacted a principle of *equality*, and equality rules out segregation.[64] The argument is important because contemporaneous understandings of the concept regarded equality as consistent with segregation.[65] Further, one may reasonably suppose that contemporaneous

[63] Unidsputed parts of the law are constraints in the same way data are constraints to theory in general. The constraining role of these 'data' is partly independent of the specifically legal basis of the constraining role of precedent, or of the special status of constitutional law and so forth. For example, a good theory of the law of the UK or the US must assign importance to past decisions. A good theory of the law of *any* jurisdiction must explain and justify past decisions (or strike them out as explicably mistaken).

[64] See *Law's Empire*, 362; *A Matter of Principle*, 48–57. In making the point in terms of the Amendment's enacting *equality*, I am making an obvious simplification. 'Equal protection of the laws' may stand for a concept more complicated than equality. I shall use the simplified version to state the general point, on order to avoid awkwardness of exposition—that is, so that I can express the distinction as holding between equality, and legislators' conception of equality. The distinction is valid for any concept, however complicated. The possible importance, in matters independent of that distinction, of the fact that the text of the Amendment uses 'equal protection', rather than equality, shall be discussed below.

[65] As Dworkin explains, that the clause did not prohibit segregated schooling was specifically mentioned during the Congress debates of the civil rights bill that preceded the Amendment; and the same Congress that adopted the Amendment also legislated for segregated schooling in the District of Columbia. See *Law's Empire*, 360. I shall discuss the contrast between objective content and legislators' subjective understanding, but the argument is meant to cover conventional understanding as well.

understanding would regard the clause consistent with gender-based discrimination or discrimination against homosexuals. So-called originalists have argued that the Framers' intention was therefore obviously to exclude all such practices or groups from the Amendment's protection, and reading the equality clause on a modern understanding of the concept that would extend its scope is politically driven 'invention' of the law, and therefore an abuse of judicial power.

Dworkin has effectively refuted the originalist argument. He has pointed out that, at most, we must attribute *conflicting* intentions to the Framers—their intention that everyone should be equally protected, and their intention that it should be permissible to deny blacks access to certain schools. We must decide which of those was the Framers' real, or dominant, intention, and the decision's grounds must be intention-independent. It would be circular to claim that one or the other was in fact the Framers' intention, because they intended that it should be.[66] The grounds for choosing the specific conviction that segregation is consistent with equal protection, rather than the abstract conviction that everyone should be equally protected, must be *theoretical*. Arguments in support of the choice must be part of a theory of law that explains why it should be better that law be individuated by specific convictions, rather than abstract ones.

Such an argument would be especially difficult to imagine, as long as it were supposed to justify identifying the law with some *mistaken conception* of equality: if it is assumed that the choice is between *conflicting* elements—equality and a misconception of it—both of which have a grounding in legislative thought, the natural conclusion seems to be that we should ignore the mistake. If I want to eat healthy food, and also think that butter is healthy, it would be bizarre to conclude that the latter thought is crucial, that my real intention is to have butter.[67]

4.2 *Avoiding Intention Problems?*

Perhaps a subtler argument for upholding the specific conviction could be built, an argument that avoids Dworkin's objection. Suppose that we have evidence that the following counterfactual is true: 'had the legislators considered the possibility that the clause would be interpreted to prohibit segregation, they would have expressly excluded segregation from its scope'.[68] If that is true, then it may seem that we

[66] See *Law's Empire*, 317–50; *A Matter of Principle*, 33–57. Note that concentrating on the choice among conflicting convictions presupposes an answer to the question whose convictions should count. That answer is not obvious—should it be the convictions of those who drafted a bill, or those who voted for it, or the groups whose political influence was reflected in the bill's adoption? Further, given that, even among each group, convictions will vary wildly (e.g. some may have voted for a bill as a result of party discipline, or in order to return a favour), should some highest common factor among the group count as the relevant conviction? Ignoring these difficulties works in favour of the originalist position, and hence strengthens the crucial argument against it that is presented in the text.

[67] This example is related to an example used by Dworkin in unpublished work.

[68] The counterfactual is due to Bernard Williams's remarks in a seminar. I do not know whether the discussion here addresses the point he was trying to make.

have some powerful reason not to apply the Amendment to segregation, a reason that avoids the complications associated with constructing real intentions out of the legislators' various beliefs. The Framers probably failed to foresee various ways in which the Amendment could be interpeted—how *could* they foresee, for example, that it could be interpreted so as to protect homosexuals? Provided that a counterfactual in the above style relevant to such proposed interpretations is supported by serious evidence, it would seem that interpreting the Amendment otherwise would frustrate what the Framers sought to achieve, simply by exploiting their (inevitable) oversight.

But neither can this argument avoid the question of concept attribution—whether the legislators sought to enact *equality*, or some other concept. For, if they did seek to do that, then their counterfactually supposed reaction over the prediction that it would interpreted in some or other way may still be *inconsistent* with their abstract project, and therefore insignificant. The counterfactual may appear to get around the problem of concept attribution by running together two very different grounds for the supposed legislative reaction. The first are *concept-dependent* grounds: they consist in legislators' beliefs about what equality requires. The second are *concept-independent* grounds: they consist in motivations for excluding something from the law's scope that are neutral with respect to the legislators' beliefs about the content of equality, and thus may well be consistent with it.

Suppose that I ask for a nutritious sandwich. Suppose further that, had I considered the possibility of being given a salmon sandwich, I would have expressly excluded it. Now I may have two different reasons for the exclusion. One could be that I thought that salmon is not nutritious, because of a confused view about what nutritious food really is. Another could be that I have some allergy, or simply hate fish, although I have no doubt that salmon is very nutritious. My request will be interpreted differently in each case. In the first case, nutrition is my sole objective, and my excluding salmon is a simple mistake: one could dispel my confusion, and then I would have no reason to reject a salmon sandwich any more.[69] In the second case, the exclusion would express, not a mistaken conception of what foods are nutritious, but a more complex objective: I want some of the nutritious foods that I happen to like. This complex objective does not make for a gerrymandered concept of the kind discussed in the preceding Chapter. The complex objective is satisfied by the combination of two conditions (nutritious and nice) in a coherent way, and the exception is principled—unlike the first case, where the exception is unprincipled *vis-à-vis* the simple objective. In the first case,

[69] Perhaps tact may require that one should not expose my confusion, and bring me something neutral, that is, both nutritious and consistent with my misconception of nutritiousness. (But what if there is no netural alternative?) The situation, nevertheless, need not carry over to legal interpretation. There, we are called to identify the law's *range*—we must be able to distinguish cases in which the law applies from those it does not—and we are bound to be tactless sometimes. A plausible theory of legislative authority proscribes dodging legislatures' political choices, not hurting legislators' feelings. Of course one may insist that a suitable conception of tact does come into legal interpretation as well; yet it takes political and moral argument to make such a conception of legislative authority plausible.

interpreting my wish so as to exclude salmon *would* make for a gerrymandered, non-genuine, concept (say, nutritious-and-not-salmon).

Of course, in both cases I assume that there is no other evidence against the proposed interpretations. It may well be the case that, in view of the apparent inconsistency between my nutrition and my salmon beliefs, and in the absence of any reason that explains it, one may research the issue further and conclude that it was not a nutritious, but a *light* meal that I had in mind—I was using the wrong word. In that case, no real inconsistency exists, since nutrition does not come into it at all. The point, then, is that some or other (genuine, non-gerrymandered) concept must be attributed in the light of the available evidence. Counterfactuals of the kind discussed belong with the sort of evidence that supports different attributions. But the exceptions set out in such counterfactuals cannot be decisive, unless they are supplemented by a general story that renders the exception principled and hence explicable.

This discussion should explain how the fact that we must often correct legislative (or judicial) misconceptions does not breach law's authority. Clearly, correcting will only take place in order to *respect* law's authority: to say that some misconception is identified is to say that the law in fact requires something different from what would appear by regarding the misconception as the law's determinant. Further, there is no pressure for finding for misconceptions, rather than finding a way to accommodate their contents as principled by characterizing them as good conceptions of some other concept. Here are some examples.

4.3 Legal Examples

First, take the 'no vehicles in the park' rule. Probably such a city ordinance should not be interpreted to prohibit ambulances taking shortcuts through the park. But that is not to say that ambulances are not vehicles. It is not the case that there is a special legal concept, related yet different to the concept of a vehicle, that picks out some but not all objects picked out by the usual concept. Rather, it is because we can think of no good reason for prohibiting ambulances, while we *can* think of good reasons for prohibiting taxis, that the ordinance should apply to the latter but not the former. Despite its apparent targeting of vehicles, the ordinance probably enacts a more complex objective—say, the regulation, rather than the outright ban, of traffic in the park. The point that some concept must be attributed does not mean that attribution must respect some word-to-concept correspondence. In fact, insistence that attribution is a substantive matter allows that some words may *not* stand for the concept they usually do. Rather, the point is that, whereas the above reasoning that justifies letting ambulances through matters, reasoning that the legislators did not have spacecraft in mind when they drafted the ordinance does not.

Stephen Munzer has criticized Michael Moore's view that natural kind concepts should be applied on the best scientific, rather than contemporaneous legislative, conception. Munzer tacitly assumes that concept-attribution questions are supposed to be settled syntactically, and sets out to prove that what legislators had in mind counts. He argues that a nineteenth century law imposing fishing quotas for environmental reasons must be interpreted to exclude whale fishing, if concept attribution is carried out without consulting mistaken legislative conceptions. But in this case the latter must be decisive, he argues, since whales cannot be excluded in a principled way.[70] However, to say that there can be no principled exclusion of whales is to say that the issue is not about what it is to be a fish. Mistaken theory of fish-hood prevalent when the statute was drafted, *explains* why the word 'fish' was mistakenly used to pick out marine life. Again, 'fish' in the statute does not stand for a special legal concept somewhat like, yet different than, fish. Rather, 'fish' stands for marine life or something to that effect. The important point is that what makes the legislators' view that whales should not be excluded count is the principle justifying the provision, in the light of which the view is not competitive with modern zoology. It is not a case of a mistaken view (as it would be if the legislative target *were* fish) that prevails so that including whales is somehow justified despite zoological error. If that were the case, the zoological error and the principle expressed in the law *would* be interdependent, and, *ceteris paribus*, the error should be discounted—*that* law should not apply to whaling.[71]

A second case of complicated attribution is illustrated by laws setting cut-off points, like the speed limit, driving or voting age, or taxable income bracket classifications. Speed limit laws are introduced to promote motorway safety.[72] However, the independent objective of having distinctions that are easy to determine and do not involve drivers' judgment also figures. Motorway safety depends on several factors like the driver, road and vehicle conditions, and speed, all of them varying together. The introduction of a speed limit is part of the project of breaking down the pursuit of safety into separate, easy to verify, requirements. This is not to say that safety is indeterminate—given the necessary information, there is no reason to suppose that all the factors that in fact make for safe driving cannot be determined. Notice that determining road safety in that fashion would result in a variable speed limit. However, the speed limit law does not refer to safety, picking it out by '70 mph'. On the most plausible interpretation, the relevant provision refers to *speed*, and enforces a technical speed limit—70 mph—specifically in order to avoid substantive disputes over safety. Even if 70 mph is manifestly bad as a mark of safety, there is no question of correcting legislative conception, because regulating traffic by means of such a strict criterion is justified

[70] 'Realistic Limits on Realist Interpretation', *58 S. Cal. L. R.*, 459–75, at 469–70.

[71] Munzer's general point that intention does count is valid: we can ignore misconceptions only on the assumption that the relevant concept is intended. Compare the point made in Ch. 2 to the effect that it is intention to pick out gold that allows discounting misconceptions of gold. It should be borne in mind nevertheless, that which intention to attribute is a theoretical matter.

[72] I ignore environmental or energy considerations for simplicity.

by safety-independent considerations.[73] This arrangement may be substantively wrong, in the sense that the law had better enforce substantive safety, rather than a technical speed limit together with other technical criteria of roadworthiness, driving ability, and so forth. But, on the most plausible interpretation, the law does the latter, and the complaint that it ought to not do so is an argument for repair, an argument about what the law should be, an argument about the *ratio* of the whole arrangement of safety management, not about the concept of safety alone, or any special legal concept—say, safety*.

Consequently, one cannot argue that the speed limit in such and such a case really was 73 mph (say, because weather conditions were especially good) or 64 mph (say, beacuse the driver was especially inexperienced), claiming that that speed was the true mark of motorway safety in the circumstances. Such an argument would ignore the law's independent objective of avoiding substantive safety evaluation, and so would not be a novel way of interpreting the law, but an altogether mistaken interpretation of the law. This is not to say, however, that no good challenge to routine understanding of the law may be raised. Suppose, for example, that car engineering improved so much that all cars were built to endure head-on collisions at 200 mph without injury to passengers.[74] It would be reasonable, then, to say that the true speed limit was now 100 mph—that proposal ***would*** respect the law's complex objective of safety and strict limits, and engage the background assumptions in the light of which the limit was originally set.

Much of tax law is typically full of technical criteria. Why should an extra £1 of income result in an abrupt bracket switch and so attract significantly more tax than its predecessor? Again, because the reason underlying the switch is not to do simply with substantive issues of how tax desert changes as income does, but also with the general justification (if any) for taxing by brackets (rather than, say, by flat rate, or by continuously progressive rates).[75] Again, arguing that the bracket system is silly or unjust is arguing about what the law should be, rather than what it is.

So none of these cases is a counterexample to the thesis that, as long as some concept is attributed to the law, mistaken understandings of that concept cannot count. In all these cases what blocks (when it does) the straightforward application of some candidate concept—vehicle, fish, road safety, and so forth—is not some view about the content of those concepts, but independent considerations within a

[73] Recall the discussion of the US Presidential candidacy limit in Ch. 5: again, making age important for maturity already renders the issue technical, moving it away form substantive questions of maturity. My argument is of course a substantive argument in legal interpretation, which is why the proposal to interpret '35' as 50 is wrong (if my argument is sound), rather than incoherent.

[74] I ignore economic considerations for simplicity.

[75] Cut-off points are related to slippery slope arguments. I cannot fully discuss slippery slopes here. See Bernard Williams, 'Which Slopes are Slippery?', in Lockwood, M. (ed.), ***Moral Dilemmas in Modern Medicine***, 126–37. Note that the use of strict cut-off points does not entail that there is no non-arbitrary point that distinguishes the top from the bottom of a slope: it may just be that the point is difficult to establish, as with the speed limit case discussed in the text. So the difficulty is epistemic, rather than substantive, but substantive reasons may dictate that we avoid the epistemic risk.

more complex legislative objective. Questions of these laws' application are not properly represented as being about those candidate concepts—attributing those concepts to the law distorts it.[76] The thesis holds about concepts that *are* properly attributed, and is not biased towards attributing any particular concept, much less towards attributing abstract or intrinsically contestable ones.

In fact, the discussion suggests an explanation for the special vulnerability of constitutional jurisprudence to revisionary challenges, as opposed to the relative security of the tax or the road traffic domain. Road traffic and tax law involve a great deal of litigation on technical issues—say, whether a vehicle's speed was properly recorded, or whether one can claim tax deduction on several schemes concurrently or disjunctively—far removed from the abstract political principles governing these areas of the law. On the other hand, the constitution sets up the most abstract political framework, and thus invites theoretical challenge. Distinguishing areas of the law in this way is almost a platitude that would not be worth repeating, if it were not for a rival explanation that could well be proposed.

On that rival explanation, the law's content is fixed in more or less the same way across the board—by sets of criteria conventionally accepted. In the constitutional domain, however, conflicting political interests are bound to break the consensus underscoring conventional application. In those cases, then, the law is bound to be largely indeterminate: the 'penumbra' will be relatively large. Further, shifting political interests are bound to erode agreement in cases in which agreement used to prevail, thus calling for a revision of the law's content. *Brown* should be seen as a *change* in the Amendment's content, brought about by the collapse of the past agreement to the effect that equal protection has nothing to do with segregation; crucially, the collapse should be seen as brought about by political pressure and expediency unrelated to the demand for equality, rather than by conceptual pressure about the content of equality.

That explanation, then, throws a special challenge to objectivists who deny that the law's content is fixed by criteria. Objectivists may be able to claim that they explain constitution-related revisions of opinion better (viz. as driven by better theories of the content of the political principles involved). But the challenge is to explain what is supposed to be a surprising fact on the objectivist account, namely that in much of the law little such revisionary activity takes place. If objectivists cannot explain the prevalence of easy cases there, then the superiority of their explanation of hard constitutional cases may be undermined. It is for this reason that an objectivist response is due, and it runs as follows: it is not the case that in some areas of the law there can be no challenge on the grounds that a concept involved in the law is misunderstood and therefore misapplied; such challenges can

[76] Again, this is not to say that problems about the concepts that *are* appropriately attributed to these laws cannot arise. For example, assuming that public interest supports allowing ambulances in the park, whether army vehicles should also be allowed may turn on what public interest properly requires. The point is that there seems to be no deep issue about the concept of a vehicle, not there there can be no deep issue at all.

be raised anywhere.[77] Rather, many cases do not concern the concepts they appear to do. They are thus not cases in which a normally contestable concept is immunized against revisionary attacks; rather they are not about such a concept at all.

4.4 Is the Distinction Genuine?

I drew a distinction concerning attempts to block the application of a concept in the way an objective account of the concept's content would require: the distinction is between trying to block by appeal to some concept-dependent consideration like some special understanding of the concept (whether the legislators' or that reflected in the extant conventions); and trying to block by appeal to concept-independent considerations like a distinct objective of the law involved. I argued that only the second kind is admissible; and that cases in which the block does go through are indeed of the second kind—that examples which appear to be cases of some concept that is, as it were, legitimately misapplied are really cases which are not, or not simply, about that concept.

The most interesting objection that can be raised is that the distinction is fake. Consider the Fourteenth Amendment again. I accepted the argument that the concept of equal protection is inconsistent with segregation, and that the Amendment should be interpreted to prohibit segregated schooling. The objection here is: what makes it the case that 'segregation' and 'equal protection' stand for inconsistent concepts? Why cannot there be an equally good description of the issue under which segregation can be allowed through in the same fashion that ambulances are allowed in the park, despite the apparent conflict with the prohibition of 'vehicles'? Perhaps segregation cannot be made consistent with equal protection, but may be made consistent with some other more complicated concept that resembles equal protection of the laws, but under which it is permissible for racially different communities to keep contact among them to a minimum—for example, some more complicated concept that would support the interpretation that the Amendment requires that there be state schools endowed with the same resources for each community, but allows the communities to keep themselves apart if either so wishes.

The point raised by the objection is not that there is some doubt whether the Amendment was in fact interpreted correctly in Brown; rather, the point is that there is no fact by virtue of which the idea that segregation is consistent with 'equal protection' must be dismissed as a mistake about *equal protection.* If interpreting the

[77] Apparently the IRS in the US has been recently challenging the 'formal' criterion of what counts as income generated in the US, and has been arguing that a substantive judgment is called for, which may neutralize some tax-avoidance schemes. I am indebted to Mark Greenburg for this example.

Notice that classifying cases as constitutional—or tax-related—involves a heuristic simplification. Cases' resolution is governed by the law as a whole; cases may raise special constitutional or tax law *issues.*

law requires attributing some concept—if, that is, which concept the law uses is not given by convention but must be substantively established—then the evidence in which we find the notion that the Amendment and segregation are consistent is *part of the basis for attributing some concept.* We could dismiss that evidence as expressing a mistake about equal protection, if we had other, independent grounds for identifying the issue as being about equal protection. But those grounds, if any, can only consist in the same type of evidence as the evidence that we treat as a mistaken conception of equal protection. Any piece of evidence can count either way, as support for attributing a certain concept or as a mistake about what some other concept requires. For example, the hypothesis that the Framers would have expressly excluded segregation from the Fourteenth Amendment's scope can count as representing legislators' error about equal protection as much as it can count as grounds for *not* attributing equal protection, properly understood, but some different concept to the Amendment's content. How can evidence, the objector continues, that can go either way make one or the other conclusion better?

The argument is partly correct: it is right to say that there is only one *type* of evidence that grounds our attribution of concepts and our accusations of error—other laws, judicial decisions, and other aspects of the legal and political background, to name a few. Consequently the distinction between attributing some concept and attributing a misconception cannot be captured in an *a priori* formula, but is a complicated, theoretical question. But this is not, however, to say that the distinction is fake.

An especially difficult case can be built around the assumption that equality requires economic equality.[78] Attributing equality to the Fourteenth Amendment should therefore imply that the Amendment must be applied to ensure that all US citizens are equal in terms of economic resources, and that we must consider what appear to be fundamental commitments to the sanctity of property, the principle of succession, and freedom of contract, among other things, as mistaken views about what equality allows or requires. We should consider, in other words, the commitment to equality as fundamental to the US political structure, and the commitments expressed in the doctrines of the freedom of contract, succession, and the rest as *interdependent* with it, as part of the same commitment that led to the adoption of the equality clause. The proposal is not *prima facie* incoherent: political theory prevalent in the past two centuries would treat economic inequality as perfectly consistent with equality, would treat, that is, equality as essentially captured by equal respect of people's *desires*, for example, as expressed in the doctrine of the freedom of contract, irrespective of the unequal size of their initial endowments. Such theories would not be independent of the concept of equality, but would consist in attempts to give content to that very concept. The prevalence of such theories would explain the existence of equality provisions side by side with contract and succession provisions that preserve or perpetuate inequalities.

[78] Ronald Dworkin suggested this example.

On the assumption that equality extends to economic equality, the principles behind contract and succession law are seen as a hangover from medieval political structure, within which no-one thought that all men are equal anyway, and confused political philosophy should not be allowed to cover the inconsistency with the proper conception of equality. Consequently, to propose that equality requires economic equality puts pressure to scrap contract, succession, and most other parts of the law, and replace them with an alternative coherent system. Such a reform would have to explain away most of the modern political structure as a vast if explicable mistake, as well as present any other parts of it that escape as instances of the 'right' practice of equality. Implausible as it is, this task is not inconceivable.

On the other hand, still on the assumption that equality includes economic equality, the law of contract, succession, and so forth may be treated as evidence that it is not equality but some other, more restricted concept that the Amendment uses, a concept under which no inconsistencies arise. The problem, however, with this conciliatory proposal is that there is no obvious candidate concept. Provided that the conciliatory proposal also accepts that the Amendment enacts some fundamental principle concerning the US political structure, that it expresses something about the relative position of citizens in that structure very close to the concept of equality, there do not seem to be many different concepts to choose from. But if a genuine, non-gerrymandered, concept can be attributed in relation to which the principles behind contract and succession are relatively independent, then the conciliatory proposal may be better.

Both ways of treating this example illustrate a general problem with outlandish interpretive proposals, namely that they create ever increasingly implausible repercussions in interdependent areas. Concept attribution is a task that typically engages an entire network of related practices that figure in novel proposals' explanatory domain. A novel proposal for the understanding of a concept must make sense, and indeed make better sense, of an array of practices that have been developing together with the target concept. This task cannot be finessed by invoking special, *ad hoc* concepts—concepts don't lie around, as it were, to be picked up in support of different interpretations.

Consider another suggestion. If it were true that fetuses are persons, then there would be a case for not attributing the concept of a person to the Amendment, rather than conceiving the fact that abortion and abortifacient contraception are not treated as murder, or that aborted fetuses have never counted in succession lines, as the result of a misconception of personhood. If fetuses are in fact persons, then the belief current during the Amendment's introduction that they are not must be treated as explaining why the word 'person' was used *mal à propos* to pick out, say, humans with rights and interests.[79] The alternative—attributing the

[79] Fortunately, there is no good reason to accept that fetuses *are* persons: as Dworkin suggests in *Life's Dominion*, everyone thinks that persons have rights and interests, but it is exceedingly difficult to claim that fetuses do.

concept of a person to the Fourteenth Amendment and treating fetuses as persons—seems unconvincing precisely inasmuch as having an abortion does not appear to be as bad as killing a child, an appearance this alternative must explain away.

Of course, the objection may be pressed by claiming that my examples are not illustrating any special difficulty—that we *can*, if we so wish, *make* the claims that I presented as preposterous—and that there could be no fact by virtue of which they would be worse than the apparently more reasonable conclusions. But then the objection would be exposed as an indeterminacy objection of the kind discussed in the preceding Chapter. It would become the claim that if interpretation is constrained by facts that are themselves interpretive—if constraints are themselves substantive and therefore open to doubt and revision—then there can be no distinction between correct and incorrect interpretation. As I argued in Chapter 5, that objection depends on the assumption that only unassailable truths—analytic or conventional—can serve as real constraints. If the conventionalist solution did work, the objector would be satisfied: there would be an *a priori* criterion of the distinction between beliefs about a concept, and beliefs about different concepts, namely whether a belief figures in the conventional specification of the content of a concept. But, as I have argued, the conventionalist solution does not work: conventional constraints cannot coherently confer determinacy upon interpretation. And anyway the belief that only *a priori* constraints are good constraints is a philosophical prejudice.

In sum, it is not true that arguing that a concept must apply objectively as long it is attributed to the law makes law hostage to ethical theory and diminishes legislative power to legislate at will. All that the argument blocks is a special type of supposed constraint—legislators' subjective or conventional understanding—not despite, but in order to respect, legislative authority. The thesis is rather commonsensical and even banal, and it can only be misuderstood for an argument to *replace* the law with politics or ethics by *assuming* that the law is identified by conventional understanding, so that failure to respect *that* amounts to failure to respect the law. But an argument that the law involves equality is an argument about what the law *is*, and the only respectable way to resist it is by engaging it in substantive criticism.

5. CONSERVATISM

The assumption that law is individuated by conventional understanding underlies another line of argument. This time, instead of arguing that the objectivist picture will tend to modernize conventional understanding of political principles in disrespect of legislative authority, it is argued that objectivism will *fail* to modernize such principles despite the fact that there is no authoritative constraint against doing so. Objectivists, on this new argument, will tend to perpetuate political arrangements where conventionalists will find themselves able to reconstruct them.

The argument is deployed in connection with the notion of judicial discretion.[80] In the context of a deeply unjust regime, the argument goes, the conventionalist view at least allows for repair to take place at the boundaries of the law by granting discretion to the judges. Objectivist models enjoin instead the judge to further the regime's unjust cause even where he has the opportunity, by virtue of the law's own vagueness, to counter it.

This form of the objection takes for granted much of what it is supposed to establish. What is to happen at the law's boundaries presupposes a way of identifying what the law's range is, and this is what the objectivist model proposes to establish. The model argues that there is no important difference between 'easy' and 'hard' cases, insofar as both depend on identifying what the law is in the same way—it simply so happens that our provisional theories match the law in a more obvious way in the former cases. Surely enough, if the content of the law were identifiable in the way the objector presupposes—on the basis of legislators' or conventional understanding—then the model would reduce to promotion of injustice, if that happens to be the mark of the regime's understanding of its laws, since the emergence of novel cases would be essentially unregulated.

The real issue, then, is how to characterize unclear cases, in which objectivism is supposed to favour deciding in a way that perpetuates injustice. For the objector's conservatism accusation to stick, it must be the case that there *is* one way to decide a case that is most consistent with past practice, one way for whose requirement by the law there exist powerful arguments. If that is accepted—if, in effect, what the law requires is given—then the objectivist has nothing further to say: the model is exhausted in finding what the law is, and is non-committal on what one will do next. Conversely, the discretion doctrine poses as a conceptual point about *establishing* the content of the law; once that is established, the injunction to ignore it is not conventionalism's prerogative.

It may be thought that we can formulate the conservatism point so that it does not presuppose that the law is already identified. It may be, for instance, that we know that the law is generally unjust by seeing the casebook, and seeing that in the (easy) cases so far the law was, say, racist; but the present case, where no clear answer seems available, gives us an opportunity to avoid injustice without supposing that the law actually requires an unjust decision. But if what the law requires (if it does require something at all) in that case is not clear, then perhaps it is not bad: perhaps the judge who perseveres will find that the law actually allows a black to win the case. If, on the other hand, we think that the contingency of finding a non-racist requirement is implausible, then this amounts to saying that we tend to accept the opposite reading (that the law is probably racist) in the case at hand.

[80] Cf. Raz, 'Dworkin: a New Link in the Chain', *74 Cal. L.R.*, 1103–19; Alexander, 'Striking Back at the Empire', *6 Law and Philsophy*, 419–38.

Of course the objector will not accept that the prediction that a case decided in a way more consistent with past cases will have racist consequences amounts to a prediction that *the law* has racist consequences in that case. He will insist that, since deciding the case thus is not *clearly*—i.e. beyond all doubt—required by the law, then it is not required by the law at all. Where the law is not clear, the judge is pictured as having a discretionary choice between deciding consistently with the past, undoubtedly racist, cases, or going for reform. But the objector must concede that the decision most consistent with past decisions is the racist one (or else there will be no question of perpetuating injustice). So he needs to show why there is no law in unclear cases, despite there being only one way of deciding that is consistent with other, clear, ones.

So we are back at the heart of the controversy. Is consistency with undisputed cases a sufficient condition for a decision's reflecting the law in a novel case; or is it also necessary that everyone agree that it does reflect the law? The conservatism objection is not a new objection, an extra difficulty for objectivism. Rather, it amounts to a restatement of conventionalism: in hard cases, there is no law.

Finally, the point may be recast along the lines of 'interpretive positivism' discussed in the preceding Chapter.[81] There is a political argument, on this version, in favour of treating controversial cases as if there were no law. Controversy marks the limits of the law, but not for semantic reasons: the objector now accepts that semantic considerations militate in favour of there *being* law in those cases—after all, what is the controversy about? Rather, the objector claims that it is an independent political desideratum not to have controversial law, and this desideratum supplies an extra constraint as to what can count as law, which is ignored by objectivists. Controversies are about the content of statutes, but controversial views on the content of statutes cannot count as law.

On one reading, anti-conservatism may pose as part of the desirability of that extra constraint. On that reading, a reason why we should not count controversial interpretations as law is precisely that we may avoid, in this way, extending wicked principles outside settled cases. But this cannot be a serious argument: if interpretive positivism avoids injustice outside settled cases, it is committed to injustice *in* settled cases. By contrast, objectivism's disrespect for consensus may work against injustice there: it may avoid counting *settled* opinion as constituting the law, and take the opportunity to cast doubt on easy decisions which have wicked results. Interpretive positivism may be worse than some form of 'conspiracy objectivism'—a thesis that it is politically desirable not to respect consensus in wicked regimes.

So interpretive positivism can get no mileage out of its supposed anti-conservative effect, and its merits must be judged independently of the point regarding conservatism. Further, if my arguments in the preceding Chapter

[81] See Ch. 5, section 11.

concerning the conceptual difficulties that mar interpretive postivism are correct, interpretive positivism does not work at all. It asks us to *pretend* that there is no law in the context of a controversy, but it fails to supply a coherent justification why this should be the case.

References

Alexander, L., 'Striking Back at the Empire', *6 Law and Philosophy* (1987), 419–38.

Amselek, P. and MacCormick, D. N. (eds.), *Controversies About Law's Ontology*, Edinburgh, Edinburgh University Press 1991.

Baker, G., 'Defeasibility and Meaning', *in* Hacker, P. and Raz, J. (eds.), *Law, Morality and Society.*

Bennett, J., *Locke, Berkeley, Hume: Central Themes*, Oxford, Clarendon Press 1971.

Blackburn, S., 'Rule-Following and Moral Realism', *in* Holtzman, S. M. and Leich, C. M. (eds.), *Wittgenstein: to Follow a Rule.*

——— *Spreading the Word*, Oxford, Clarendon Press 1984.

——— 'Errors and the Phenomenology of Value', *in* Honderich, T. (ed.), *Morality and Objectivity.*

——— 'Morals and Modals', in McDonald, G. and Wright, C. (eds.), *Fact, Science and Morality.*

——— 'How to Be an Ethical Antirealist', *in* French, P. A., Uehling Jr., T. E., Wettstein, H. K. (eds.), *12 Midwest Studies of Philosophy*, Minneapolis, University of Minnesota Press (1988), 361–76.

Brink, D. O., 'Legal Theory, Legal Interpretation, and Judicial Review', *17 Philosophy and Public Affairs* (1988), 105–48.

——— *Moral Realism and the Foundations of Ethics*, Cambridge, Cambridge University Press 1989.

——— 'Semantics and Legal Interpretation; (Further Thoughts)', *2 Canadian Journal of Law and Jurisprudence* (1989), 181–91.

Brint, M. and Weaver, W. (eds.), *Pragmatism in Law and Society*, Boulder, San Francisco, Westview Press 1991.

Burge, T., 'Individualism and the Mental', *in* French, P. A., Uehling Jr., T. E., Wettstein, H. K. (eds.), *4 Midwest Studies in Philosophy*, Minneapolis, University of Minnesota Press (1979), 73–121.

——— 'Two Thought Experiments Discussed', *23 Notre Dame Journal of Formal Logic* (1982), 284–93.

——— 'Other Bodies' *in* Woodfield, A. (ed.), *Thought and Object.*

——— 'Individualism and Psychology', *45 Philosophical Review* (1986), 3–45.

——— 'Intellectual Norms and Foundations of Mind', *83 Journal of Philosophy* (1986), 697–720.

——— 'Cartesian Error and the Objectivity of Perception', *in* Pettit, P. and McDowell, J. (eds.), *Subject, Thought, and Context.*

——— 'Wherein is Language Social?', *in* George, A. (ed.), *Reflections on Chomsky.*

Burton, S., 'Ronald Dworkin and Legal Positivism', *73 Iowa Law Review* (1987), 109–29.

Cavell, S., *The Claim of Reason*, Oxford, OUP 1979.

Chang, R., 'The Frege–Geach Point and Non-Cognitivism', unpublished manuscript.

Child, W., *Causality, Interpretation, and the Mind*, Oxford, Clarendon Press 1994.

Dancy, J. (ed.), *Perceptual Knowledge*, Oxford, OUP 1988.

Davidson, D., *Essays on Actions and Events*, Oxford, Clarendon Press 1982.

——— *Inquiries Into Truth and Interpretation*, Oxford, Clarendon Press 1984.

——— 'A Coherence Theory of Truth and Knowledge', *in* Le Pore, E. (ed.), *Truth and Interpretation*.

——— 'Knowing One's Own Mind', *60 American Philosophical Association Proceedings and Addresses* (1987), 441–58.

——— 'The Structure and Content of Truth', *87 Journal of Philosophy* (1990), 279–328.

Dennett, D., 'Real Patterns', *88 Journal of Philosophy* (1991), 27–51.

——— *Consciousness Explained*, Boston, Little, Brown 1991.

Dummett, M., *Frege: Philosophy of Language*, London, Duckworth 1973.

Dworkin, R. M., *Taking Rights Seriously*, London, Duckworth 1978.

——— 'Law as Interpretation', *60 Texas Law Review* (1982), 527–50.

——— 'My Reply to Stanley Fish (and Walter Benn Michaels): Please Don't Talk About Objectivity Any More', *in* Mitchell, W. J. T. (ed.), *The Politics of Interpretation*.

——— *A Matter of Principle*, Oxford, OUP 1985.

——— *Law's Empire*, London, Fontana Press 1986.

——— 'Legal Theory and the Problem of Sense', *in* Gavison, R. (ed.), *Issues in Contemporary Legal Philosophy*.

——— 'Bork's Jurisprudence', *57 Chicago Law Review* (1990), 657–77.

——— 'On Gaps in the Law', *in* Amselek, P. and MacCormick, D. N. (eds.), *Controversies About Law's Ontology*.

——— 'Pragmatism, Right Answers, and True Banality', *in* Brint, M. and Weaver, W. (eds.), *Pragmatism in Law and Society*.

——— *Life's Dominion*, London, Harper Collins 1993.

Evans, G., *The Varieties of Reference* (edited by J. McDowell), Oxford, OUP 1982.

——— *Collected Essays*, Oxford, OUP 1985.

Fish, S., 'Working on the Chain Gang: Interpretation in Law and Literature', *60 Texas Law Review* (1982), 551–67.

——— 'Wrong Again', *62 Texas Law Review* (1983), 299–316.

——— 'Still Wrong After All These Years', *6 Law and Philosophy* (1987), 401–18.

——— *Doing What Comes Naturally*, Oxford, OUP 1989.

——— 'Almost Pragmatism: the Jurisprudence of Richard Posner, Richard Rorty and Ronald Dworkin', *in* Brint and Weaver (eds.), *Pragmatism in Law and Society*.

Frege, G., *Logical Investigations*, transl. by P. T. Geach and R. H. Stoothoff, Oxford, Blackwell 1977.

Gavison, R. (ed.), *Issues in Contemporary Legal Philosophy: the Influence of H. L. A. Hart*, Oxford, Clarendon Press 1987.

Geach, P. T., *Logic Matters*, Oxford, Blackwell 1972.

George, A. (ed.), *Reflections on Chomsky*, Oxford, Blackwell 1989.

Gibbard, A., *Wise Choices, Apt Feelings; a Theory of Normative Judgement*, Oxford, Clarendon Press 1990.

Goldstein, L. (ed.), *Precedent in Law*, Oxford, OUP 1987.

Goodman, N., *Fact, Fiction and Forecast*, Cambridge, Harvard University Press 1979.

Greenawalt, K., 'How Law Can Be Determinate', 38 *UCLA Law Review* (1990), 1–86.

Greenberg, M., 'The Nature of Law: the Role of Values in Legal Interpretation and Implications for Dworkin's Legal Theory', Oxford B.Phil. thesis 1990.

Hacker, P. and Raz, J. (eds.), *Law, Morality and Society: Essays in Honour of H. L. A. Hart*, Oxford, Clarendon Press 1977.

Hart, H. L. A., 'Ascription of Responsibility and Rights', *49 Proceedings of the Aristotelian Society* (1948–49), 171–94.

——— *The Concept of Law*, Oxford, Clarendon Press 1961.

——— *Essays on Bentham*, Oxford, Clarendon Press 1982.

——— *Essays in Jurisprudence and Philosophy*, Oxford, OUP 1983.

Holtzman, S. H. and Leich, C. M. (eds.), *Wittgenstein: to Follow a Rule*, London, Routledge and Kegan Paul 1981.

Honderich, T. (ed.), *Morality and Objectivity*, London, Routledge and Kegan Paul 1985.

Hornsby, J., 'Descartes, Rorty and the Mind–Body Fiction', *in* Malachowski, A. (ed.), *Reading Rorty*.

Hurd, H., 'Sovereignty in Silence', *99 Yale Law Journal* (1990), 945–1028.

Hurley, S., *Natural Reasons*, New York, OUP 1989.

——— 'Coherence, Hypothetical Cases and Precedent', *10 Oxford Journal of Legal Studies* (1990), 221–51.

Jackson, F. and Pettit, P., 'Functionalism and Broad Content', *97 Mind* (1988), 381–400.

Kermode, F., *History and Value*, Oxford, OUP 1988.

Kress, K., 'The Interpretive Turn', *97 Ethics* (1987), 834–60.

——— 'Legal Indeterminacy', *77 California Law Review* (1989), 283–337.

Kripke, S., *Naming and Necessity*, Oxford, Blackwell 1980.

——— 'A Puzzle About Belief' *in* Margalit, A. (ed.), *Meaning and Use*, reprinted *in* Salmon, N. and Soames, S. (eds.), *Propositions and Attitudes*.

——— *Wittgenstein on Rules and Private Language*, Oxford, Blackwell 1982.

Kroon, F., 'Theoretical Terms and the Causal View of Reference', *63 Australasian Journal of Philosophy* (1985), 143–66.

Lane, J., 'The Poetics of Legal Interpretation', *87 Columbia Law Review* (1987), 197–216.

LePore, E. (ed.), *Truth and Interpretation: Perspectives on the Philosophy of Donald Davidson*, Oxford, Blackwell 1986.

Lear, J., 'Leaving the World Alone', *79 Journal of Philosophy* (1982), 382–403.

——— 'The Disappearing "We"', *58 Arististotelian Society Supplementary Volume* (1984), 219–42.

Lewis, D., *Convention*, Oxford, Blackwell 1969.

——— 'New Work for the Theory of Universals', *61 Australasian Journal of Philosophy* (1983), 343–77.

——— 'Putnam's Paradox', *62 Australasian Journal of Philosophy* (1984), 221–36.

Lockwood, M. (ed.), *Moral Dilemmas in Modern Medicine*, Oxford, OUP 1985.

Luntley, M., *Language, Logic and Experience*, Open Court, La Salle, 1988.

Lycan, W., *Judgement and Justification*, Cambridge, Cambridge University Press 1988.

MacCormick, D. N., *Legal Reasoning and Legal Theory*, Oxford, OUP 1978.

——— *H. L. A. Hart*, London, Edward Arnold, 1981.

McCulloch, G., *The Game of the Name*, Oxford, OUP 1989.

McDonald, G. and Wright, C. (eds.), *Fact, Science and Morality*, Oxford, Blackwell 1986.

McDowell, J., 'On the Sense and Reference of a Proper Name', *86 Mind* (1977), 159–85.

——— 'Are Moral Requirements Hypothetical Imperatives?', *52 Aristotelian Society Supplementary Volume* (1978), 13–29.

——— 'Non-Cognitivism and Rule-Following', *in* Holtzman, S. H. and Leich, C. M. (eds.), *Wittgenstein: to Follow a Rule.*

——— 'Criteria, Defeasibility and Knowledge', *68 Proceedings of the British Academy* (1982), 455–79; extended version *in* Dancy J. (ed.), *Perceptual Knowledge.*

——— 'Aesthetic Value, Objectivity and the Fabric of the World', *in* Schaper, E. (ed.), *Pleasure, Preference and Value.*

——— '*De Re* Senses', *34 Philosophical Quarterly* (1984), 283–94; reprinted *in* Wright, C. (ed.), *Frege: Tradition and Influence.*

——— 'Wittgenstein on Following a Rule', *58 Synthèse* (1984), 325-63.

——— 'Values and Secondary Qualities', *in* Honderich, T. (ed.), *Morality and Objectivity.*

——— 'Singular Thought and the Extent of Inner Space', *in* Pettit, P. and McDowell, J. (eds.), *Subject, Thought, and Context.*

——— 'In Defence of Modesty', *in* Taylor, B. (ed.), *Dummett: Contribution to Philosophy.*

——— *Mind and World*, Cambridge, Harvard University Press 1994.

McGinn, C., 'Charity, Interpretation and Belief', *74 Journal of Philosophy* (1977), 521–35.

——— 'Rigid Designation and Semantic Value, *32 Philosophical Quarterly* (1982), 107–15.

——— *The Subjective View*, Oxford, OUP 1983.

——— 'Radical Interpretation and Epistemology', *in* LePore, E. (ed.), *Truth and Interpretation.*

——— *Mental Content*, Oxford, Blackwell 1989.

Mackie, J. L., *Problems from Locke*, Oxford, OUP 1976.

——— *Ethics: Inventing Right and Wrong*, Harmondsworth, Penguin, 1977.

Malachowski, A. (ed.), *Reading Rorty*, Oxford, Blackwell 1990.

Margalit, A. (ed.), *Meaning and Use*, Dordrecht, D. Reidel 1979.

Mitchell, W. J. T. (ed.), *The Politics of Interpretation*, Chicago and London, Chicago University Press 1983.

Moore, A. W. (ed.), *Meaning and Reference*, Oxford, OUP 1994.

Moore, M., 'A Natural Law Theory of Interpretation', *58 Southern California Law Review* (1985), 277–398.

——— 'Precedent, Induction and Ethical Generalization' *in* Goldstein, L. (ed.), *Precedent in Law.*

——— 'The Interpretive Turn in Modern Theory; a Turn for the Worse?', *41 Stanford Law Review* (1989), 871–957.

Moser, P. (ed.), *A Priori Knowledge*, Oxford, OUP 1987.

Munzer, S., 'Realistic Limits on Realist Interpretation', *58 Southern California Law Revieew* (1985), 459–75.

Nagel, T., *The View from Nowhere*, Oxford, OUP 1986.

Nelken, D., 'The Truth about Law's Truth', UCL Working Papers 7, 1989 (mimeo), University College, London.

Nozick, R., *Philosophical Explanations*, Oxford, OUP 1981.

Peterson, G. (ed.), *The 10 Tanner Lectures on Human Values*, Salt Lake City, University of Uteah Press and Cambridge, Cambridge University Press, 1988.

Pettit, P., 'Realism and Response-Dependence', *100 Mind* (1991), 587–626.

Pettit, P. and McDowell, J. (eds.), *Subject, Thought, and Context*, Oxford, OUP 1986.

Postema, G., 'Coordination and Convention at the Foundations of Law', *11 Journal of Legal Studies* (1982), 165–203.

——— 'The Normativity of Law', *in* Gavison, R. (ed.), *Issues in Contemporary Legal Philosophy.*

——— '"Protestant" Interpretation and Social Practices', *6 Law and Philosophy* (1987), 283–319.

Putnam, H., 'Meaning and Reference', *70 Journal of Philosophy* (1973), 699–711, reprinted *in* Moore, A. (ed.), *Meaning and Reference.*

——— *Mind, Language and Reality*, Cambridge, Cambridge University Press 1975.

——— *Reason, Truth and History*, Cambridge, Cambridge University Press 1981.

——— *Realism and Reason*, Cambridge, Cambridge University Press 1983.

——— *Realism with a Human Face*, Cambridge and London, Harvard University Press 1990.

——— 'Sense, Nonsense and the Senses: an Inquiry into the Powers of the Human Mind', *91 Journal of Philosophy* (1994), 445–517.

Quine, W. v. O., 'Two Dogmas of Empiricism', reprinted *in* Moser, A. (ed.), *A Priori Knowledge.*

——— *Word and Object*, Cambridge, MIT Press 1960.

Raz, J., *The Authority of Law*, Oxford, Clarendon Press 1979.

——— 'Authority, Law and Morality', *68 The Monist* (1985), 295–324.

——— 'Dworkin: a New Link in the Chain', *74 California Law Review* (1986), 1103–19.

Rorty, R., *Philosophy and the Mirror of Nature*, Oxford, Blackwell 1980.

——— *Contingency, Irony and Solidarity*, Cambridge, Cambridge University Press 1989.

Ruben, D.-H., *The Metaphysics of the Social World*, London, Routledge and Kegan Paul 1985.

Salmon, N., *Reference and Essence*, Oxford, Blackwell 1982.

Salmon, N. and Soames, S. (eds.), *Propositions and Attitudes*, Oxford, OUP 1988.

Schaper, E. (ed.), *Pleasure, Preference and Value*, Cambridge, Cambridge University Press 1983.

Seabright, P., 'Explaining Cultural Divergence: a Wittgensteinian Paradox', *84 Journal of Philosophy* (1987), 11–27.

Strawson, P. F., *Individuals*, New York, Methuen 1959.

——— *Skepticism and Naturalism: Some Varieties*, London, Methuen 1985.

Stroud, B., 'Wittgenstein and Logical Necessity', *in* Moser, A. (ed.), *A Priori Knowledge.*

——— 'The Study of Human Nature and the Subjectivity of Value' *in* Peterson, G. (ed.), *10 The Tanner Lectures on Human Values.*

Taylor, B., *Dummett: Contribution to Philosophy*, Dordrecht, M. Nijhoff 1987.

Tushnet, M., 'A Note on the Revival of Textualism in Constitutional Theory', *58 Southern California Law Review*, (1985), 683–700.

Vesey, G. (ed.), *Idealism: Past and Present*, Cambridge, Cambridge University Press 1982.

Wiggins, D., *Sameness and Substance*, Oxford, Blackwell 1980.

——— *Needs, Values, Truth*, Oxford, Blackwell 1987.

——— 'Moral Cognitivism, Moral Relativism and Motivating Moral Beliefs', *91 Proceedings of the Aristotelian Society* (1990–91), 61–86.

Williams, B., *Descartes: the Project of Pure Enquiry*, Harmondsworth, Penguin 1978.

——— *Moral Luck*, Cambridge, Cambridge University Press 1981.

——— *Ethics and the Limits of Philosophy*, London, Fontana Press 1985.

——— 'Which Slopes are Slippery?', *in* Lockwood, M. (ed.), *Moral Dilemmas in Modern Medicine.*

Williams, M., 'Coherence, Justification and Truth', *34 Review of Metaphysics* (1980), 243–72.

Woodfield, A. (ed.), *Thought and Object*, Oxford, OUP 1982.

Wright, C., *Wittgenstein on the Foundation of Mathematics*, London, Duckworth 1980.

——— 'Anti-Realist Semantics: the Role of Criteria', *in* Vesey, G. (ed.), *Idealism: Past and Present.*

——— 'Second Thoughts About Criteria', *58 Synthèse* (1984), 383–405.

——— (ed.), *Frege: Tradition and Influence*, Oxford, Blackwell 1986.

——— *Truth and Objectivity*, Cambridge, Harvard University Press 1992.

Index

adjudication
  classification and 49
  Hart's semantics and 55
altruism 97
anti-realism 5–6, 77–80
appearances 100–2
Archimedes 102–3

Baker, G., 53, 65, 69, 78
beliefs
  ethics and 104–5, 107, 112–13, 120
  Fish and revision of 171–72
  knowledge as 111
  Kripke's semantics and 25, 27
  Moore and 184
bias 188 *see also* discrimination, equality, prejudice
Blackburn, S. 97–100, 130
  Wittgenstein and 151, 157–8
Brink, D.
  artifacts and 89
  Kripke-Putnam semantics and 5
  realism and 6–7
Burge, T.
  characterizations and 75
  classification and 50
  common nouns and 8, 9
  community and 123
  criteria and 37
  Criterial Model and 3
  Descartes and 39
  designatum and 87
  individualistic contents and 39
  social context and 34–8
  social environment and 34, 36
Burton, S. 141

cases
  easy 12, 140–3, 147n., 194, 199–200
    Wittgenstein and 157–9
  hard 139–40, 140–3, 194, 199–200
causality
  choice and 98
  explanations and 104, 105, 107, 111, 122
  naturalism and 105
  relations and 104
  scepticism and 98
circularity 117–21
choice
  causality and 98
  necessity and 98
charity 42–4
civil rights
  intention and 188–90
  USA, in 4
classification 48–51
  adjudication and 49
  criteria and 49
  evaluation and 93, 95
  Hart's semantics and 53
  judgments and 51
  legal entities and 48
  legal reasoning and 48
  reification of law and 48
  revision of 50
cognitivism 83–124 *see also* non-cognitivism
  counterfactual independence and 111
  culture and 114
  mind-dependence and 90
  objectivity and 100
commitment 130
communal practices
  ethics and 187
  interpretation and 166–79
  legal practice and 176
communication 134–6
competing conceptions
  ethics and 117–18
  non-cognitivism and 115
concept attribution
  bias and 188

concept attribution (*cont.*)
discourse autonomy and 186
equality and 190, 195–7, 199–200
economic 196–7
ethics and 187, 198
evaluation and 187
evidence and 196
independence and 190, 192–3
syntax and 192
concepts *see also* concept attribution, legal concepts
beliefs and 44–6
complex 50, 144
conditions and 50
content of 146, 195
Criterial Model and 2–3
culture and 114
definition of 1–2
determination of range of 2, 46–8, 190n.
disagreement and 125–6
discrimination and 101
equal protection and 195–6
evaluation and 93
extension 2
Hart's semantics and 53
inconsistent 195
independence and 106–7
interpretation of 125
legal reasoning and 51
revision and 50
semantic assumptions and 1,3
senses and 2
substantive disagreements and 144
theory and 15, 44–7, 73–6, 159–60, 177–9
use and 54–5
conditions *see also* criteria
concepts and 50
Hart's semantics and 52, 62–6
theoretical terms and 45
conservatism 136, 198–201
judicial discretion and 199
objectivity and 198
positivism and 200–1
content
concepts and 146, 195
intention and 135
conventionalism
discourse autonomy and 186
Dworkin and 141–4
Fish Stanley and 165
foundationalism and 145
indeterminacy and 159
interpretive constraints and 157
Moore and 180
Wittgenstein and 148–51, 157, 161
convergence 115–17
counterfactual independence 109–11
cognitivism and 111
ethics and 109
metaphysical necessity and 109
criteria
Burge and 37
classification and 49
conditions and 62–5
Criterial Model and 3
objectivity and 194
relevant 3
Criterial Model
challenges to 4
concepts and 2–3
Dworkin's criticism of 126, 129
expressions and 129
properties and 129
relevant criteria and 3
culture
cognitivism and 114
concepts and 114
ethics and 113–14, 117–20, 122
Fish and 175
non-cognitivism and 114–15
values and 122

Davidson, D. 3, 16, 30, 32, 150
charitable ascription and 43–4
mental events and 71
physical events and 71
scepticism and 41
deceit 174
defeasibility 54, 62–4
Descartes, R.
Burge and 39
Putnam's semantics and 39
descriptions
ethics and 90
Kripke's semantics and 17, 19, 23
Putnam's semantics and 33
discourse autonomy
concept attribution and 186
conventionalism and 186
equality and 187
Moore and 179–86
discretion
Hart's semantics and 66–7
judicial 199
discrimination
concepts and 101
experience and 101
intention and 189
Moore and 186
doubt 37, 80–1, 123–4
Dworkin, R.
civil rights and 188–9
commitment and 130
communication model and 134–6

Constitution and 188–9
conventionalism and 141–4
conviction and 130
Criterial Model and 126, 129, 136
equal protection and 189
Fish and 128, 166
indeterminacy and 136–7
Kripke-Putnam semantics and 48–9, 129–35, 160–2
legal interpretation and 129
metaphysics and 160–2
Moore and 180, 182
paradigms and 129, 141, 142
positivism and 3, 127–8, 166
pre-interpretive agreement and 137–43
Raz and 12, 126, 128
scepticism and 161
sources thesis and 141
substantive disagreement and 130–1

equality *see also* discrimination prejudice
bias and 188
civil rights and 4, 188–90
concept attribution and 190, 195–7, 199–200
discourse autonomy and 187
Dworkin and 189
economic 196–7
error 84, 117–21
ethics
assumptions and 187–8
beliefs and 104–5, 107, 112–13, 120
causal explanations and 107, 111, 122
circularity and 117–21
commitment and 130
communal practices and 187
competing conceptions and 117–18
convergence and 115–17
culture and 113, 114, 117–20, 122
descriptions and 90
error and 84, 117–21
events and 104
facts and 104, 113
identifying 104
independence and 113, 115
knowledge and 112, 116, 121
mathematics and 111
non-cognitivism and 113
objectivity and 119–20
personal interest and 113
projection and 90, 96–100
properties and 107, 111
real options and 117–21
reductionism and 95, 111, 121
scepticism and 83
semantic depth and 90
standards and 113
superstition and 119
truth and 112, 115, 119
evaluation
classification and 93, 95
concept attribution and 187
concepts and 93
Hart's semantics and 60–1
Moore and 180
non-cognitivism and 92, 95
non-evaluative terms and 94–5
projectivism and 96–100
realism and 97
reductionism and 93–4
scepticism and 98–9
subjectivity and 92–3
value-free world and 94
experience
appearances and 101
concept of 101
discrimination and 101
ideas and 101
non-cognitivism and 100–1
subjectivity and 101
values and 101
expressions 17, 129

Fish, S. 114, 165–79
beliefs and 171, 172
concepts and 12–13
constraints and 165, 176
conventionalism and 165
culture and 175
Dworkin and 128, 166
formalism and 165
foundationalism and 166, 167
indeterminacy and 176
interpretation and 166–79
community and 167, 170
truth of 168
legal realism and 178
Moore and 184
objectivity and 170, 176
politics and 168
pragmatism and 166, 172, 173, 175
preferences and 173
radical indeterminacy and 169
scepticism and 167, 169–72, 178–9
theory and 177–9
truth and 175
Wittgenstein and 168, 169
formalism
Fish and 165
interpretation and 166–7
scepticism and 167
foundationalism
conventionalism and 145
Fish and 166, 167
representations and 40

Gavison, R. 141
Geach, P.T. 91
Greenawalt, K. 141

Hart's semantics 52–82
  adjudication and 55
  anti-realism and 77–80
  classification and 53
  concepts and 10, 53
    cases of 54
    use and 54–5
  conditions and 52, 62, 66
  conformity and 57–8
  counterparts and 68–9
  defeasibility and 62–4
  definitions and 53
  discretion and 66–7
  domain of inquiry and 77
  epistemic distance and doubt and 80–2
  evaluation and 60–1
  force and 55–61
  individuation and 79–80
  Kripke-Putnam semantics and 52
  legal concepts and 54
  legal statements and 52
  ontological liberalism and 77–80
  performance and 54, 56
  positivism and 127
  preferences and 58–9
  projectivism and 82
  property and 57, 74
  realism and 69–70
  reductionism and 52, 69–76, 79
  Rule of Recognition and 127, 130, 136–8
  rules and 61
  scepticism and 79
Hurd, H. 134–5
Hurley, S.
  causal explanations and 104–5
  causal relations and 104–5
  centralism and 137
  distributive justice and 144
  non-cognitivism and 91
  quantifiers and 110
  scepticism and 112–13

ideas *see* concepts
illusion 40
independence
  concept attribution and 106–7, 190, 192–3
  conceptual 106–8
  counterfactual 109–11
  ethics and 113, 115
indeterminacy 136–7, 159–60
  conventionalism and 159
  individualism and 159–60
  interpretation and 159
  Wittgenstein and 147–8
individualism
  Burge and 39
  indeterminacy and 159–60
  Wittgenstein and 148–9, 161
intention
  civil rights and 188–90
  content and 135
  counterfactuals and 191
  discrimination, racial and 189
  legislative 1, 65–8, 134–5, 188–91, 195–8
  semantic 184n.
interpretation *see also* legal interpretation
  community and 166–79
  concepts and 125
  Fish and 166–79
  formalism and 166–7
  indeterminacy and 159
  statutes, of 1
  truth and 168
  Wittgenstein and 155, 157–8
interpretive constraints 129, 132, 155–9
  conventionalism and 157
  ethics and 156
  meaning and 156
  substantive disagreement and 156

Jackson, F. 108
judgments
  classification and 51
  evaluative 100, 102
  objectivity and 100, 102
  pre-interpretive agreement and 138–9
judicial discretion 66–8, 138, 199

knowledge
  belief as 111
  ethics and 111–12, 116, 121
  Kripe-Putnam's (K-P) semantics and 32
Kress, K. 131–3
Kripke-Putnam's semantics. *See also* Kripke's semantics, Putnam's semantics
  abstract properties and 83
  anti-realism and 77–8
  anti-reductionism and 73
  application of 7
  Brink on 5
  classification and 50
  concepts and 109
  Dworkin and 48–9 129–35, 160–2
  Hart and 52, 54, 76
  legal concepts and 79, 83
  legal positivism and 133
  McGinn's objections to 79
  metaphysics and 125
  mind-dependence and 84–5

Moore's theory on 5–6
necessity and 74
physical entities and 48
prejudice and 7
semantic depth and 83
synonymy and 74
thought and object and 44
Kripke's semantics
names on 8, 16–29
bearerless names and 38
beliefs and 25, 27
classical theory and 17–19, 22–3
chain and 25
descriptions and 17, 19, 23
designators and 18
epistemic contexts and 22–4
modal contexts and 18–22
natural kinds and 29–34
object-independence and 26–7
referents and 17, 21–3
rigidity and 18, 20
scope-sensitivity and 19–20
semantic rules and 22
sense and 26
substitution and 38
Semantic Assumption and 3
Wittgenstein and 147

legal concepts
arbitrary nature of 48
argumentative character of 47
complexity of 50, 144
conditions and 47
content of 47
depth of 47
empirical counterparts and 53
Hart's semantics and 54
Kripke-Putnam's semantics and 79, 83
legal consequences and 54
legal practice and 165
mind-dependence and 83
properties in 47
semantics of law and 47
substantive disagreement on 125
theories and 46
legal interpretation
constitutional 4
Dworkin and 129
objectivity of 1
morality and 165
prejudice and 145
semantics and 1
statutory 4, 135n.
substantive disagreement and 126
legal practice 165–201
community and 176
deceit and 174
legal concepts and 165
Moore and 180–2
pragmatism and 165
scepticism and 165
legal realism
Fish and 178
reductionism and 72
legal reasoning
classification and 48–51
empirical investigation and 49–50
ethics and 49, 50
legal entities and 49
politics and 49, 50
properties and 49
Lewis, D. 153
limits of the law
meaning and 128
positivism and 163
substantive disagreement and 127
Locke, J. 87, 88
Luntley, M. 78

MacCormick, N. 58, 61
Mackie, J.L. 86, 87–8
theory of error and 116
values and 104
mathematics 111
meaning
doubt and 37, 80–1, 123–4
interpretive constraints and 156
limits of the law and 128
problem of 40
theory of 15, 38
Wittgenstein and 147, 149, 152, 157–8
McDowell, J. 16, 26, 28, 96, 147
non-cognitivism and 100–1
subjective properties and 102
Wittgenstein and 157
McGinn, C. 79
mental
autonomy of the 40–1
irreducibility of 71
representations 41
Wittgenstein and the 147–8, 152, 157
counterfactual independence and 109
Dworkin and 160–2
Moore and 5–6
mind and 71
necessity and 109
objectivity and 84
realism and 5–6
reduction and 69–75
mind-dependence 83–124
artifacts and 86–9
cognitivism and 90
evaluative properties and 83
ethics and 84, 89, 90

mind-dependence 83–124 (*cont.*)
  legal concepts and 83
  morality and 84
  objectivity and 84–5
  semantic depth and 84, 88–90
  subjectivism and 89–90
  values and 83
Moore, G.E. 70, 103, 109
Moore, M.
  beliefs and 184
  conventionalism and 180
  discourse autonomy and 179–86
  discrimination and 186
  Dworkin and 180, 182
  evaluation and 180
  external criticism and 181–4
  Fish and 184
  Kripke-Putnam's semantics and 5–6
  legal interpretation and 179–80
  legal practice and 180–2
  metaphysical realism and 5–6
  natural kinds and 191–2
  practice-dependence and 13
  pragmatism and 180
  relativism and 180
  scepticism and 185
  theory and 180
morality 84, 165
Munzer, S. 191–2

natural selection 97
naturalism 103–11
  causal explanations and 104, 105
  causal relations and 104
  causation and 105
  evaluative reasoning and 103
  legal 3
  science and 103
  values and 103–4
necessity
  choice and 98
  conceptual 109
  epistemic 39
  metaphysical 109–10
  scepticism and 98
  supervenience and 110
Nelken, D. 183
non-cognitivism
  appearances and 100
  competing conceptions and 115
  culture and 114–15
  dependence and 114
  ethics and 90, 92, 97, 106, 113
  evaluation and 92, 95
  experience and 100
  objectivity and 92, 95–6
  scepticism and 97
  subjectivity and 92
  values and 94, 95
Nozick, R. 111–12

object-dependence 8, 26–8, 38, 45–6
objectivity
  anti-realism and 5–6, 77–8
  cognitivism and 100
  conservatism and 198
  criteria and 194
  epistemology and 84
  ethics and 119–20
  evaluative judgments and 100, 102
  Fish and 170, 176
  legal interpretation and 1
  metaphysics and 84
  mind-dependence and 84–5
  non-cognitivism and 92, 95–6
  projectivism and 100
  realism and 6
  truth and 5
  values and 100, 102

paradigms 31, 34, 46, 129, 137–8, 141, 142
Pettit, P. 102, 108
politics 49, 50, 168
positivism
  challenges to 5, 163
  conservatism and 200–1
  Dworkin's criticism of 127, 128, 140–2, 166
  Hart's rule of recognition and 127
  interpretive 162–4, 200–1
  limits of the law and 163
Postema, G. 76, 79, 159
pragmatism
  Fish and 166, 172, 173, 175
  legal practice and 165
  Moore and 180
preferences
  Fish and 173
  Hart's semantics and 58–9
pre-interpretive agreement
  centralism and 137
  Dworkin and 137–43
  judgments and 138–9
  legal positivism and 137–8
  meaning and 138
  Rule of Recognition and 138
  substantive disagreement and 137–43
projectivism 93, 97–100
properties
  abstract 83
  Criterial Model and 129
  ethics and 107, 111
  evaluative 83
  legal concepts and 6, 47
  legal reasoning and 49

mind-dependence and 83
Putnam's semantics and 83
Putnam's semantics
artifacts and 86
competence and 32–3
Descartes and 39
descriptions and 33
external environment and 30
knowledge and 32
linguistic labour and 185–6
natural kinds and 8, 16, 35
Semantic Assumption and 3

Quine, W.v.O. 39–40

radical indeterminacy 136–7, 143–6, 148, 169
rationality
charity and 43–4
Raz, Joseph 12
Dworkin and 126, 128, 136–7, 142–3
realism
Brink, David, and 6–7
Moore, Michael, and 5–6
objectivity and 6
reification 48
reductionism
ethics and 95, 111, 112
evaluation and 93–4
legal realism and 72
metaphysical of 69–75
supervenience and 71, 74, 110–11
values and 124
referents
Kripke's semantics and 17, 21–3
theoretical terms and 45
relativization 123, 180
revision
classification and 50
concepts and 50
truth and 39
Rorty, R. 26, 114
Rule of Recognition 127, 130, 136–8

scepticism
anti-realism and 77
causality and 98
domains of 77
Dworkin and 161
ethics and 83–4, 113
evaluation and 98–9
Fish and 167, 169–72, 178–9
formalism and 167
global 111–15
Hart's semantics and 79
indubitability and 39–42, 143–6
legal practice and 165
Kripke-Putnam's model and 40–2, 162
Moore and 185
necessity and 98
non-cognitivism and 92, 97
selective 84, 111–15
truth-tracking and 111–12
Wittgenstein and 147–51
science
conceptions and 102
naturalism and 103
scope-sensitivity 19–20
semantics *see also* Criterial Model, Hart's semantics, Kripke semantics, Kripke-Putnam's semantics, Putnam's semantics, semantic assumptions
challenges 36–7, 139
concepts and 1
criterial 3, 129–31, 133
defective 1
depth 90
law and 47
legal concepts and 47
legal interpretation and 1
precedent and 4
prejudice and 4
realism and 114
substantive disagreements and 139
traditional theory of 1–2, 17, 19–22, 26, 28, 30, 37, 38–9, 148, 152
semantic assumption
concepts and 3
disagreements and 4–5
legal naturalism and 3
legal positivists and 3, 5
originalist-interpretivist controversy and 4
self-evidence of 4
senses 2, 17, 25–6
sources thesis 141
standards 113
statutes
canonical text of 1
intentions of legislature of 1, 65–8, 134–5, 188–9, 195–8
interpretation of 1
purpose of 1
Stroud, B. 94
subjectivity 92–6
appearances and 102
attachment and 93
Dworkin and 130–1
ethics and 102
evaluation and 92–3
experience and 101
interpretive constraints and 156
legal concepts and 125
non-cognitivism and 92
values and 122

substantive disagreement 125–64
  commitment and 130
  complex concepts and 144
  consensus and 139
  convention and 143
  inventing the law and 127
  limits of the law and 127
  legal interpretation and 126
  realism and 130
superstition 119
supervenience 71, 74, 161
  reductionism and 74, 110–11
syntax 192

theoretical terms
  belief, different concepts and 44–6
  compliants and 44
  concepts and 44–5
  conditions and 45
  natural kind terms and 44
  referents and 45
theory *see also* theoretical terms
  concepts and 15
  Fish and 177–8
  Kripke's semantics and 17–19, 22–3
  legal concepts and 46, 73–6, 137–8, 142, 144, 146, 157–8, 159, 161–2, 177–8
  meaning and 15
  Moore and 180
  properties and 46–7
  Putnam's semantics and 5–6, 31, 34
  semantics and 1–2
thought
  objects and relation between 40
  Putnam's semantics and 44
truths
  analytic,
    confirmation and revision of 39
  ethics and 112, 115, 119
  Fish and 168, 175
  interpretation and 168
  objectivity and 5, 77
  scepticism and 111–12

United States
  civil rights in 4
  Constitutional interpretation in 188–90, 195–8
  originalist-interpretivist controversy in 4

values 121–4
  culture and 122
  evaluation and 94
  experience and 101
  mind-dependence and 83
  naturalism and 103–4
  non-cognitivism and 94, 95
  objectivity and 100, 102
  reductionism and 93–6, 110, 124
  social practice and 122
  subjectivity and 122
veridical perception 40

Wiggins, D. 106, 115
Williams, B. 102, 117–20
Wittgenstein, L.
  Blackburn and 151, 157–8
  community consensus and 148–53, 157
  content and 12, 16
  conventionalism and 149, 157, 161
  easy cases and 157–9
  ethics and 158–159
  Fish and 168, 169
  individualism and 148–9, 161
  interpretation and 155
  Kripke and 147
  McDowell and 157
  meaning and 147, 149, 152, 157–8
  patterns and 148
  psychological mechanisms and 147
  rules and 147–9
  scepticism and 147–51
  theory and 157–8